We Can Take It!

The Roosevelt Tree Army
At
New Jersey's
High Point State Park
1933-1941

Peter Osborne

1st Books Library
Bloomington, Indiana

© 2002 by Minisink Valley Historical Society.
All rights reserved.

No part of this book may be reproduced, stored in a retrieval system, or transmitted by any means, electronic, mechanical, photocopying, recording, or otherwise, without written permission from the author.

ISBN: 1-4033-0241-3 (e-book)
ISBN: 1-4033-0242-1 (Paperback)

This book is printed on acid free paper.

1st Books - rev. 09/16/02

The following publishers have generously given permission to use an extended quotation or illustrations from these copyrighted works. Reprinted by permission of Pictorial Histories Publishing Company. From *The Tree Army: A Pictorial History of the Civilian Conservation Corps, 1933-1942* by Stan Cohen. Copyright 1980 by Stan Cohen. From *We Can Take It: A Short History of the CCC* by Ray Hoyt. Copyright 1999 and reprinted by permission of Basil Nickerson. From *High Point of the Blue Mountains* by Ronald J. Dupont, Jr. and Kevin Wright. Copyright 1990 by Ronald J. Dupont, Jr. and Kevin Wright and reprinted by permission.

Dedications:

TO
Dr. Eliot Rosen
My mentor and the person who gave me my love
of FDR so many years ago.

Albert Mastriani
Whose phenomenal memory provided me with so
much information and insight
into the CCC era at High Point.

and

Melvin Gemmill
The project superintendent and designer of most
of the projects at High Point,

The army officers, National Park Service foremen
and
The C Boys of Company 216 and Company 1280
who gave us so much of what we still use in
High Point State Park
some 69 years after the first C camp was
established.

CONTENTS

PREFACE ix
CHAPTER 1 1
CHAPTER 2 26
CHAPTER 3 67
CHAPTER 4 98
CHAPTER 5 129
CHAPTER 6 171
CHAPTER 7 186
CHAPTER 8 209
CHAPTER 9 225
CHAPTER 10 240
CHAPTER 11 270
CHAPTER 12 287
CHAPTER 13 324
CHAPTER 14 336
CHAPTER 15 355
APPENDIX 390
NOTES 421

BIBLIOGRAPHIC ESSAY 463
BIBLIOGRAPHY 470
ACKNOWLEDGMENTS................................. 486

PREFACE

In the fall of 1975, I began my first semester at Rutgers, the State University of New Jersey, with the hope of becoming a forest ranger. One of my first classes was with a professor who often described himself as having been the meanest military police officer in the U.S. Army. He forced those who were not serious about history out of his classroom with his difficult course outline and expectations. He carried a worn leather briefcase, wore tweed jackets and was all business. I remember the first American History class I had with him and listening to his lectures with hundreds of other students in a huge lecture hall.

Dr. Eliot Rosen taught American history as I had never heard it taught, through broad sweeps of historical movements and not the date-based recitations we all remember from high school. I decided I wanted to be a historian just like him. Dr. Rosen was a Franklin Delano Roosevelt (FDR) scholar having begun his career working with Raymond Moley on his book called *The First New Deal*. Moley was one of the original informal group of advisors FDR called the brains trust. Rosen made his own contribution to the Roosevelt field by publishing his book called

Hoover, Roosevelt and The Brains Trust: From Depression to New Deal in 1977.

By the time I graduated from college, I had taken all his courses and acquired a serious interest in and a profound respect for President Franklin D. Roosevelt. With the publication of this book, the torch passes from Dr. Rosen to me. It is now my duty to promote the FDR legacy and what it means.

In the years since I left college, I have worked in the public history field, and my interests have taken me far away from FDR and the New Deal of the 1930s. Several years ago, I came back to FDR quite by accident and revived my long-standing interest in the Civilian Conservation Corps (CCC), one of FDR's most popular New Deal programs. With the 1990 publication of *High Point of the Blue Mountains* by Ronald J. Dupont, Jr. and Kevin Wright and my trail maintaining duties at Stokes State Forest, I realized I was at ground zero of CCC history. The CCC camps at High Point and Stokes were typical of those once spread across the country. The CCC statue of a young man ready to go out into the forest at Stokes was one of the first of its kind to be dedicated east of the Mississippi River.

Since my arrival in Port Jervis more than twenty years ago, I have acquired a great love for High Point State Park. I often eat lunch there and walk in the park a couple of times a week. I can see the sun rise over the High Point

Monument from my dining room window, and my wife and I got married at High Point in 1994 on a snowy and icy Christmas Eve. We had planned to be married on the Appalachian Trail, but the weather turned bad and by accident, others would argue by fate, we wound up in the beautiful stone CCC-era Iris Inn or Visitors Center as it is now known. What a serendipitous turn of events.

We live in a time of great cynicism and anti-government feelings. As such, we forget there was a time when leaders thought the federal government could perform great deeds and that two Roosevelts, Theodore and Franklin, both of whom would become president, were very much at the center of the synthesis of those ideas.

When FDR announced the creation of the CCC, there were critics who would later call it a government "boondoggle" but the most amazing thing is the legacy of the CCC at High Point and at parks and forests around the country, is by and large, still with us. We continue to drive on roads, admire the stonework at Sawmill Dam, hike on the trails, camp at sites they built and fish on lakes they created. Taxpayers in the 1930s paid some $3 billion dollars for these projects across the country. Seventy years later, we are still benefitting from that investment, a bargain indeed.

As a nation, we have often debated since the 1930s what to do for people who have fallen on what were then called "hard times." We have argued about how to help them and to make them more self-sufficient. I believe part of the answer is found in the likes of the Civilian Conservation Corps. It gave young men hope, exposed them to the outdoors and hard work and got them prepared for an uncertain future, which in their case meant fighting a world war just as many were moving on to manhood.

I have met many CCC boys over the years and almost to a man they said their days in the *Roosevelt Tree Army* were some of the best of their lives. Others, brothers, sons or nephews of C boys, remembered the money sent home at a time of great need. Even more remember a C camp just a few miles down the road or over in the next county. Interestingly, whenever I speak about FDR and the CCC, everyone agrees we need another version of it again. As you read this book you will see the need is not only for the benefit of our young people, but for our parks and forests which need the loving care, maintenance and nurturing the CCC gave them seventy years ago.

CHAPTER 1

The Dirty Thirties

The country needs, and unless I mistake its temper, the country demands bold, persistent experimentation. It is common sense to take a method and try it. If it fails, admit it frankly and try another. But above all do something.
-Governor Franklin D. Roosevelt, May 22, 1932

Freedom from Fear: The American People in Depression and War 1929-1945

I propose to create a Civilian Conservation Corps to be used in simple work, not interfering with normal employment, and confining itself to forestry, the prevention of soil erosion, flood control and similar projects.
-President Franklin D. Roosevelt, Address to the Congress, March 21, 1933

The Tree Army: A Pictorial History of the Civilian Conservation Corps, 1933-1942

This is the story of a national organization called the Civilian Conservation Corps, created by one of the last century's leading figures, Franklin Delano Roosevelt. He was our nation's 32nd president and one of the most beloved and one of the most reviled men of his day. It is also the story of one the most effective and important efforts ever undertaken by our nation to combine relief efforts, as welfare was then known, with major conservation projects in our parks and forests in the 1930s and early 1940s. It is the story of three million young men who served in the *Roosevelt Tree Army*, as it was known. Their motto was "We Can Take It!" because of the hard work they undertook. Finally, it is about the young men who served in New Jersey's most famous state park of the 1930s, High Point State Park and how High Point came to be developed.

The Great Depression

As we begin the twenty first century in unparalleled prosperity, it is almost impossible to imagine what America was like when Franklin D. Roosevelt took the oath of office for the first time, in 1933. In the closing weeks of February, America was gripped by the worse economic depression it had ever seen. Rural America had been suffering through economic calamity since the end of World War I. The stock market crash of 1929 was only a symptom of what was fundamentally wrong. The market lost, in less than a month, $26 billion, more than 40 percent of its face value. In 1929, new capital issues in the United States had totaled $10 billion and in 1930 they had declined to $7 billion.[1]

Corporate profits fell from $8.4 billion in 1929 to $3.4 billion in 1932. Over one hundred thousand businesses failed from 1929-1930 and the banking system was slowly collapsing of its own weight. Almost seven hundred banks with deposits of $200 million disappeared in 1929. In 1930, 1,352 banks went out of business and in 1931, the number rose to 2,294 with deposits of almost $2 billion. As each bank collapsed, so went the life savings of millions of Americans who had no other financial resources.[2]

Other numbers were grim reminders how bad things had become. Industrial production had declined 26 percent from 1929 to 1930 and by 1932, it was only 51 percent of its 1929 level. Unemployment rose in numbers never before seen in American history. Nearly 4 million were unemployed in 1930. Seven million were unemployed a year later and 11 million were without work by the fall of 1932. By 1933, that number stood at 15 million.[3] At one point, it is estimated unemployment was between 25-30 percent, numbers that would create sheer panic today when unemployment hovers around 5 percent. Some estimates suggest as many as 20 million Americans were out of work. National income in 1929 was $81 billion and by 1932 it was down to $49 billion.[4]

Unemployment among young men aged 18-25 hovered around 25 percent. About 5 million of them were unemployed. About 29 percent of men that age were working in part time jobs.[5] About two hundred and fifty thousand of these "teenage tramps of America" as they were called were simply wandering around with no sense of roots or place.[6] It was a segment of the population thrust into an economic calamity not of their own making, and they had little ability to change the course of the economy.

Andrew Mellon, President Herbert Hoover's Secretary of the Treasury, said for the country to get out of the depression, it had to "liquidate labor, liquidate stock and liquidate the farmers."[7] These comments seem to sum up best what was happening across America and culminated with a great fear sweeping the land as the middle class lost their savings, farmers lost their farms and millions were put out on the streets with no where to go because they had no money to pay the rent. Mellon's comments also represented what many Americans thought President Hoover's policies were doing to them personally. Bread lines sprang up across America and Hoovervilles (towns of the homeless) and Hoover blankets (yesterday's newspaper) and Hoover flags (pants pockets pulled out) became common sights.

The voluntary and locally based system of taking care of the needy which had worked well in decades past was simply overwhelmed by the multitudes of those in need in the 1930s. States loaned tens of millions of dollars to provide "relief" and soon those funds were gone. President Hoover tried several programs that loaned money to the states, only to see it quickly swallowed up.

Hoover created the Reconstruction Finance Corporation with an ability to loan $1.5 billion for public works and an additional $300 million in loans for supplementing local relief funds. Pennsylvania Governor Gifford Pinchot asked for a loan of $45 million even though that amount would only provide $.13 per day per jobless person for food for a year.[8]

Rural America was also in desperate straits and, in fact, had been in trouble since the end of World War I. Prices for commodities had simply collapsed. In the summer of 1919, wheat sold for $2.16 a bushel. By 1929 it dropped to $1.03 a bushel, and in 1932 the price was $.38.[9] Deflation, not the inflation that has been the focus of our recent economic policies, was widespread and prices rapidly declined. Road blocks were set up to stop food from moving to market. Farmers in Nebraska burned corn as fuel and judges were thwarted in their efforts to carry out farm auctions. One was almost lynched.[10]

Peter Osborne

Not only was the economic front collapsing but the American landscape was damaged considerably by generations of waste and poor and unproductive use of the land. At one point, 800 million acres of the United States had been covered with forests. In 1933, only about 100 million acres of timber were left. The wholesale cutting of forests had encouraged severe soil erosion and literally billions of tons of soil were washed away in the famous "dust bowls" of the 1930s.

It has been estimated 300 million acres had washed away or was in danger of being swept away by wind. Soil, in some cases, lacked moisture to a depth of three feet. Huge clouds of dirt, known as "black blizzards," moved across the country towards the cities in the East.[11] Millions of farmers were moving off the land and were recorded by photographer Dorothea Lange and author John Steinbeck in his book *The Grapes of Wrath*. The decade came to be known in history as the "Dirty Thirties."

The depression not only affected the United States but was a financial and political calamity for the industrialized countries around the world. The economic catastrophe had its roots in World War I, which lasted from 1914-1918 and brought mass destruction to Europe along with the deaths of 10 million people. From this turmoil came new and competing political systems that were totalitarian in nature. Russia underwent a bloody revolution in which the

Communists took over and Benito Mussolini came to power in Italy as an anti-communist Fascist. Germany was the worse hit by the depression as it feared Communism, but it like Italy used complete government control of the economy to try and deal with collapsing economies. It witnessed the rise of Adolph Hitler and his National Socialism to power.[12]

The New Deal

It is against this backdrop of despair and fear that New York State Governor Franklin Roosevelt was elected to the presidency in 1932 with 57 percent of the popular vote. His Democratic Party carried both houses of Congress which gave him a strong mandate for action. His campaign theme song was *Happy Days are Here Again* and he promised action - any and all kinds of action to end the depression. He would treat it as the moral equivalent of war. Because of his own fight with polio a decade earlier and the active role played by his wife, Eleanor, he understood the sufferings of the "forgotten man" as he so aptly called him, and his programs would endear him to millions of Americans for decades afterward.

On Inauguration Day, March 4, 1933, with banks collapsing around America and with some believing the country was on the verge of anarchy, the nation held its collective breath as President Roosevelt said in his first inaugural address - "The only thing we have to fear is fear itself."¹³

Within hours of his inauguration, Roosevelt began a whirlwind of legislative activity never before seen nor duplicated since. In his first one hundred days in office, the American political and economic landscape was radically transformed. Legislation dealing with the banking crisis, the agricultural crisis and the National Industrial Recovery Act all sailed through Congress.

Among the laws passed in those extraordinary times was one called the Emergency Conservation Work (ECW). It created an organization called the Civilian Conservation Corps (CCC) which was to employ a quarter of a million men in forestry, flood control and beautification projects. It ultimately became one of the most popular of the New Deal programs and would come to impact the creation, use and appearance of hundreds of state and federal parks and forests across the country. It would also provide employment for three million young men. It was up until that time the most extensive peacetime project ever attempted by the federal government.¹⁴

The CCC was, along with the Federal Emergency Relief Administration, part of FDR's move toward direct involvement by the federal government in relief for the unemployed. For the first time in American history, individuals would get money directly from the federal government in a time of economic crisis. This whole concept had been soundly rejected by Herbert Hoover who believed responsibility for relief for the unemployed should be left in the hands of the state and local governments.

Within a short time, a plethora of government agencies and programs had grown up where few existed before. Collectively they became known as the "alphabet soup" agencies of the New Deal. Critics charged Roosevelt was taking America down the road of socialism and communism but millions were represented by the one farmer who, in the middle of a parade in which FDR was passing by, shouted out, "Thank You Mr. Roosevelt, you saved our farm." A new era in the American experience had begun.

FDR & Conservation

The idea of using men on relief in conservation-related tasks that culminated in the creation of the Civilian Conservation Corps did not begin in 1933 with FDR but was the result of ideas and developments that began with many people he admired. They included his cousin, President Theodore Roosevelt (TR), and TR's first chief of the United State Forest Service, Gifford Pinchot.

Early on, FDR was influenced by Gifford Pinchot, America's first professional forester and friend of his cousin Theodore Roosevelt. It is worth remembering Gifford Pinchot's family home, Grey Towers, is located in Milford, Pennsylvania, and was within sight of High Point State Park. At the Pinchot home, countless conversations took place on the great conservation issues of the day. Pinchot's leadership in promoting the wise use of the nation's forests and natural resources contributed greatly to Theodore Roosevelt's legacy as the conservation president. During TR's presidency, the national forests increased in size from 56 million to 175 million acres.

FDR had a long interest in conservation issues and wildlife dating back to his boyhood. His endeavors in conservation began in 1911 when he was elected to the New York State Senate.[15] FDR chaired the Forest, Fish and Game Committee and helped to pass a new fish and game law in 1912 and an additional piece of legislation, known as the Roosevelt-Jones bill, included a number of suggestions and recommendations made by Pinchot that called for the professionalization of the state's forest system. FDR was considered to be a major ally of conservation forces in the state for the two years he was in the Senate.[16]

After leaving the Senate, he maintained an active interest in conservation affairs, assisting the grange in Hyde Park in purchasing trees, lobbying highway officials not to cut down historic trees along new road projects and dealing with abandoned farms. Even when he ran for vice president in 1920, he made conservation an issue.17

While he was governor, from 1928-1932, he continued to promote conservation issues. He successfully sponsored an amendment to the state's constitution that gave the government the ability to purchase land and reforest it. And, as governor, he took ten thousand men off relief rolls to plant trees as temporary employees.

There was a constant flow of correspondence about conservation issues that crossed his desk, not only from New York residents but from nationally known figures. M. L. Wilson, head of the Department of Agricultural Economics at Montana State College in Bozeman, requested copies of Roosevelt's pamphlet entitled "Acres Fit and Unfit." Wilson was one of the leading scholars on the state of the nation's agricultural economy and would later become the Under Secretary of Agriculture in the Roosevelt administration.18

Twice in his term as governor, FDR received proposals for CCC-type organizations, one from F. A. Anderson, who served on the Executive Committee of the Mississippi Forestry Association and the other from Francis Cuttle, who was chairman of the Tri-Counties Reforestation of California.

Anderson's proposal called for the purchase of 1 million acres of cut-over forest land in the South and having each state enlist forty thousand unemployed men through the U.S.

Army to serve for a period of six months, being paid $30 per month and maintenance. Cuttle's proposal was similar. It would pay men $1 a day and maintenance. Cuttle's organization had been promoting this approach since 1907.[19]

The Intellectual Origins Of The CCC

In FDR's presidential nomination acceptance speech at the Democratic National Convention in 1932 he said, "It is clear that economic foresight and immediate employment march hand in hand in the call for the reforestation of these vast areas. In so doing, employment could be given to a million men."[20] Throughout the 1932 presidential campaign, Herbert Hoover attacked the idea of this plan to reforest the country, even as professional foresters lauded it. During the campaign FDR communicated with many men in the field gathering ideas and thinking about how a national program could be implemented.

Other sources of inspiration for youth work camps that were operating at the time came from Europe and Africa: Bulgaria, the Netherlands, Norway, Sweden, Denmark, Austria, South Africa, Poland and Germany. The youth conservation camps program in Germany, created in 1931 during the Weimar Republic, was later called the Labor Service and became distinctively military in its focus after the rise to power of Adolph Hitler.[21] In Russia the participants were called the "Young Pioneers;" in

Italy they were named the "Sons of the Wolf" and in Germany they were called the "Hitler Youth."[22]

It has been suggested FDR found inspiration for the CCC in this effort, a connection he always denied vehemently. This was especially the case after the German program became a puppet for the Nazis' propaganda machine. However, some provisions of the German program, including the term of enrollment and the token wage paid to participants, were remarkably similar to the features that were used in the CCC in America.[23] Perhaps that is why the word "civilian" is so prominent in the name of the organization.

Finally, the idea of federal agencies working collaboratively with states on conservation projects, where men were housed, fed and directed by a government agency, was already being done in the states of California and Washington through joint efforts with the United States Forest Service.

The CCC Legislation

Thus it was only natural in the early days of 1933, with his inauguration fast approaching, FDR contacted Gifford Pinchot for advice on putting the unemployed to work in the forests, something Pinchot was already doing as governor of Pennsylvania.

On January 20, 1933, Pinchot described a plan that outlined what the CCC would ultimately become and what the core of its mission would be. He wrote "By utilizing the unemployed, highly necessary and productive improvements could be made in the forests thus acquired at substantially no cost to the public."[24] When the CCC legislation was passed, Pinchot was the first governor to get CCC camps approved for his state. In a 1935 speech, FDR gave credit to Pinchot for the employment of five hundred thousand young men who were in the CCC in every state of the union. He even called Pinchot the first of the brain trusters.[25]

While the intellectual origins of the CCC are found in the work of Theodore Roosevelt and Gifford Pinchot, the Mississippi and California proposals and a variety of other projects and experiences, it was FDR who would bring together for the first time in a national program two wasted resources: millions of unemployed young men and a landscape that lay in ruin from past practices. He was enthusiastic about a program that would take urban boys and put them out in the country and to work.

One of the most critical elements of the CCC was that it was meant to give work in high numbers to an important segment of the American population, young unemployed men who represented the next generation of American workers. Another key element of the program was that it was designed to benefit the enrollee and his family financially with money the enrollee was required to send home. And, finally, the state of the nation's natural resources would be improved.

With the election of FDR, a number of meetings and developments occurred that culminated in the creation of the Civilian Conservation Corps. In November 1932, Henry Wallace, the soon-to-be Secretary of Agriculture, and Rexford Tugwell, one of FDR's brain trusters, began to conceptualize a plan for putting twenty-five thousand men to work in the national forest system. Chief Forester Major Robert Stuart believed the program could be handled by the United States Forest Service. A month later the number of enrollees was increased ten-fold to two hundred twenty-five thousand. In January 1933, a Congressional hearing was held on using the army to help in relief schemes. It was quickly dismissed, but in a few short weeks it was back on the table.

Initially, discussions about a *civilian conservation corps* were held at staff level. The idea of a corps was not even mentioned by FDR in his inaugural address. The first meeting of what would become the major players in the CCC took place March 9, 1933. Attending was the president, the Secretary of War, Secretary of Agriculture, Secretary of Interior, the Director of the Budget, the Judge Advocate General of the Army and the Solicitor of the Department of Interior. FDR sketched out his plans and turned over to his advisors the task of coming up with a plan by that evening.

In the weeks that followed, FDR devoted significant amounts of time and thought to the CCC. Additional meetings of various cabinet secretaries regularly took place in what would become the CCC's Advisory Council. Conferences with state foresters and officials from the United States Forest Service and the National Park Service presided over by Henry Wallace and Rexford Tugwell, another of FDR's brains trusters, were also held. Input from those meetings would be incorporated into the final program.[26]

On March 21, 1933, the president sent a message to Congress outlining his plans for "Relief of the Unemployed." He outlined an organization that would draw upon the resources of existing agencies and undertake forestry projects, erosion and flood control. He said two hundred and fifty thousand men could be given work by the summer. Bills were then introduced in the House of Representatives and the Senate. The Senate version, S.598, was only one page long. Today, a bill is typically 600 pages long.[27] The legislative bodies took only eight days to create a *civilian conservation corps* through the Emergency Conservation Work.[28]

Little press was focused on the CCC bill. National interest was on an agricultural bill and events in Germany where Hitler was beginning his persecution of the Jews. Labor was opposed to the bill for several reasons, first, because of the army's proposed involvement in running the program and second, because the wage rates at "a dollar a day" generated fear the private sector would be hurt. Others argued wages should be more than doubled. The Socialist Party also argued against the bill because of the fear it was Fascist in its focus.[29]

There were other hurdles to getting the bill passed in such a short time. Some in the Congress wondered if the program was just a dole or handout. Some said it was a way for young men to take "a vacation in the woods at government expense."[30] FDR remembered the "ribald laughter about planting trees," and his "crazy dream" and that it was just a "political gesture."[31]

The Labor Department testified at hearings through its secretary Francis Perkins that it did not have the experience nor the manpower to conduct CCC enrollments. Perkins said that her department would have to rely on state unemployment relief agencies to sort out the eligible men because they knew the population better.

Hearings in Congress were not particularly troubling, and the debate was mainly favorable although some Republicans were against giving broad authority to the president. Opposition in the House was much more notable, but in the end, a bipartisan vote allowed the passage of the legislation by large margins.[32] By March 31, 1933, the president had received the power to enact the legislation. The broad-based support by members of both parties was a hallmark of the CCC's entire existence and lasted until the final year of its operation.

The Creation Of The CCC

Within weeks, an entirely new government organization and program was created that managed to put hundreds of thousands of young men to work in the country's national and state parks and forests. The legislation that passed Congress so quickly empowered the president to organize and manage this huge undertaking. For Roosevelt, the most immediate and critical need was getting the program up and running.

On April 3, 1933, a meeting was held of the Advisory Council with the principals and the basic plan for the operation of the CCC was essentially created. While there would be changes in years to come, the essential design of the agency was created that day. The plan called for the Department of Labor to process the young men who would participate. The army would transport the men to the camps and the departments of Agriculture and Interior through the United States Forest Service and National Park Service would build the camps, create work projects and manage them.

The terms of enrollment, pay scales and the focus of employing a specific segment of the population were all decided. The budget official would oversee the finances, and the legal officers would deal with legal issues. On April 5, President Roosevelt issued Executive Order 6101, and the CCC was in business.[33]

The enabling legislation included hiring a director at a salary of $12,000 per year and creating an Advisory Council with which cabinet heads would meet regularly to debate policy matters and make decisions about the program. The official announcement of Robert Fechner's being appointed as the first director of the ECW was announced the same day the Advisory Council was meeting for the first time.

Robert Fechner was a vice president of the American Federation of Labor and a former machinist union official for thirty-seven years. Fechner had been active in efforts to create a nine-hour work day and, later an eight-hour work day. Born in Tennessee in 1876, he was from Quincy, Massachusetts. He had worked as a machinist as a young man. He was a lecturer in labor relations at Harvard University, Brown University and Dartmouth.[34]

He met FDR during World War I as a special labor advisor. Fechner campaigned for FDR in 1932 and got the support of the Machinists Union for him. He was unlike the other men who came to Washington to implement the New Deal. He was described as "a simple, homely man who still wore in 1933 the high topped hooked shoes fashionable around the turn of the century. His idea of a good time was to shed his boots and read a magazine, lying on a bed in a moderately priced hotel room he always occupied when in Washington."[35]

He was in many ways the perfect candidate for the job - a negotiator and a simple man among the many large egos of FDR's other advisors. His appointment mollified labor organizations. Because of his experience in negotiations, he was able to chart the shoals of the established bureaucracy. He was beloved by his staff and the enrollees. One can easily see from his simple lifestyle why the enrollees liked him.

He visited camps regularly therefore his knowledge of what was going on was without parallel. While there has been some criticism leveled at him by CCC historians for his lack of vision, he headed a complicated multi-agency project that in the end served 3 million men and the nation remarkably well.[36] His low-key leadership style kept the CCC from public relations problems that were common to some other New Deal agencies.

His biggest trouble came from the Department of Interior's Secretary Harold Ickes, who was one of the most difficult men in FDR's cabinet. They did not get along, and Ickes saw himself as a "Secretary of Conservation." In the closing years of the CCC, Ickes even recommended the abolition of the office of CCC director.[37]

Fechner chose as his assistant James J. McEntee who was from Jersey City, New Jersey. He, too, was a machinist and also involved during World War I in union affairs, negotiations and disputes in munitions plants. He was involved in various negotiations to end several newspaper and railroad strikes. McEntee and Fechner had been friends for a long time and together they ran the CCC until Fechner's death.[38]

The Advisory Council was composed of the secretaries of Interior, Labor, Agriculture and War, each of whom appointed representatives to work with the director. Fechner listened to and often acted upon the advice of cabinet officials, and a significant part of the success of the program can be attributed to their input. The council remained in place until the termination of the CCC program and met as needed, sometimes weekly and sometimes not for months.

While legislation was being debated in Congress, plans were made by the various agencies that were going to participate. In spite of the complexities and challenges, the army sent orders to begin enrolling men. The first enrollee was signed up at the first CCC camp, Camp Roosevelt, near Luray, Virginia on April 7, 1933, just a week after the legislation passed Congress.

By early May it was apparent the army was going to be the only agency capable of meeting the July 1 deadline of managing and operating thirteen hundred camps across the country. The army did not relish this new role. States which had selected their quotas were not able to send enrollees anywhere. FDR changed course and ordered the army to assume control of the camps and that technical services would take control of the work day and work projects.[39] Decisions regarding the appointment and pay of project superintendents finally were resolved, and camps began to undertake projects.[40] All this happened against the backdrop of camps with dissatisfied enrollees who had nothing to do and who feared public criticism.[41]

On May 12, a new plan was approved by the Advisory Council giving the army broad authority over the camps. The army saved the day as it began to process eight thousand five hundred men per day and created twenty-six camps every day.[42] By July 1, about two hundred and seventy five thousand young men were enrolled in camps nationwide, including the one at High Point State Park.

The last major decisions that affected the entire corps were made on August 17 and November 2, 1933. The August decision called for the use of CCC boys in firefighting details in Montana, an action that would ultimately be put into practice throughout the country. It would also set a precedent for C boys to be used for all kinds of local and national emergencies and would forever endear local citizens to the CCC. The second decision called for an education program to be instituted in the CCC nationwide. This action would begin a long-running dispute among the major players as to what should be taught and who would do it or if it should be done at all.

The Emergency Conservation Work, which was the actual name of the program that created the CCC, lasted from 1933 until 1937. In June 1937, the Civilian Conservation Corps was established as an official government agency and the program was extended for three more years. The conservation work reached its peak in 1936 when five hundred thousand enrollees were in the program. In 1939, at the direction of FDR, a major federal government reorganization took place, and the CCC came under the Federal Security Agency, a move Fechner vehemently opposed. In late 1939, Fechner, in poor health and suffering the effects of a heart attack, died, and assistant director McEntee took over the program. He ran it until it closed in 1942.

President Roosevelt personally approved camp locations and equipment purchases in the early months of the CCC.[43] It was certainly one of his "pet projects" as a congressman called it during a series of public hearings in 1937. FDR continued to follow the work of the CCC with great interest, especially through reports and meetings with Fechner. When his schedule permitted, he visited CCC camps, and he was often invited to camps although his hectic press of duties did not allow for many visitations. He delivered speeches on the anniversary of the CCC's creation and wrote at least one article for its national in-house newsletter called "Happy

Days." FDR's forest restoration efforts were rewarded by the Society of American Foresters in 1935 when they presented him with the Sir William Schlich Memorial Medal.[44]

Roosevelt always hoped for the CCC to be a permanent government agency, and of all of the New Deal programs, it was the most popular and enjoyed the greatest support with the general public, bipartisan support in Congress as well as in the media.

The Value Of The CCC To The Army

In one cabinet meeting, George Dern, Secretary of War, remarked that he thought the experience of handling the initial CCC organization was the most valuable achievement the army ever did.[45] It was also the first time in American history when a number of cabinet officers had been able to work across agency lines. In all, twenty-five different agencies in the federal government played a role in creating or administering the CCC.[46]

The CCC was a larger mobilization of forces than what had occurred during the Spanish-American War, and it was the most extensive peacetime operation of the army in history. The army created the largest peacetime government labor force the United States had ever known.[47] In addition to the mobilization, the army had to feed and clothe two hundred and fifty thousand men within several weeks. Orders went out for millions of pieces of clothing, tents and equipment, and within weeks, C boys were being clothed with their own uniforms and work clothes and living in tented communities.[48]

There were not only enormous pressures to get the CCC up and running quickly, but there were also turf battles within the various government agencies involved. However, in the final analysis, the creation and implementation of the CCC legislation occurred in about three months, and as FDR promised, hundreds of thousands of American boys were in the camps and sending much needed money to the folks back home.

Location Of CCC Projects

Each state made its own decisions as to where the CCC boys would actually work and what their duties would be. The program expanded very quickly, and some states, like Massachusetts, planned for seven camps but got thirty-one instead.[49] In mid-1933, there were eight camps operating in the state of New Jersey with about twelve hundred enrollees. By year's end, there were twenty-two camps and over four thousand enrolled with 217 supervisory personnel.[50]

CHAPTER 2

The Boys Are Coming

For the boys are coming, the boys are coming ... They are here! The boys of the Civilian Conservation Corps, who have been sent out from city, town and village to protect and [re]construct the forests of these United States. If you know boys, you need no other introduction to these young men. They are the youth of America, taken from the streets, the homes, the business offices of America.

Sussex Independent, Sussex, New Jersey, July 21, 1933

The Civilian Conservation Corps arrived at High Point State Park in northwestern Sussex County, New Jersey in the late spring of 1933. On average, during the life of the CCC, twenty-five camps would operate within the state of New Jersey and all of them would operate in much the same fashion. They were located in state parks, state forests and on private property.

The typical CCC camp was organized like an army camp. The "company" was the basic unit of operation. At full strength, a company had two hundred young men in addition to army officers and cooking staff. The company was given an identification number to use until projects it was working on were completed and the company was disbanded. There were two companies at High Point, 216 and 1280. The company numbers were chosen because the camp was located or created in Army Corps District No. 2. Numbers ranging from 200-299, 1200-1299 or 2200-2299 indicated the company was from the Second Corps area which included New York, New Jersey and Delaware. In all, there were nine corps areas covering the entire country.[1]

Because of the large number of camps, on average more than sixteen hundred per year, the designation helped the administration keep track of enrollee records, payroll, projects list and sundry items. The company number stayed with it even if it were moved somewhere else within the state.

An additional numerical designation was indicated by the type of facility in which the company was operating. In the case of High Point, Company 216 was at SP-1 and Company 1280 was at SP-8, both indicating a camp at a state park with projects being created by the National Park Service (NPS). Other designations included "MC" for mosquito control, "A" for Bureau of Animal Industry, "F" for National Forest or "S" for state forest.[2] If asked where he was assigned, a CCC boy at High Point would say, Company 1280, SP-8, or Company 216, SP-1.

Camps and companies were moved quite regularly. Some were operational for only a few months and then went out of business. The process of locating a camp was part practical - where the work needed to be done - and part political - some camps being located in certain areas because a congressman or governor wanted it. When camps were closed, there usually was a lobbying effort to keep the camp open because of the economic benefit it brought to the community.

Each company at High Point was distinct and separate from the other and involved in different projects. Company 216, SP-1 operated from June 9, 1933 until June 30, 1937, and was mainly involved with forestry, landscaping and road projects.[3] Company 1280 was initially formed as a forestry company and worked in Idaho from June 1933 until November 1933.

When the first enrollment period ended, a small cadre of remaining 1280 enrollees returned to New Jersey in November to make up Camp SP-8 that operated until November 15, 1941, and was mainly involved with the large construction projects in the park.[4] Surprisingly, enrollees from both companies while living across the street from each other, did not intermingle.[5]

Enrollees, Allottees & LEM's

The young men who served in the CCC had to voluntarily enroll in the program, hence the name "enrollee" for those who served. A CCC man had to be a U.S. citizen, of good character, unmarried, and out of school. In the early years, enrollees were between eighteen and twenty-five and general enlistment was for six months with the possibility of serving for an additional six months. Men had to be of sound physical condition. Physical disabilities were reason for refusal and some included "running ears, hernia, flat feet, bad eyesight, marked deafness, etc.," according to a 1937 *New Jersey Herald* newspaper article. There was an occasional exception however.[6]

Typically, an enrollee was "between eighteen and nineteen, had completed eight years of school and had been without a job for seven months prior to entering the corps. He weighed 147 pounds, was 5'8" tall and served in the CCC for nine to twelve months."[7] His parents and family usually had to be on "relief" as welfare was then known. In most contemporary literature they were known as the "CCC boys," or "C boys" and the camps were described as "C camps."

As the years went by and the economy improved, requirements were eased. Age limits were expanded to seventeen to twenty-nine. Men could reenlist for another six months if they were honorably discharged and then had to wait a year if they wanted to enlist again. Requirements changed over the years and the locations from which the men signed up changed as well.

After 1937, it was not required for one's family to be on relief to get into the CCC although if an enrollee was going to send a prescribed portion of his salary home, he had a better chance of getting into the program. It was also around this time that a system of promotion was announced by the Federal Civil Service that allowed enrollees to apply for more permanent positions. By 1940, restrictions were eased so much that young men could simply sign up at the C camps including High Point and did not need to wait for enrollment periods.

For the most part, enrollees in the CCC tended to be young men but some were older and in their 30s. Of the potential two hundred fifty thousand unmarried men who were to be taken into the program, President Roosevelt authorized the enrollment of twenty-eight thousand military veterans, and they made up about 10 percent of the CCC. Over the life of the CCC some two hundred and twenty five thousand veterans of World War I served.[8] Veterans could be married as long as they were willing to send their allotment to dependents.[9]

There were separate camps for African-Americans, reflecting racial prejudices of the time and camps for Native Americans on or near reservations. Black CCC camps were controversial because neighboring communities, which were largely white, feared large groups of young black men.[10] There were three "colored" camps, as they were then known, at Wawayanda, New York. At High Point, the camps were entirely white although the ethnic makeup of the camp was diverse. It is possible that an occasional African-American served there, but that seems unlikely. In 1941, the enrollment for the 2nd Corps area included fifteen hundred enrollees who were white and 250 who were black.[11]

In general, enrollees from the East and Midwest were assigned to camps in the West although that was not always the case. The reason was that western states had smaller populations and many of the national parks and forests were located there. There were relatively few state parks and forests across the country at that time. As a result, there was initially difficulty getting projects lined up in the East. Only Pennsylvania, home to Governor Pinchot and his relief conservation projects already operating was capable of having CCC camps from the very beginning.[12]

The state of Idaho was home to a number of New Jersey companies including company 1280, for a short time, because in the summer of 1933 it was determined that 25,200 workers were needed to undertake projects there.[13] It also had more camps, 163, than any other state except California. The camps were closed in winter because of the severe weather.[14] Idaho also became home to many New Jersey boys after their enlistment in the CCC was done and they married local girls and established new lives there.

In the case of the C camp at High Point and in many camps in New Jersey, men were mainly from metropolitan areas in northeastern New Jersey. From newspaper accounts, interviews and other records, it is known that the enrollees at High Point came from Newark, North Arlington, Jersey City, Camden, Trenton, Hoboken, Paterson, Passaic, Garfield and Clifton. The military officers were from army bases scattered throughout New York and New Jersey. At least one 1933 estimate showed 95 percent of the enrollees at High Point were from New Jersey.[15] In the next enrollment period, a 1934 estimate determined 60 percent of seventy-five recently enrolled men in both companies at High Point were from Newton, New Jersey.[16]

About 10 percent of men enrolled nationally or about thirty-five thousand men, were called "LEMs" or locally enrolled men. There were no age restrictions and both single and married men were accepted. This policy was initiated because it was believed the men would be more mature and bring leadership to the companies. There was concern that enrollees who were coming from urban areas needed supervision by men who had experience in the outdoors. Because the USFS and NPS did not have enough employees to provide this supervision, they looked to the LEMs.[17]

LEMs also addressed the concern that local communities might resent companies of men from other places who were being given jobs in their area while their own men remained unemployed. Some had worked for logging companies and others were unemployed state foresters.[18] In the case of High Point State Park, 10 percent of the work force were LEMs drawn from Sussex County. LEM's were chosen by the Department of Labor until 1935, and after that, the process was turned over to the National Park Service.[19]

Compensation

Enrollees were paid $30 a month, bi-weekly, $25 of which was sent home to dependents or "allottees" as they were called. Allottees were not allowed to send back any funds they received and enrollees were subject to discharge if it happened. LEMs received the full sum.

In the later years of the CCC rules were changed and if men had no dependents, they would deposit $22 of their monthly pay into a savings account that would be given to them when they left the CCC. Room and board was part of the compensation package as well as clothing and supplies. The government provided transportation to their assignments and for the return trip home when their enrollment ended.

It cost approximately $1,000 per enrollee per year in 1940 for food, clothing, overhead and allotments to dependents. The cost of feeding and clothing an enrollee was about $1.92 per day.[20] In 1933 as the CCC was being organized, Duncan K. Major of the War Department wrote that an "allowance of $3 per man per day was to be made available for purchase of all necessary material, equipment, supplies and overhead as well as wages and subsistence."[21] About one half of the total expenditures of $300 million went directly to enrollees in the form of food, housing, medical attention and clothing. One third of the total was paid to enrollees and their dependents for their monthly allotment. A quarter of total CCC expenses went for the men's food and clothing. About 40 percent of the total budget was used for supplies, equipment, technical services, building and maintenance.[22]

We Can Take It!

Signing Up For The Three C's

Enlistment periods were conducted twice a year, in the spring and in the fall. Later, they were conducted four times a year. Upon filing an application, enrollees were accepted into the program. Depending on each state's allotment and the CCC's needs, enrollees were sent to camps either in that state or across the country. The process was supervised by the U.S. Department of Labor and program requirements stated the number of available slots were rationed by the Federal government. Rules stated that men who had worked in the CCC for twenty-four months were ineligible for further enlistment. If a man worked just short of that time and had been honorably discharged, he could apply for another six month period after a year.

In Sussex County, potential enrollees applied to the program by going to the County Welfare Office at the Hall of Records or the Newton Town Committee rooms in Newton, New Jersey. Overseers of the Poor in all of the municipalities took applications elsewhere in the county. Enrollments were also taken at public schools and public buildings across the state. Men from families on relief were given preference.

During the first enrollment period in 1933, in spite of the severity of the depression, Sussex County had trouble finding young men to fill the slots. Some did not qualify. Others did not want to enroll, and in some cases parents simply would not give permission. Sussex County was given a quota of thirty-nine men. The men were loaded onto public buses and sent to Newark for a physical and given their assignments.[23]

Leaving The CCC

Enrollees who were honorably discharged at the end of their term were provided with a certificate. If they deserted and failed to return after fourteen days without permission, they were said to have "gone over the hill" and dishonorably discharged. If they got into serious legal trouble or were an especially bad enrollee in terms of behavior or work habits, they were also dishonorably discharged. The desertion rate in 1939 was more than 20 percent.[24] One of the biggest reasons for desertion was homesickness. This issue was addressed in the CCC enrollee's handbook in an effort to stem the tendency. After 1940, desertions came about because enrollees thought they might be drafted directly from the CCC into the military. Other factors included the rapidly expanding economy with better job opportunities which diminished the quality of enrollees.

There is very little evidence to suggest that desertion was a major problem at High Point, probably because most of the men could get home on weekends. In 1934, there were 177 men in Company 1280, and there had been twenty-two "elopements" or desertions. That was about 12 percent, the national average, in the early years of the program. Another interesting statistic concerns honorably discharged men. In the same 1934 period, of the same seventy three men who were discharged, eleven had accepted employment and sixty-two came to the expiration of their terms.[25]

A different analysis can be made by looking at the 1934 camp inspection report for Company 216. In the period from June 1933 to April 1934, 293 men were honorably discharged, seven were dishonorably discharged and seventy-three men eloped or went "over the hill." At the time of the report sixty-six men were on forest work duty, ninety-five recruits were being reconditioned and ninety-five men came from the local community.[26] In later years, elopement figures were not included in inspection reports as the format changed so it cannot be determined if the number of elopers was rising or remained consistent at High Point.

Another way to see how the camps were doing in serving the boys is to consider re-enlistments. At Stokes State Forest, about fifty of the two hundred enrollees left the service in 1933. About half got their old private sector jobs back or got new jobs. The rest, about twenty-five, were discharged for refusal to work. In fact, a local 1933 newspaper article reported that some enrollees believed it was supposed to be "a vacation for which they would be paid."[27] For many from urban areas, the physical labor and being isolated in the outdoors proved to be too much.

At High Point, only three enrollees were dismissed during the same period and the majority in the camp expressed a desire to enroll again. The power to discharge was in the hands of army officers, and the difference may have been in the styles of leadership or management.[28] Also, the first six months of the CCC's operation at High Point, as in all camps across the nation, were a decidedly different experience than the following seven years. After the first enrollment period passed, procedures for operating camps were set up and there was a much better organization in place.

Re-enlistments at High Point occurred at a high rate in the beginning, and remained so. In October 1933, at the end of the first six month enlistment, fifty-one enrollees left, presumably to return to private sector jobs. A number of enrollees from Sussex County left the camp when a new paper mill opened in Hamburg, New Jersey. Ninety three enrollees re-enlisted for another six months.[29]

Assignments for enrollees varied, and an attractive feature of the program was the opportunity to see and work in various parts of the country, particularly in the West. Many signed up because they would be far from hot cities during the summer months. Participants were from all social-economic levels and represented all layers of the population. The common denominator was destitution and lack of employment.

Camp Administration

The administration of the CCC camps was accomplished with the dual authority of the army and either the Department of Interior (DI) or Agriculture (DA), depending on the projects. The relationship worked remarkably well. While there were occasional personality conflicts and institutional turf struggles, the leadership of both agencies completed the greatest number of conservation projects in our nation's history.

The army supervised the camp's operations, acted as paymaster and was in charge of discipline, education, recreation and record keeping. Other functions performed by the military were to accept the enrollees into service, transporting men, providing a command structure, clothing, food preparation, overseeing the mess hall, on-site recreation and medical services, including an infirmary and doctor at each camp. The army was responsible for the men when they were not working.[30]

Courtesy High Point State Park

The administration of Company 1280 in the early years of the company's existence.

Courtesy High Point State Park

Company 216's army officers and NPS personnel about 1936-1937. The man with the gloves is 1st Lt. Clyde Marion, the man next to him is Leigh Saltzman and in the lower right corner, George O'Neill. NPS foreman Melvin Gemmill is in the second row, on far right.

The role of the army in C camps was interesting because the camps were not military installations. There were no military drills, instructions, no saluting or military regulations. A contemporary newspaper account said, "They learn to respect those in authority, their fellow men and, above all, to respect the flag of their country. The aim of the CCC is not to train soldiers but to train youth in good citizenship."[31]

The army served as the purchasing agent for supplies, clothing and food. They were responsible for maintaining sanitary conditions, sending allotment checks home each month, keeping discipline and providing education and recreational programs.[32] Commanders were also required to file monthly reports to corps area leaders. Their office at High Point was located in a small building at the southern end of the camp, near the flagpole and parade grounds. Operational files were kept here and a senior enrollee generally served as company clerk.

Each camp or company was led by a commander who was responsible for the enrollees and operations, following army regulations. A large manual was prepared for each corps area that was two inches thick and dealt with details of running the camp.

Generally, a captain served as camp commander although both camps were led by lieutenants occasionally. At least one, and sometimes two, lieutenants served under the captain and were known as subalterns. Many army officers came from the reserves. A tour of duty was supposed to be six months, but that was usually extended especially in the early years. For the most part, captains and lieutenants at High Point served for a year and then moved on to the next assignment or left the service. All officers wore uniforms when on duty.

Lieutenants served as financial officers, mess officers, quartermasters and transport officers and they filled in when captains were transferred. There were often medical officers on hand as well. As in the military, officers were loved and loathed. Some came to CCC camps thinking they would make a name for themselves. Others had long service in the military and some had been in World War I. Some camp commanders were fondly remembered when they left while other's departures were barely noticed. When Maj. Richard Cooksey, the original commander at High Point left after the construction of camp facilities, he was given a pair of silver-mounted spurs and a clock.

Some officers participated in company affairs while at least one captain was remembered for his desire to be left alone. Officers tried to promote morale, and some were well-liked for their efforts to make enrollees lives easier. The company newsletters reflected this appreciation and reported on improved facilities. They used creative ways to get more equipment or clothing from the larger corps area. Capt. W.C. Halbert of Company 216, for example, worked on improving camp life and the physical appearance of the camp. Officers lived at the camp and single officers often dated local women when off duty.

In the winter of 1936, Capt. Benjamin Perricone and Lt. Scott left Company 216. Perricone was the commanding officer for three months and moved over to Company 1280. Company 216 responded to the transfer by saying, "We believe that competition will be quite keen from now on, but Company 1280 will have to do plenty to catch up with the best company in the district."[33]

Perricone had a reputation for worrying about CCC boys and trying to make their experience a good one. He personally solicited household items for the camp's buildings and for use by enrollees. His arrival and introduction to SP-1 was not particularly auspicious as Oswald Brown, the company's project superintendent, described it in his November 1935 report, in which he said: "So far, he has shown little or no disposition to cooperate with ECW personnel, but he may calm down after he has been here awhile. It makes it rather mean to have new commanding officers coming into the camp at such frequent intervals. They invariably try to rearrange the whole routine of the camp, which has been established after many experiments in trying to determine what will work the best."[34]

In Brown's next report, things had changed considerably: "The new camp commander Capt. B. Perricone, whom I mildly complained about in my last narrative report, has settled down and no one could complain of the cooperation which he has lately given us."[35] By May of 1936, Capt. Perricone was transferred to Company 1271 at Hasbrouck Heights, New Jersey. He was replaced by Russell Westerhoff, who came from the same camp.

In the first six months of operation, almost all officers in CCC camps came from the regular army including four enlisted men who were also included in each company. At the time of the CCC's organization, there were twelve thousand regular officers in the entire army, three thousand of whom were sent to the CCC camps. After 1933, the army began to call up reserve officers to run the camps. By 1936, only 3 percent of the camp's commanders were from the regular army; the rest were from the reserves.[36]

Officers brought with them a variety of life's experiences. Several of the officers were engineers, others were from the infantry reserves and even a Coast Guard warrant officer served at High Point after Navy and Marine reservists were authorized to serve in the CCC. Some had worked at other CCC camps, others were transferred to different CCC camps around the region. Captains Covert, Woyton and Hotton, and Lt. Kuhn were all transferred to other C camps after their service at High Point. A least one,

Capt. Halpert, was a professional architect and was sympathetic to the needs of NPS officials.

Several officers were promoted from their positions at High Point to more important jobs. Maj. Cooksey was promoted to supervisor of the 6th district camps of the 2nd corps area in New York City after his tour at High Point was over. Capt. Donald McGrayne, one of the officers in charge of the original advance cadre of Company 1280, became an inspector in the sub-district High Point was located in. He originally came to High Point with the rank of lieutenant. Lt. Louis Ebert went to camp S-54 at Peekskill, New York, and after a tour of duty there, resigned from active service.

One of the most interesting officers who served at High Point was Capt. Samuel Loyd. He was the son of a famous mathematical puzzle originator and his mother was a well-known actress. He attended the Clauson Point Military Academy, went to West Point Military Academy for two years and graduated from New York University in 1931.

Loyd had worked for the U.S. Engineers for seven years and for the New York Central Railroad as a surveyor for one year. He was stationed at S-54 at Peekskill, New York after having served at camps in Cornwall, New York and Hackettstown, New Jersey. He was married and had two daughters who lived in Brooklyn. His family regularly visited him at High Point.

Beginning in 1940, camps across the country were commanded by civilian officers. This was done because Congress gave full disability benefits to reserve officers, and FDR, seeing the enormous cost of such a policy, ordered the change. At High Point, Captain Loyd, who had been in the army and then placed in the reserves, was made its first civilian commander.

Another officer who was remembered by CCC boys was Lt. Gregory Keenan. It was under his command that the winter quarters at High Point were built. He was from the southern part of New Jersey and a flashy man. Florence Fuller, a member of a family long associated with the park, remembered him flying an airplane over the park so low that he could clearly be seen.[37] Keenan was host to Countess Felix VonLuckner and Capt. Julius Lauderbach when they visited High Point in November 1933. Count VonLuckner was well known for his military exploits with the Germans during World War I. Both came to High Point to inspect the facilities.[38]

The last camp commander, Capt. Louis Smith, attended public schools in New York City and went to the Ethical Culture School. He enlisted in the cavalry in 1905 and was stationed in a variety of places including Fort Slocum, New York; Hawaii, Montana, the Philippines and Japan. He was an army instructor during World War I and left the service after that.

In 1933, Smith's service resumed as a captain commanding CCC camps in the state of Tennessee and Fort Dix, Toms River, Woodbine, Branchville and Tompkins Corner, all in New Jersey. He served until 1936. In 1940, he returned to the CCC and became camp commander at High Point. In intervening periods he had also been a police officer and a guard.

The relationship between enrollees and officers was formal and the army officers reflected the overall desire of the CCC program to create hard-working and moral citizens of these young men. Their missives in company newsletters reflect their efforts to instill in the CCC boys the highest moral values. There was no fraternization between officers and enrollees. In interviews for this book, former enrollees remembered run-ins with officers that diminished their chances of being transferred to camps out West, and some were discharged.

Technical Services

Technical Services, which included supervisors from the Department of Interior or Department of Agriculture, were responsible for the men during working hours. To the enrollees, they were teachers and counselors and worked side by side with them. Technical services undertook the planning and oversight of conservation projects. In all, 2,106 camps in 1936 came under Department of Agriculture and

Peter Osborne

690 under the Department of Interior. In 1937, 20 percent of the camps were engaged in work on park areas, 46 percent on forestry projects, 23 percent on erosion control and farm drainage and 10 percent on grazing work. Because High Point was a state park, the work projects came under the jurisdiction of the Department of Interior's National Park Service and its State Park Division.

The Department of Interior provided the equipment to conduct work projects. This included not only picks and shovels but dump trucks, bulldozers and a steam shovel. During the first year of operation at High Point, the acquiring of equipment for work projects was made difficult by the fact there simply was not enough equipment.

We Can Take It!

Courtesy High Point State Park

NPS equipment had special license plates designating they were owned by the CCC. On the front of this bulldozer, which is pulling part of a stone crusher, is a license plate which reads USCCC 80936 Department of the Interior.

There was no central NPS warehouse where equipment could be found, and some equipment like shovels and tractors came from the army. Supplies for the work projects also had to be scavenged. At least one CCC camp commander was told where to find grass seed and soon a memo went out telling what federal agency had a storehouse of surplus grass seed.

Initially, NPS officials could only encourage local camp officials to rent or borrow trucks because they were in short supply, and it was not known if the CCC was going to be a long-term project or not. Another problem especially in the early months at High Point was acquiring license plates for the new vehicles. As state and NPS officials debated whether state or federal license plates should be used, trucks necessary for the hauling of shale sat idle.

Some items were obtained in time. In 1934, there was a 1.5 ton Chevrolet pickup truck and eight 1.5 ton Chevrolet stake body trucks available for Company 216. By 1937, there were thirteen trucks at the camp. Eight were in good condition and five were in fair condition according to an inspection report. The army generally had two trucks on hand for its use. In the first year, the NPS rented a gas-powered shovel for Company 1280 to use.

The Technical Services staff included a project superintendent, assistant project superintendent, designers and foremen. The project superintendent was in charge of the work project. In later years, an assistant project superintendent was appointed. There were a varying number of designers and foremen, all considered temporary employees of the NPS even though many served for a number of years. All were paid with CCC funds administered by the army.[39] Designers created plans for projects including working drawings, construction lists and final reports to regional inspectors. It was the foremen's responsibility to oversee projects, to be sure they were kept on budget, to provide job training and to be sure safety rules were enforced.

Their office was at the western side of the entrance to the camp. It was a small building divided into three rooms and a small storage area. One room served as an office for the project superintendent, another as a drafting room and the third as a room for the clerk, who came from the ranks of enrollees. The clerk served as a secretary, answered the phones, dealt with the mail, did the company newsletter and kept track of daily temperatures. He served at the superintendent's pleasure.[40]

The superintendent's pay was $225 per month and the foremen earned between $150 and $170 per month which increased with their rating. Mechanics were paid $120 per month. The position of superintendent was an important one and often obtained through political connections. By and large, superintendents were well qualified for their jobs and were responsible for all of the required reports including a monthly work progress report sent to regional and national headquarters.

The reports contained data on the camp's operation, weather problems and general news including complaints about operational matters and problems with army officers. Curiously, the reports are not based on expenditures of funds, but rather developed in terms of man-hours and man-days spent on projects.

Foremen were evaluated for work performance and had to file project reports monthly.[41] They were also required to keep time books in which they recorded the hours worked by enrollees, what the tasks were and what training was received. They turned in time sheets each day. Foremen were given a book called *CCC Foremanship* which provided a wealth of information about their jobs. It included a job overview, methods for accomplishing their tasks, tips and even likely scenarios foreman might encounter.

The most significant NPS official at High Point during the CCC-era was Melvin Gemmill. He came to the park in 1933 as a foreman on a field crew and worked his way into the design office. He became the camp superintendent of Company 1280 in 1939. He was a graduate of Penn State University, and most of the projects built at High Point were designed by him and constructed to blend in with the natural features of the park.[42]

Many of his drawings done in a beautiful hand remain in the park's archives. His most significant contribution was the master plan for the park. He was a talented photographer and owned one of the premier cameras of the day, a Leica. His brother, R. M. Gemmell, worked at the CCC camp in Vorhees State Park in High Bridge, New Jersey. R. M. Gemmell's drawings of park projects are just as beautifully done as his brother's. He died in 2000.

For the first six years of Camp SP-8's existence, Howard Platt served as the camp's project superintendent and was said to be an authority on railroad bridges.[43] He was originally from Jersey City, New Jersey, but lived in Colesville, New Jersey, and commuted to the camp every day. He was married and had a daughter.[44] He arrived in the camp early on and was responsible for some of the biggest projects including Sawmill Lake and Steenykill Dam.

Oswald Brown served as project superintendent for Company 216 at Camp SP-1 for the entire time of its existence (1933-1937) and was considered to be the senior superintendent. Little else is known about him except he was a federal forestry official and was well regarded by the men in both camps and somewhat aloof.

Designers were often brought in on a short-term basis to work on specific projects like landscaping or in the case of the two dams to design the complex structures. Most served for a year or two, or as in the case of Eric Flemming just the fall of 1933 when he created the initial drawing of High Point State Park that was the basis for future planning and provided an inventory of what was already there. At least two foremen were promoted into the design office.

Foremen were classified as either landscape or cultural foremen, landscape foremen being graduate landscape architects. The foremen came to the National Park Service from a variety of backgrounds and probably had some political connections as well. For example, Albert Mastriani had completed two years of engineering school before he arrived at High

Point. H. W. Lewis, who was an older man and one of the original foremen, became too sick to work and was taken by ambulance to New York City.

Frank Clark was an excellent craftsman from Highland, New York. Larry Jones was the principal dynamite man from Snowhill, Maryland, and Herman Hornecker was an expert tree surgeon. Charles Henkle was a former surveyor for the Erie Railroad. He was remembered for the unusual habit of eating out of cans and throwing the cans out the window of his room.[45]

John Bowblis, a popular foremen among the enrollees, taught elementary photography. Enrollees who worked for Morrie Atkin's crew called themselves the "Atkins Chain Gang" because they were assigned the task of breaking up shale at the pit by hand. Of the men who worked for Oliver Wells, it was said that they were the "WAW's" - "Wells Ass Wipes." Raymond Evans was a landscape architect from Massachusetts and a graduate of Massachusetts State College. He had worked in other CCC camps.

Several foremen were transferred to other C camps temporarily to undertake new or short-term assignments including Theodore "Tommy" Turner and Albert Mastriani. Mastriani was sent to Orange, New Jersey to work at the South Mountain Reservation. He returned several months later. Tommy Turner was reassigned to

Camp SP-5 at High Bridge, New Jersey in 1939. In his place arrived Frank Clark who worked at SP-12 in Alpine, Englewood Cliffs, New Jersey where he was the camp carpenter.

Herman Hornecker was transferred from SP-7 at Orange, New Jersey to High Point and Arthur Parker was transferred from High Point to the Mohawk Trail camp in Massachusetts. At least two foremen were transferred between companies including Charles Henkel and Oliver Well who both started in 216 and were then assigned to 1280. Emmett Paige, a designer at High Point from 1935-1936 worked for the Public Roads Administration after his tour of duty.

Frank X. Clark, a NPS foreman, is typical of the kind of men who worked for the NPS during the CCC era and Albert Mastriani wrote: "Frank X. Clark was a foreman who came on board about 1938. He had a daughter who worked for the U.S. government in Washington D.C., who was about my age, so it figures that he was old enough to be my father. As I noted before, he was an excellent craftsman in both stone and wood and was a great teacher for the enrollees. In his spare time, with the help of the men, he built a wonderful alter in the Camp Meeting Hall.

"He had a habit of needling Mr. [Howard] Platt by taking out a notebook whenever he was given any instructions and copying them down. This was his way of backing himself up in case of a dispute."[46]

Nicholas Hanisak, an enrollee who served as a clerk in the Technical Services offices from 1939 until the camp closed in 1941, remembered Clark's background which reflects not only on the important kinds of projects that he had worked on but also his political connections which reached the highest levels. He said: "Frank X. Clark worked on some of the buildings at West Point ... He was from that area ... He was a friend of Roosevelt's postmaster general, James Farley ... Somebody told me when Frank Clark came up there [High Point] he took one look at the place and said, 'Oh My God, this forsaken place, this God forsaken place.' He wired, I understood, James Farley's office and said 'Get me out of here get me out of this God forsaken place.' Well maybe less than a week or so Farley, Roosevelt and the rest of the gang went out to Africa or one of those safaris, drinking parties. So it was a couple months by the time Farley gets back to the office ... Frank wired him back, 'Cancel that, I like it up here.'"47

After leaving the NPS and overseeing the CCC projects at High Point, the foremen went on to other work. Melvin Gemmell became a prolific illustrator and Albert Mastriani became a consulting civil engineer working in his profession until well into his eighties. Mastriani, who was at High Point for almost the entire time SP-8 was in existence, remembered the life of a typical foreman:

We Can Take It!

"As for the foremen, many of them already had families before coming to High Point and established residences in Port Jervis, Sussex and Milford. Some, however, left their families where they were and went home weekends. Most of them had cars. I did not start off with one. Our week was similar to the enrollees as far as work was concerned. At first I spent many evenings in the rec hall with the enrollees playing table tennis and trying to play pool. I could beat them at ping-pong but they beat me at pool.

"We took turns at weekend duties in the event an emergency arose, such as a forest fire. I finally bought a car in the spring of 1934, a 1930 Ford Model A. The foremen who were single, and maybe even some married ones, attended affairs in Port Jervis such as dances and church dinners, and being a young, single man myself, began to do some dating.

"One place where they held dances was the Village Barn [at 162 Ball Street in Port Jervis]. I suspect after all this time it has been demolished. My friend Mel [Gemmill] met a beautiful girl in PJ whom he married and they are still together after sixty-five years."[48]

While enrollees from both companies do not appear to have intermingled, foremen did associate with each other and ate in the same dining room.[49] Army officers and NPS supervisors who were single, or whose families were elsewhere, lived full time at the camp in the officer's quarters.

The relationship between army officers and the NPS employees was congenial but separate as NPS employees did not work under the command of the army. In the early years, there was some fraternization between them but after many of the foremen got married or moved into surrounding communities, there was little contact between them except during the day.[50]

While foremen and C boys did not fraternize, it is interesting to note that, when interviewed, many enrollees referred to the foremen as rangers even though that position was actually held by permanent NPS employee in the field. The reason they may have seen them as rangers is that after the initial organization of the CCC, foremen were required to wear a uniform that was olive gray in color, included long pants or breeches and a campaign hat.[51]

Enrollee Leadership

Among enrollees there was a system of authority that facilitated the leadership of the army and National Park Service. The system began in June 1933. If a young man showed promise he was promoted or "rated." Under CCC regulations, for a company of two hundred, there were ten leaders and sixteen assistant leaders. Eight leaders were assigned to the army and eighteen were assigned to technical services. These leaders saw that orders were obeyed, were in charge of discipline in the barracks and served in a leadership capacity on work projects.[52]

Leaders received $45 per month and assistant leaders received $36 per month. The appointment of leaders was made by the company commander and leaders for work projects were advanced on the advice of the project superintendent.[53] The senior leader was the highest ranking enrollee in camp. Uniforms of enrollees who had been rated included insignia patches on their shoulders representing their position which might be 1st or 2nd cook, baker, mechanic, company clerk or medical assistant. Each patch had its own unique symbol. The baker's patch, for example, was a rolling pin while the cook's patch had a large kettle.

From the few remaining records at High Point, it can be determined there was a smaller number of leaders, perhaps reflecting a company not at full strength or a commander's discretion. For example, enrollees were sent to army schools for cooking and baking. Cooks, second cooks, orderlies, mess stewards, clerks, truck drivers and assistant educational advisors all were chosen from the enrollees. Once trained, cooks were in demand in the private sector and the CCC had a hard time keeping them on the staff.

Enrollees could be promoted to the position of "Junior Assistant Technician" which brought an increase in salary to $85 per month. The promotion came as a result of consultation between officials of the Departments of Agriculture and Interior and army officers. Additional promotions were possible beyond that.

By The Numbers

The CCC kept voluminous records and from those documents a more complete history of the agency can be gleaned. President Roosevelt loved to meet with CCC director Robert Fechner and discuss what was going on in his conservation organization. For CCC officials, reports quantified what was being done as a permanent record but also as a tool in promoting the organization with the public. From the work progress, camp inspection and superintendent's reports, one can follow in great detail what was happening in the camps. The camp at High Point was typical in the statistics compiled about it.

The two companies at High Point never reached the maximum of two hundred enrollees per company consistently. Most of the time they were well below maximum strength. In the last year of Company's 1280's existence, the number of enrollees dwindled to a point where the camp could not be sustained. In the final report of Company 216, Oswald Brown, who was required to keep a running total of the man-days, was able to show enrollees had worked 26,138 man days from June 1933 until June 1937.[54]

Typically, monthly reports provided a detailed accounting of the men's time. By June 1937, men from Company 216 building the Appalachian Trail shelters used 314 man-days to do it. In the same report they spent 2,885 man-days building 5,349 feet of guard rails, spent 384 man days building twenty-three table and bench combinations and 258 days building eight camp fireplaces.[55]

Company 1280's records are equally detailed. In the June 1937 report, the superintendent calculated the company used 10,664 cubic yards of fill for dam projects and 2,350 man-days were expended. Six hundred and forty man-days had been expended building twenty-one seats on the Sawmill Lake beach, sixty-one man days were taken up with fire fighting and 106 man-days used searching for and rescuing lost persons. By June 1937, enrollees from 1280 worked 26,433 man-days for the year.[56]

After setting up permanent quarters, on average, about 70 percent of the men of a company worked on various forestry and construction projects and about 20 percent worked in the camp. About 10 percent were either sick, on detached duty or away without leave or away on leave. When those numbers fell out of the prescribed range, there were questions from corps officials.

In April 1934, for example, Company 216 had only sixty-six men available to undertake forest work while thirty-nine were assigned to camp duty. In addition, ninety-five recruits were being reconditioned for active service. A little more than a month later, James McEntee inquired of the army why so many men were assigned to camp duty. Lt. J. King Wallace apparently provided an answer that did not wholly satisfy McEntee.[57]

The following table illustrates how a typical camp staff was deployed. The data comes from various camp inspection reports from both companies.

Year	Total Co. 216	LEM's	Camp Duty	Project Duty	Total Co. 1280	LEM's	Camp Duty	Project Duty
1933	192		90	101	184	7	29	109
1934	200		39	66	177	16	29	145
1936	157	11	21	129				
1937	126	12	23	99	118	8	22	91
1941	—	—	—	—	96		24	42

Camp Inspections & Problems

Among the reports that are in the National Archives are yearly inspection reports, filed by a high ranking official from the CCC who gave each camp across the country a thorough review of its operations. This review included paperwork, salaries of foremen and superintendents, the camp's health and safety programs, food menus and costs, work projects, enrollee complaints, morale and an analysis of how enrollees were being used.

It is known that James McEntee and Robert Fechner made at least one unannounced inspection at High Point and were gone before NPS officials knew they were there. Charles Kenlon, a special investigator for the CCC, also made several unannounced inspections of the camp. At least one representative of the German government, Major von Wrenchstern, an officer in the German army who was in charge of the youth camps in his country, inspected the camp in the fall of 1935 to study its management. This is particularly interesting because the Germans already had a form of a youth work program in place. It was compulsory and the next step before military training.[58] He was accompanied on his trip by Captain Donald McGrayne who was then commanding a veteran's camp in Morristown, New Jersey, after being commander of 1280 at High Point.

On the whole, Company 216 seems to have been the better managed of the companies on the administrative side. There appears to have been no major problems during its four years of existence. Other than complaints about the frequent changes of commanders and a rare complaint by an enrollee, inspection reports reveal a well-run company. However, both companies went through cycles where they rated high and then regressed. The factors in these shifts may be attributed to the type of enrollees at different times and also the quality of the army officers.

Inspection reports and other data also reveal there were people who abused their positions or were subjected to abuse. In Company 1280 there were more problems at the army and administrative levels than in Company 216. For example, in one three-year period, there were six different officers in command. During that period, 1280 was at the bottom of the rankings in the sub-district. The command at 216 was much more stable after the initial organization of the company.

After Company 216 closed in 1937, 1st. Lt. Clyde Marion was transferred to command Company 1280. According to the inspection report, the intense rivalry between the two camps did not make his transfer a happy one, and within a short time, he was relieved of his command and discharged. He was a veteran of World War I having served in France and Germany. Marion served longer than any of the other army officers at High Point, having been stationed there for three years. He served at two other CCC camps as well. In both camps he uncovered "dishonest grafting" by camp officials.[59]

From the moment he arrived at Company 1280, there were problems. Project superintendent Howard Platt made what Marion called "exceedingly unjust charges" against enrollees and while a trial was held to resolve the charges as per CCC regulations, they were not proved to Marion's satisfaction. In a letter he wrote to Charles Kenlan at the Office of the Director of the CCC, Marion discussed several encounters with Howard Platt including one instance where Kenlan, who was on an inspection trip of the camp, ordered Marion to have trucks stopped because of the poor condition of the tires and the shape of the men's uniforms. Platt was obviously upset at being upbraided in front of a CCC inspector and blamed Marion for it. Platt was also infuriated with a former designer at 1280, Edwin Taubert, a corps inspector who was also there.[60]

Not long after, Marion became concerned with the number of accidents occurring in the field in Company 1280. He inspected their job site finding at least one man operating a stone crusher who should have been on medical leave. Again Platt angrily protested Marion's involvement. Marion also submitted testimony from three different cases Platt brought against enrollees. In all three cases it is apparent Platt could be an extremely difficult man to work for and in some cases treated enrollees with total disregard for their physical well being.[61]

Not long after, Marion received orders continuing his active duty for a year. Several days later, he learned he would be relieved of his command instead. While some correspondence in the inspection files indicate he was not liked by officials higher in the Army's command, the poisoned relationship between him and Platt may have had some bearing on his dismissal. No reasons were given for his discharge.

Lt. Marion was succeed by Capt. Harry Ryskind who had been a junior officer in a veterans CCC camp in Rahway, New Jersey. In 1937, Ryskind was relieved of his command of Company 1280 when he was charged with misusing camp funds. A report said he "spent too much time around the office and let too much rest with his mess sergeant and did not give due attention to his work and reports. Investigation revealed mess funds and other funds were not properly checked."[62]

An additional comment by the inspector said Ryskind "did not handle mess funds properly and ran the camp into a financial hole."[63] While Ryskind was never charged with fraud, he faced a trial, and it was thought that he would lose his commission. The outcome of the trial is not known.

In 1939, Howard Platt was relieved of his duties after he stole government property. He wrote off a vehicle from the camp's inventory, but enrollees restored it to working order. His relationships with people he worked with had always been troubled and strained. In this case, James McEntee personally intervened as he investigated the case and met with other camp personnel and then dismissed Platt.[64]

CHAPTER 3

Life At Camp Kuser

The Civilian Conservation Corps had a triple value: it gave the boys a chance to see different parts of their own country, and to learn to do a good day's work in the open, which benefitted them physically; also, it gave them a cash income, part of which went home to their families. This helped the morale both of the boys themselves and of the people at home.

-Eleanor Roosevelt

This I Remember

Men of the Civilian Conservation Corps, I think of you as a visible token of encouragement to the whole country. You - nearly three hundred thousand strong - are evidence that the nation is still strong enough and broad enough to look after its citizens.
-President Franklin D. Roosevelt, July 17, 1933

The Tree Army: A Pictorial History of the Civilian Conservation Corps, 1933-1942

The camp at High Point was initially known as New Jersey No. 2 or CCC Camp No. 2. During the first week of June 1933, Charles P. Wilber, the state forester, and John Stanton, the executive secretary of the High Point Park Commission, scouted out the list of potential locations for a camp to be used by the company at High Point and one from Stokes State Forest in Branchville, New Jersey.[1]

In previous weeks, consideration had been given to the Lusscroft Farms where the North Branch Experiment Station in Beemerville was located. The station, which became a world famous dairy research center, was donated to the state of New Jersey in 1931 by James Turner, a New York stockbroker. Turner acquired four smaller farms and created a large eleven hundred acre farm.[2]

The Tent Camp At Lusscroft Farm

A final decision was made to go to Lusscroft because the federal government preferred to use publicly-owned lands rather than private property. The camp was located on what is now a former 4H camp on Neilson Road in Wantage Township. It is believed the tented camp was in a large open field east of the main road. The men could then be transported easily in trucks to the forest and the park.

An advance cadre of about twenty-five men and army officers arrived, and by June 9, 1933, a tented camp was being set up.³ In all, there were thirty-six large tents on the site and the camp was completely finished by July 17, 1933.⁴ A group of 167 young men soon joined the "reforestation army," as it was called in a contemporary newspaper account. The men were brought from Fort Dix in Wrightstown, coming from urban areas including Newark, North Arlington, Jersey City, Camden, Trenton and Hoboken. They were the original members of Company 216.

Company 1280, also made up of New Jersey boys, was formed in June 1933 and they were sent to work in a privately owned forest (P-211) near Elk River, Idaho, performing blister rust control work.⁵ It was not uncommon for government workers to assist private forest owners because fire, insects and diseases knew no boundary lines. Cooperative agreements with private landowners were common at the time and the basis for which the CCC went into such areas.⁶

Company 1280's mission in Idaho was similar to many other companies. However private landowners were severely criticized by Rodney Brink, the editor of a newspaper in the state. In June 1933, around the time of 1280's arrival in Idaho, Brink wrote a letter to FDR complaining that the work being done was to benefit large timber interests under the guise of building fire trails and scenic roads. The work was done with full approval of Forest Service employees. It is not clear how this was resolved, but work continued as more than twenty-five thousand men were sent to Idaho.[7]

After that work project was completed, the company was divided up with most of the men going to Fort Lewis. Only eight men returned to Camp Dix, where they were joined by seventeen others. The newly reconstituted Company 1280 arrived at the Lusscroft farm on October 30,1933, to prepare for arrival of the remainder of the company which was being organized.

It must have been difficult for army officers and NPS officials to get the work projects organized. There had never been anything like the CCC, and the the remarkably successful organizational structure that was the hallmark of the CCC in later years was not yet developed. The camps were usually placed in open fields which exposed them to the elements and made for difficult living arrangements for many of the men who came from urban environments. In one of the earliest official reports, SP-1, Company 216 Superintendent Oswald Brown noted there were minor revolts early on and that better clothing, food and quarters alleviated many of the morale problems of the first months of the CCC at High Point.[8]

The camp was initially commanded by Major Richard Cooksey of New York City and his first lieutenant was E. A. Merkle, who was a regular army instructor at Fordham University. Meals were served in military style, and a first aid and hospital tent was constructed to attend to medical needs.[9]

In the early weeks, plans were being made for forestry projects under the direction of Oswald Brown, who was a federal forestry official. He created a list of timberlands to be cleared, repaired and replanted in the vicinity of the camp and in the state park. Enrollees began clearing a parking area for trucks and a new drainage system for the camp area.

As winter approached, Robert Fechner selected winter quarters for sixty-seven camps across the country. By the early fall of 1933, CCC and NPS officials were looking for a permanent site at High Point to create winter headquarters for Company 216 and for a company from New York State.[10] The new facility would replace the tented camp at Lusscroft which would not be suitable for the harsh winters. A small detachment of surveyors and engineers scouted and then laid out the site.[11] The site was leveled, and was bisected by present-day Cedar Swamp Drive (then known as Laurel Drive). The road was improved and came to be called Company Street.

The Construction Of CCC Camp No. 2

Construction of the permanent camp began in the first week of October 1933 under the direction of lieutenants Gregory F. Keenan and Donald McGrayne. The plans were of a standard design and created by the army. The camp was built by local private contractors as was done at other camps. On December 8, 1933, the construction of CCC Camp No. 2 was completed.[12] While the National Park Service extensively documented its work at High Point, the construction of the two camps was overseen by the army, and there are no known surviving pictures of the construction of the camp.

The thirty-six tents on the Lusscroft site were taken down, and the first CCC camp at High Point was closed. During the first week of December 1933, enrollees moved into permanent headquarters at the park.[13] At some point, it was decided Company 1280 would also be moved to the new camp, and there was no more discussions of bringing in a company from either New York or Stokes. Company 1280, now at full strength, moved into its new quarters and reported for their first day of work on December 4, 1933.[14] At the same time, a fleet of twenty Ford trucks arrived via railroad at Branchville for use at High Point and Stokes State Forest.[15]

After the C boys left Lusscroft, participants in the Civil Works Administration (CWA) moved into the Lusscroft site to undertake an experimental farm project. The CWA was created for unemployed men to work in various municipal projects across the country.[16] This camp was closed in the summer of 1934 because the transient nature of the enrollees caused difficulties locally.

Why the permanent site for the CCC camp was chosen is not known, but a number of issues were considered. Foremost was accessibility. A road system was already in place at that location and most of the park's facilities were centered around Lake Marcia. The camp's administration was close to the park's administrative buildings where efforts were coordinated between the two organizations.

The need for an adequate water source was important, and Lake Marcia fit the bill. A wooden aqueduct was constructed from the lake into the camp. The state park drilled a 112-foot deep well for the camp's use.[17] The camp's chlorinated water system was regularly checked by army officers who sent the water samples to the army's testing facilities in New York City.

The CCC camp was appropriately called "Camp Kuser" in honor of Col. Anthony Kuser and his wife Susie Dryden Kuser, who donated the park area to the State of New Jersey a decade before. The camp was known by this name early on but it did not achieve widespread acceptance. A substantial and large gateway with the name emblazoned on it was constructed over the front entrance at the southern end of the camp. In fact, there is no mention of the name in later years although the name was on the gateway as late as 1937. After 1937 the sign simply read "United States Civilian Conservation Corps." While none of the enrollees interviewed for this book could remember the Kuser's name being used, most remembered the generosity of the man.

Courtesy High Point State Park

A large gateway was constructed at the entrance to the camp on Cedar Swamp Drive that designated it as CCC Camp 2, the second camp created in the state. Here, Ernie, Bud and Hurd stand under the sign with the view looking down Company Street.

The camp was more usually described as SP-1 or SP-8 and even the license plates of the army trucks used a designation that had on its first line USCCC, on the second line the plate number and on the third line Department of Interior. Included in the upper left corner was the CCC logo.

Camp Kuser was a "double camp" which meant it was designed to house between four hundred and fifty and five hundred men and was divided into two divisions, known as Camp 2A or Kuser "A" and Camp 2B or Kuser "B." Company 216's facilities were on the eastern side of Company Street and Company 1280's facilities were on the western side. Altogether there were twenty-six buildings, ten sixty-man barracks, two 275-man mess halls, two shower rooms, two infirmaries, two storehouses, a large recreation hall where there was an enormous fireplace and a headquarters for each company and two officers' quarters. The officers' quarters had nine private rooms for the army officers and technical services employees.[18] As time passed, enrollees improved the appearance of the camp lining the sidewalks with rocks, placing garbage cans along walkways and maintaining the grounds immaculately.

The camp's electricity was first provided by a generator unit located near Cedar Swamp, but a central service was ultimately installed by a local utility company. The camp had two telephone systems. One was internal which went to all major buildings like the recreation hall, mess hall, infirmary and offices. The second went outside via a multi-party rural line. The outside line was not installed until 1934 and the camp's phone number was Sussex 22-F-187. There was a centrally located latrine which serviced more than four hundred men at its peak of operation. The waste was processed through a chlorinator that dumped effluent over the western bank of the camp. An incinerator was used to burn garbage and was operated by enrollees. It was located in the former shale quarry just off of New Jersey State Route 23 and demolished several years ago. All that remains is the concrete foundation.

The recreation hall, or as it was known then, the "rec hall," included a large open fireplace and each company had a room for its headquarters.[19] Here men could spend their leisure time and particpate in a variety of activities including pool, ping-pong and cards. The CCC enrollee's handbook referred to it as the CCC Man's Club. Another building was set aside for movies, religious services and educational programs.[20]

There was a canteen where things like cigarettes, ice cream, soft drinks, candy and toiletries could be bought at certain hours. Post cards of the camp were also sold. Some canteens even had matchbooks with the company number on them. Profits from sales were used to buy sports equipment, magazines, and to make repairs to items like the pool tables. The canteen was overseen by an officer, but an enrollee ran it.

Enrollees could also purchase scrapbooks entitled "*My CCC History*" to record their time in camp. It included a short history of the CCC, humorous comic strips about the organization, the men and "*Kodak Snaps*" where pictures could be mounted. Group photographs of the camp and company were sold that featured enrollees, exterior building shots, interior shots and a listing of the men. At least one of those survives from High Point for 1940.

Induction Into The CCC

Enrollees today have different recollections about what happened to them after they signed up at a centrally located government building in their hometowns. Some remembered being taken directly to High Point while other references say that enrollees were sent to Fort Dix where they spent a week receiving conditioning training. Some said they anxiously expected to go to the West, only to find they were to be stationed in New Jersey, a short bus or train trip from home.

Enrollee Neil Thiede recalled how he wound up at High Point:

"So it was in the fall of '36 I went down to the armory in Paterson and they were enlisting or enrolling a bunch of new enrollees for High Point. We were there a good part of the day in the armory. I can still remember the ride up to High Point. They had these, what they called stake body trucks, long flat body with stakes on the side. They had tarpaulin over and benches inside, and we had that ride, and I think that it was getting dark ... I guess it was October or November, I don't remember exactly.

"But they stopped at that diner, and it's still there on [Route] 23 just before you make the turn to the left to go up to High Point. We stopped there. I don't think I had any money. I don't think I went in. But we got up to the camp in the dark, and they processed us ... we had been physically processed in Paterson, but they took us through the supply house and threw a lot of clothing at us, and I don't remember if we ate anything or not. I guess not. I don't remember that but that was the beginning of it."[21]

At least one enrollee, William DeGhetto, remembered how he got to High Point after he signed up. He said: "I got on a bus and ... we go on up the old Route 23. The old Hamburg Turnpike. I said ... we should be going to Warwick if we're going to get on the train to go out West. First stop, Butler. It was a camp right off Route 23. So many guys got off the bus. You, you, you, you and you, whoever came out of the camp, so many went there. The next stop was Branchville, and me and about twenty other guys were left on the bus and we ended up here at High Point."[22]

Another enrollee, Frank Seddio, remembered his bus trip as a little more exciting when he said: "Well we got up here, [High Point], naturally we enjoyed the scenery getting up here, but when we got up to the mountain, the bottom of the mountain, we wondered how the heck we were going to get up the mountain. But then eventually the bus couldn't make it so we had to get out and walk and eventually the bus made it to the top of the mountain."[23]

We Can Take It!

Upon arrival at High Point, usually by bus, the "rookies" as new enrollees were called were given a meal and then met with the camp's administration. The commanding officer made a presentation on camp policies and life and Melvin Gemmill made a presentation on safety procedures. The education advisor gave an overview of the library and the availability of educational courses in camp. Introductions were made to leaders and assistant leaders, and the next day, enrollees began their assignments.

They made a stop at the infirmary and were given a booklet entitled *Your CCC: A Handbook for Enrollees* which provided them with information on how to carry out duties and obligations and how to benefit from their stay at the camp. They were issued a shaving kit, soap, soap dish, toothpaste, toothbrush, safety razor and sewing kit. Clothing issue included socks, underwear, overcoat, cap, work clothing and a uniform. The work outfit was blue denim, and the uniform until 1939, was light khaki, similar to World War I military issue. After 1939, the CCC designed its own uniform which was spruce green with black shoes. When clothing became worn out, replacements were issued. Upon leaving the CCC, enrollees were given the clothing they needed for "immediate use."[24]

Rookies were the subject of occasional pranks like being sent to the High Point monument with coal for night guard duty. Some were ordered to stand at the monument and wait for an air-mail delivery. They were told it was dropped from a plane. Rookies were often given a tour of K.P. duty for a week at a time.

Rules And Regulations

The following rules were posted, and enrollees were expected to follow them:

In the Barracks

Beds must be made each morning; aired on Wednesdays. The floors and lockers must be kept clean. Obey your leaders. Each man is expected to do his share in helping to make the barracks a fit place to live in. All fire equipment must be kept in its place and kept clean. Lights will be put out at 10:00 p.m. sharp. One window at each end of the barracks will be kept open at all times.

On the Job

We rise in time to be washed, have our barracks cleaned and beds made and be on line in time for reveille at 6:53 a.m. except Sundays and Saturdays when there is no work. O. D. clothes will not be worn out on the job - denims are provided. Men improperly dressed or late for work are AWOL.

Rules and regulations laid down by the Superintendent, the Foremen or your strawbosses will be closely followed.

Relations with the Staff

Always address Officers, Foremen, Superintendent, Education Advisor and Leaders as "SIR."

Always report when addressing an Officer. When an Officer enters a barracks or other building, the man who first sees the Officer will call "Attention." All men in the building will then rise and stand at attention wherever they are until the Officer says "Rest."[25]

Men were required to wear uniforms at special formations and when away from camp. Photographs from the High Point archives show men did not always wear denims, but sometimes, civilian clothes. On at least one occasion, there was an inspection by a district official who cited camp officials for enrollees wearing dress uniforms to work. This seems to indicate clothing regulations were not always enforced by army officials.

Overall, discipline was not a major problem in the camp, partly because of the difficulty of getting a job on the outside and the presence of army officers. There were dismissals to be sure, but there were not some of the major disciplinary problems that did occur in other camps across the county. Albert Mastriani recalled that: "As I remember, there were very few disciplinary problems. Only one time did I have to bring anyone in from the field for refusing to work. The punishment was meted out by the army personnel but, I forget what it was now."[26]

One of the most important goals of the CCC was to develop character, good physical habits and citizenship in its enrollees. Charles Wilber, the state forester, said: "The development of young men and boys of this nation into the physical timber so necessary in the building of good citizenship is without a doubt of great importance. The building of these boys into men of good physique is inspiring if you follow them from their entrance into camp, hardly able to do a full day's work, to the men they finally become after a stay in the open, eating wholesome food and getting proper exercise. They are preparing themselves for the future to give dollar for dollar to their employer and able to cope with the best. The Civilian Conservation Corps is making a richer nation in respect to manpower and building the finer characteristics to enter human society."[27]

Newton LeFevre, an enrollee, wrote in a Company 1280 newsletter in February 1938: "Your government has established your camp to help you and your family. You are off the streets, you are eating good food, you have body-building work to do, you are feeling better than ever. Your government is helping you through the lean years and keeping you fit through your early manhood so that you will be able to fight the battle of life during the normal years to come."[28]

Company newsletters also promoted clean living and high standards. The following appeared under the title of "This Spicy-Snappy Stuff;"

"Would you eat mud? Would you sleep in a gilded puddle? Would you be satisfied to wear clothing that is all spotted and soiled? ... NO. You think more of keeping your body clean.

"What about your mind, your thoughts, the very center of your being, the real inside you? Do you keep that clean too? Think it over. Soiled thoughts and dirty habits of mind are just as unpleasant and just as repugnant to others, as any other kind of filth.

"There is too much thrilling, inspiring and instructive good reading in the world for any man to spend time reading such trash as Spicy This and Snappy That, but the Quintessence of Poisonous Tripe is the sensationalized detective story."[29]

On bad language, the following missive was issued: "From time to time, as one goes through camp, he hears foul and vulgar language freely used. There is a tendency to encourage, indulge and approve of that kind of talk on several counts. The most outstanding reason is that we think it manly, masculine, or regular to 'swear.' Think it over, men, and you will all agree that such reasoning is blundering and stupid. Why should the CCC lad be distinguished from other groups by his ugly language? If for no other reason than because of the monotony of its use, we should work towards the hasty elimination of the 'common patter.'

"Let us give consideration to the quotation from Shakespeare: 'Mend your speech a little, let it not mar your fortunes.'"[30]

The men at High Point learned valuable lessons they might not have been exposed to ordinarily. They learned to live in the company of men, how to live by a set of rules and schedules, how to take care of themselves and their equipment and how to obey orders. Many men came to the CCC undernourished. Work, exercise, army food and work in the outdoors brought their physical toughness and mental alertness back. It was believed their time in the CCC was worth a year of military training.[31]

Many quickly became homesick because they had never been away from home, and many missed the various attractions and forms of entertainment so accessible to them before they signed up. Men who had never seen livestock were being exposed to chickens and cows for the first time and outdoor living and were unaccustomed to sleeping in tents or building roads or cutting fire breaks.

A contemporary newspaper account suggested for the first time in American history city boys and country boys were interacting in a way that had never happened before.³² That seems to be an overstatement considering the huge numbers of men who served in both the Civil War (1861-1865) and World War I (1917-1919). However, it was probably correct in terms of our nation's peacetime history.

A Day In The CCC

A typical day at High Point saw men rise early at 6 a.m. After a meal, a barracks inspection was done. Some enrollees remembered doing calisthenics outdoors, weather permitting, for about fifteen minutes before heading off to work. If the weather was bad, the exercises were done indoors.

After breakfast a work whistle blew, and the men reported to the Department of Interior garages which were at the far northern end of the camp. They boarded their assigned trucks and proceeded to the field under the direction of the foremen. The rest of the day was taken up with "work, good hard work, solid work, work that produces twice, building up the objects worked on and the person doing the work" as a local newspaper account said.³³

Courtesy High Point State Park
Enrollees gathered in front of the DI garages every morning for work assignments.

NPS foreman Albert Mastriani, remembered a typical day for an enrollee: "The enrollees worked from 8:00 a.m. to 4:00 p.m. every day, Monday through Friday, unless there was inclement weather in which case we worked on Saturday to make up the time lost during the week. Noonday lunch was generally taken out by each individual in the form of sandwiches although occasional hot meals would be provided.

"There was no reveille like in the army, but there was a top enrollee, similar to a top sergeant in the army, who got the men out on work days and inspected the barracks with an officer ... meals were not spirited times but they were not like meals in a prison either. I never saw any fights or rowdiness going on and the enrollees were very well mannered and had a great deal of respect for the army officers and foremen."³⁴

After work assignments were made, enrollees and foremen were transported to the work site in flatbed trucks with high sides. Foremen Albert Mastriani remembered the size of the crews:

"There was no typical work crew. The size depended on the particular job to be performed. For instance, a road gang would consist of anywhere from twenty to twenty-five men as that many could be used efficiently. Also, on the dam projects, usually large crews could be used, especially in the early stages when a lot of earth work by hand was employed. Frank Clark [NPS foreman], who built the comfort stations [at Sawmill Lake], could not use that many men at a time so that he might of only had eight or ten men. Incidentally, Frank was a great craftsman, and many of the men that worked under him, I am sure, went on to be good stone masons and carpenters.

"Also, when I had the quarry duty, only about ten men could be used at one time. Two men would always be on the rock drill rotating turns as that was extremely tiring work and some men were on the dynamite squad. Once in a while, we might of taken an enrollee in the design office to teach him drafting, but never had much luck with that."³⁵

Lunch was at noon and continued for an hour. Meals were served in several ways. Early on, when the camp was still located at the

Lusscroft farm, meals were served outdoors in the first picnic shelter near the main entrance of the park. When work projects were in distant parts of the park, a portable dining unit was brought to the work site, and meals were served outdoors.

After a long day in the field, men returned to the mess hall and had their evening meal at 5:30. After dinner, they were free for the evening unless they had other duties. There were many activities for them including recreation and education classes. A full time recreation director created a variety of activities, or the men went into Port Jervis, Franklin, Sussex or Milford.

Courtesy High Point State Park
The interior of the mess hall of Company 1280 at Camp Kuser, set up for a meal.

Enrollees worked on average sixteen to twenty-two days per month, weather permitting and depending on holidays. Project superintendents occasionally noted in their reports that the weather was so bad at High Point, that a higher than average number of work days were lost. Men could not work outside if the temperature was five degrees or lower, or if rain impacted on the work project.[36] Albert Mastriani remembered how time was made up: "An enrollee ... had the weekends off unless there was a day during the week when it rained or the temperature was too low to go out in the field."[37]

Lights were put out at 10 p.m. There were discussions in the camp newsletters whether it should be earlier or later depending on what radio shows were on and what the officers wanted. At 11 p.m., a final bed check was made.

The barracks typically housed forty men, and each man was assigned a bed and, in some cases, a footlocker or a small makeshift closet in which to put personal belongings. The barracks measured 20 x 112 feet and were lighted by electric lights. Interiors were covered with a plain paneling and painted white. Some barracks had curtains on the windows; others did not.

Enrollee Neil Theide remembered: "The barracks that we lived in ... they were between 50-60 feet long, a stove here and a stove there [at either end]. It burned coal, soft coal. And while we were there putting coal on it watching the fire, they were pretty warm. We'd stand around the fire, the stove and talk, whatever, smoke. In those days, almost everybody smoked."38

Courtesy High Point State Park

A typical barracks building at High Point. This is Barracks 2B in 1937.

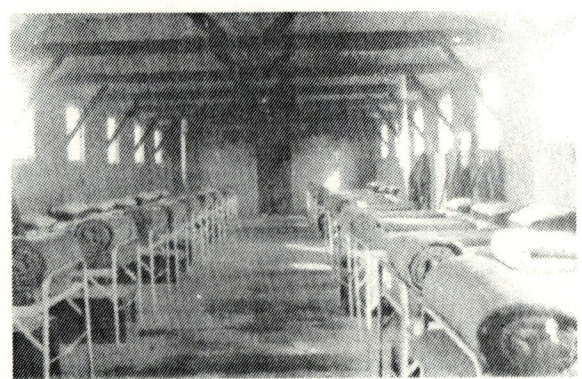

Courtesy High Point State Park

The barracks housed about forty men and measured 20' x 112'. Each man was assigned a bed and, depending on the time they were there, a footlocker or closet was provided. This photograph is of the interior of Barracks 5 which was at the northern end of the camp and housed enrollees of Company 1280.

Building exteriors were covered with a vertical barnboard siding, and a ladder hung on the outside for use in the event of fire. A small shed was attached to the outside to store coal. The buildings were not insulated. Neil Theide remembered: "I slept in an end bunk. There was the fire barrel with a pail of water on top of it. Sometimes there was a little ice on top of that pail of water and we slept with four army blankets and a comforter. I imagine it was close to thirty degrees in the barracks quite often. Because the night guard would go around and keep the fires burning ... He would make sure they were burning and that was all you know, it got pretty cold at night ... But of course, when the thing would bank at night there wasn't much heat at all. You might have had a little bit if you were close to it, but not much."[39]

Albert Mastriani remembered the facilities where the men lived: "The enrollees had barracks no different than I was in when I was drafted into the army in 1942. The barracks lived in by officers and foremen at High Point were partitioned off into rooms with a shower room and a rec room with card tables and a Ping-Pong table down on one end. It was quite comfortable."[40]

Barracks inspections were done, and there was competition among the barracks to be the best. Camp commanders made other inspections weekly and enrollee Frank Seddio remembered:

"We had inspection once a week, every Saturday morning ... When I was cooking on Saturday morning, that was my job. Well one of my jobs was to see that the kitchen was spic n' span ... they were very particular on that [be]cause they were afraid of dysentery. And if the pots and pans and equipment wasn't clean, hey then you'd have problems."[41]

Seddio also remembered if enrollees' personal areas did not past muster, they would be given K.P. duty. Peter Lutz remembered the importance the army attached to clean quarters: "Clean up, oh yeah. You had to have your barracks straightened up before you went to work. And they have what you call barrack orderlies in each one ... he would keep the fires going all day long and then if your bed wasn't straightened up, he would hurry up and straighten up before the commanding officer would come in ... [He was] a retired officer from the U.S. Army ... every morning he'd go right on through!"[42]

If things were not clean, Lutz said: "That means the weekend, you sit home and you scrub the floors! ...We'd have to clean up the barracks ... Whether you were a good boy or a bad boy, you scrub the barracks until those boards were white! They put salt on them ... There'd be somebody designated to take turns at this... Also, there was what they call a latrine orderly. He took care of the showers after the fellas got done ... like shaving, shampooing ... pieces of soap, all articles of underwear ... pieces of paper, cigarette butts, whatever. But it would be his job to clean up after that so then when the officers came to inspect everything was [good] - you better believe it!"[43]

The camp was inspected monthly by district commanders and officers, corps headquarters and even by officials from Washington. Camp Kuser was rated on occasion as among the best in the Sub-District. Technical services were regularly inspected for the progress of their work, equipment and foremen.

Mealtime At Camp

The quality and quantity of food at High Point was well remembered. There was good reason for these memories because substantial percentages of men enrolling in the CCC were malnourished in the early years. This was one of the devastating side effects of the economic turmoil of the time. In describing a group of incoming enrollees, project superintendent Oswald Brown wrote: "The boys taken in during the October enlistment period are pretty generally a young and frail looking lot of boys and it will be some time before they can turn out a good days work."[44] One camp inspection report in 1934 said enrollees at High Point gained between ten and fifteen pounds during their six month tour.[45] When enrollees returned home after their enlistment, they were healthier and had a better appreciation for a good diet.

An early newspaper account said: "Army officers and civilian foremen in charge of the Civilian Conservation Corps camps in New Jersey continue to be dumbfounded at the appetites of the boys in the camps in New Jersey. The healthy out-of-door living has done nothing to diminish the capacity of the boys in the mess line ... State Forester Charles T. Wilber of the Department of Conservation and Development who is in charge of the work ... said that it is not uncommon for boys to line up three and four times in the mess line before they are satisfied. Mr. Wilber reports that the appearance and spirit of the boys indicates that the environment and the life they are living is unquestionably doing wonders for them."[46]

Perishable food was purchased locally. Staples and non-perishables were brought from Fort Wadworth, New York and meat was purchased on contract. In a typical month, September 1940, the camp spent about $1,800 for food, $327 in local purchases, $302 in quartermaster purchases and $1,175 on contract for 178 enrollees. In that report, it was also noted ice cream was served twice a week and that forty-one gallons had been consumed.[47] Rations for one man averaged between $.40 and $.50 cents per day and cooks had some discretion as to what they could serve as long as it did not exceed the budget.⁴⁸ Strict regulations were in effect to maintain high quality.

The camp was supplied by local vendors and enrollee Carl LoGrand remembered the deliveries: "Some big truck used to come and he used to unload at the mess hall … once, twice a week he'd bring a good load …"⁴⁹

Michael Sagursky, the 1st Cook for Company 1280 remembered:

"The meals we had were, oh God, our menu. We cooked the best … we had a mess officer, T. F. Sullivan. He was a warden, a warrant officer of the Coast Guard, and he would always say that nothing was too good for our boys, and this is true … many a time different things came into camp, and he would look at it and he'd reject it, tell them they've gotta take it back … Meat was mixed in with a lot of fat. Different grades of hind quarters and fore quarters, he would check them out and, of course, I knew enough about it because I learned at school, but it was his OK or rejection. And he would reject it and they would have to take it back. Bread, the same way. We'd get bread, and just feeling it, it was stale … Like I say, nothing was too good for our boys. And nobody ever went out of the mess hall hungry. We had a battle with the boys that wanted to be KPs … we used to give them $3.00 extra a month and give them a stripe."⁵⁰

Another enrollee, Edwin Jakobowski, remembered some of the meals: "[For lunch] they'd bring out coffee, peanut butter and jelly and a bologna sandwich and a little apple. That was the worst meal. Or, [a] sardine sandwich ... But then you come back and you get a good meal ... they'd have a nice hot meal waiting for you. Potatoes, and you know, [a] good nice meal. Sundays wasn't bad, it was a good meal if I stayed, but, I was usually home on Sunday ... But I'd stay Friday and we always had fish on Friday."[51]

Peter Lutz, remembered lunches: "The lunch was brought out to us. They had a couple cans about so big, resembling something like a thermos bottle ... And then ... they had some hot food. That was in the winter time, they had maybe hot food. But most of the time there was sandwiches ... like peanut butter ... They were very healthy, they really were excellent. Like bologna and cheese and some of that stuff was on good solid bread, it wasn't that bread you would squeeze up into a bite, [be]cause these guys were hungry ... Then there was an apple ... And you would sit out there in the cold and sometimes you'd have this little container of soup which was good. Then you'd toast your sandwich on the fire."[52]

Enrollee Carl LoGrand remembered: "The food was good ... I enjoyed the food. They gave me good food and they had a cook there that did his own baking. Always remember he loved to bake cherry pies. I always remember that ... We had big tables and about eight or ten at a table. And more or less like family style ... Breakfast was either eggs, pancakes, which I enjoyed, French toast. Lunch was jam sandwiches, peanut butter and jelly ... Dinner, you got roast beef or stew. We used to have a lot of stew. And something else, they called it [unintelligible] on shingles. You know. It was toast and we had a name for it."53

Enrollee Neil Theide remembered you had to get to the chow line quickly or go without: "The food was very good ... I had been thin all my life. I gained a little weight ... the healthy mountain air, the food. And one interesting thing about the food. We got a box of cereal and a half a pint of milk and a regular breakfast ... But I learned to eat my cereal last, because if I ate my cereal first the other stuff would all be gone by the time I got to them ... If it was pancakes, or whatever I ate that first and ate the cereal last."54

Not all enrollees liked the food. Robert Wilbert remembered: "We had a few that went over the hill ... from Jersey City ...They said they weren't gonna eat that garbage. So they went over the hill. But I liked the food myself ... The only thing I didn't like was liver and there aren't too many people who like liver anyway!"55

CHAPTER 4

Education
&
Recreation

As you came of working age, the hard work, regular hours, the plain wholesome food, and the outdoor life of the CCC camps brought a quick response in improved morale. As muscles hardened and you became accustomed to outdoor work you grasped the opportunity to learn by practical training on the job and through the camp educational facilities. Many of you rose to responsible positions in the camps. Since the corps began some 1,150,000 of you have been graduated, improved in health, self-disciplined, alert and eager for the opportunity to make good in any kind of honest employment.

-President Franklin Delano Roosevelt,
Radio Address, April 17, 1936

The Essential Franklin Delano Roosevelt:
FDR's Greatest Speeches, Fireside Chats, Messages and Proclamations

CCC enrollees had a fair amount of free time but the federal government, early on, had a say in what they did in their time off. The government provided educational programs, job training efforts and medical care as well as some forms of recreation. It was a unique experiment in light of the fact the government insisted the CCC was not the military. In spite of the government's public position, it had a major influence in determining what men did during their enrollment periods. It was also one of the few aspects of the CCC that generated controversy during its existence.

Educational & Job Training Programs

One of the major goals of the CCC was to provide general education instruction, vocational training, eliminating illiteracy, correcting deficiencies in previous education, providing for cultural events and encouraging moral character and good citizenship.[1] Nationally, the program was known as "The School of the Woods" and there was a belief better educated men would have an easier time getting a job after leaving the CCC. Those national goals were pursued at High Point as well.

On average nationally, about 45 percent of inductees had never been employed and only about 13 percent had graduated from high school.[2] Some 40 percent of the enrollees had some high school education. Slightly less than

30 percent had passed the eighth grade and only about 4 percent had attended college. Less than 1 percent had no schooling and 3 percent were illiterate.[3]

There was no formal education component in the CCC at the outset. But in May 1933, the first proposal was made for some kind of education program. In October 1933, the National Association of State Foresters urged that instruction be started in camps. By December 1933, a director of education was hired and by June 1934, the program was up and running in the camps.[4]

The education component of the CCC was controversial, and it is generally agreed while it was not a total failure, it never reached its potential. The army was against it because it feared radical elements would find their way into the education program. Colonel Stuart Major who was in charge of the army said: "Instead of teaching the boys how to do an honest day's work, we are to be forced to the wishes of long-haired men and short-haired women and spend most of the time on some kind of an educational course."[5]

As the years went by, his feeling was somewhat vilified as many people wanted to make the CCC more of an educational program and less of a work outfit geared towards conservation. Others were concerned that cutting back on work hours would diminish the value of the conservation work. Talk of shortening the work day was considered, and in the end, the army's feelings on the matter were borne out.

To standardize education programs, the War Department with input from the Department of Interior's Office of Education (OE), created a program where education advisors would be hired and under the supervision and payroll of the army. An adviser selected by the OE was appointed to each camp and served under the camp commander. Generally, they were experienced teachers who worked full time to provide educational programs, not only in academics but avocational interests, recreation and hobbies as well. The education advisor also coached various sports teams and found volunteer coaches.

Early on, camps created programs that reflected the individual tastes of the officers. At High Point, a school was instituted at Company 216 in the early winter of 1933, and regular classes were taught by lieutenants Kuhn, Wesley Guptill, William Sullen and Wilfred Baetz. This school, the first in the country, was in session three nights a week in the mess hall. Textbooks were obtained from local schools and also from New York City and primers were used to teach enrollees to read.[6]

Education Advisors at High Point included M.E. Young (1934), G.D. Smith (1934-1936) and Edwin H. Wintermute (1936-1937). Wintermute was from Point Pleasant, New Jersey and attended Barringer High School and Brown University. He was a journalist for ten years and had been an instructor of journalism at the University of Washington in Seattle. After his time at High Point, he was promoted to Assistant Education Adviser for forty-three CCC camps in New Jersey. The final advisor at High Point was David E. Traub (1937-1941), who also served the longest period of time. Two enrollees served as assistant advisors.

Twenty-three year old enrollee Michael Sagursky remembered: "[Mr.] Wintermute. He had ... whatever you were interested in. He had a big list on the bulletin board. I never paid attention to it but he had youngsters in on it ... different things ... writing, reading, math. I'm trying to think of the stuff because the kids would tell me ... 'I'm going to Wintermute. He's terrific and he's helping me out and what have you.' And these were young kids that probably couldn't even go to high school. They were here and they were up to learning something."[7] Besides academics, courses included carpentry, masonry, mechanical drawing, auto mechanics, elementary electricity, surveying, radio, stamp collecting, steam engineering, navigation, model craft, truck driving, auto mechanics and forestry.[8] Primers on forestry, carpentry and cement work were available for CCC boys to use in camp. They were small booklets with instructions, diagrams and tests. Enrollees were encouraged to attend these programs to improve themselves and many enrollees took advantage of the classes.

Photography classes were among the most popular courses given at C camps across the country. A photography lab and darkroom was built in the education building and was available for teaching photography. It was considered one of the best in the district. Many enrollees had photographs taken to send home and for their scrapbooks. Some enrollees were enterprising enough and sold pictures to their colleagues.

Edwin Jakobowski, an enrollee from 1937-1939 remembered the classes: "They had different classes every night ... there were all kinds of things you could pick up. Mechanics, like I said photography - I took mechanics too. I took a little bit of everything. And I didn't go to swimming school from here. I went from Greenwood Lake. And where I got that was, I was diving off the bridge and the girls were coming in a canoe and I wet them and they made a complaint. And the captain says, 'I got a complaint about you jumping off the bridge' ... He says 'but you're lucky. I need a couple guys to go down to Camp Norman, New Jersey to become life guard instructors.' So I went down there for a few weeks, swimming eight hours a day, to become a lifeguard."[9]

Classes were also held at Port Jervis High School on East Main Street and at Sussex High School in Newton. The New Jersey State Board of Vocational Education also sponsored courses, including auto mechanics. Courses were created by the WPA authorities at the College of Forestry at Syracuse University in Syracuse, New York. In some cases, teachers volunteered to teach courses and others were paid by the federal government.

Courses were also given by foremen including Larry Jones, who taught a current events class and one on forest fire fighting. Occasional lectures were given including one by Dr. Pauline Doppler, a renowned world traveler and the first woman to receive a salary from the Turkish government. Her presentation was called the "Economic and Historical Basis for the Present European Situation."[10] Another was given in May 1940 by Bohemian Glass Blowers, much to the delight of the C boys.

Camps were given funds for educational programs, but they did not cover the entire cost so that enrollees were asked to pay $.25 to take courses that had twelve lessons. It took on average one week to complete a lesson. In one of the few references to the number of men taking courses at High Point, a newsletter writer said it was 25 percent of the men.[11] Across the nation, about 60 percent of the enrollees took part in the courses offered.[12]

Some men were sent to various schools or training workshops. Michael Sagursky's enlistment took a decidedly good turn when the following sequence of events caused him to go to the U.S. Army's School for Bakers and Cooks. He said: "At the time, we were building two dams and a couple of bridges at intervals and on the third day, when I lined up in the morning, I was advised by my sergeant ... to step forward two steps and the rest of the company went about their business. He told me to go to the barrack and get my barracks bag. And I'm shoving off. I didn't know where I was going. I went into the captain's office; I got the orders that they were sending me to Fort Slocum Cooking and Baking School.

"And I told him I knew nothing about cooking, and they said, 'you'll learn.' We'll give you a six-week course, and you'll come back as a good cook. And I did have six weeks of cooking. It was, baking, butchering and cooking. There were weeks of each. And while I was there, I was the shift leader on all the classes."[13]

The camp also had a well equipped library. One newsletter described it as mainly fiction although it had books on history, biography, travel, fiction, social problems, civil service, forestry and mechanics. Books of interest were simply checked out by enrollees. Six daily newspapers, four weekly magazines, four monthly magazines and periodicals were available to enrollees and a traveling library which contained recent editions that made its way around the other 2nd Corps C camps. The circulating library stayed for 2 ½ months.

The education building used by the CCC at High Point burned in March 1938 and soon after, plans were formulated to use the former Company 216 mess hall for that purpose. In the new building, partitions were put up to create classrooms, a darkroom, shop, library and office for the education advisor.

Beginning in 1937, there was a greater emphasis placed nationally on job training and that effort was reflected in the camp at High Point. Regular features appeared in the company newsletter about job training including how to pick a job vocation and at least one feature on why men could not hold jobs. In one report prepared for CCC inspectors, fourteen courses were given relating to jobs going on in the park, including roads, surveying, construction, excavation and landscaping.

Courtesy High Point State Park

Newspapers and radios were the major news sources for enrollees. Here, enrollees are on their time off in a barracks.

Increasingly, former CCC enrollees were sought after by the private sector because of their job training, work experience and the disciplined environment in which they worked. After 1940, classes were taught to reduce deficiencies in English. During World War II, former CCC enrollees were sought because they had already proved adept at living in a military-type situation.

For many enrollees, training and education equipped them with skills they would use for the rest of their lives. Cook Sagursky remembers coming across other C boys after their time of service: "There's some that I've met as time went on, and they said that 'what I learned in the C's I'm using now as part of my occupation' ... Construction, mostly construction ... some of my guys in the kitchen, there's a couple of guys that became chefs that were second cooks with me ... Others opened restaurants and have ... been running their restaurants. And then of course there's a few of them that are truck drivers, which we've had here [at High Point]."[14]

Nicholas Hanisak turned his experiences at High Point into a long and varied career. A resume he put together some time after his service in the CCC included the following citation:

"CCC High Point State Park, Sussex, New Jersey

July 11, 1939 - November 17, 1941

Duties: Consolidate daily time sheets and progress sheets, which data was used as the basis for our weekly and monthly progress reports submitted to the district office in New York City. Costs were kept for all jobs and each piece of equipment. There were at least ten different jobs and fifteen trucks (dump and stake body), one Austin grader, one Allis Chalmers bulldozer, one power shovel, one stone crusher, two pickup trucks, and several centrifugal pumps. For each piece of equipment, we had a separate record booklet in which was recorded the number of hours used or mileage, fuel consumption, repairs and other maintenance data. I prepared the payroll for the supervisory personnel of nine men. I had one man directly under my supervision. I worked directly under the Superintendent, Mr. Melvin H. Gemmill, who was assistant Art Director at Fairchild Aircraft for part of the latter years of World War II. Since the war, he has been a free lance artist, illustrator and designer. Some of the things he does is that he designs housing developments, designs other buildings, designs turnpikes, and illustrates catalogs and books."[15]

Medical Benefits & Cleanliness

Another major benefit of enrollment in the CCC was access to quality medical care including dental care and coverage under the compensation laws. Enrollees were encouraged to see the camp doctor to prevent getting and spreading diseases. Most doctors were army officers and lived in the camp. They visited sick enrollees twice a day. The infirmary at High Point was manned by an enrollee and minor medical problems were dealt with by a medic in the infirmary. A sick bay with separate quarters was available to enrollees.

Men with major medical problems were usually sent to military medical facilities like the Naval Hospital in Brooklyn, New York. High Point had an ambulance on hand for emergency transport, and doctors taught first aid courses. At the end of the course, a card was given to successful participants. The doctors also inspected the camp to lessen the chances of contracting diseases and to eliminate unsanitary conditions.[16]

One of the problems of so many men living together was the possibility of contracting contagious diseases. In February 1937, the camp was quarantined because of influenza and scarlet fever. Monthly checks were made of enrollees for venereal diseases and if an enrollee was found to have syphilis or gonorrhea he would be discharged. Kitchen staff were checked twice a month.[17] Overall the C boys contracted venereal disease at 18.3 per thousand. The regular army rate for World War I was 87 per thousand while during the Spanish-American War it was 140 per thousand.[18]

Men were also discharged for causing problems or "public disturbances." These problems usually occurred on weekends or when enrollees were on leave. Camp administrators often noted that the bad behavior of one enrollee reflected badly on the whole camp. Homosexuality was forbidden in the CCC as it was the regular army. Admission of being a homosexual was cause for dismissal.[19]

There was an overriding concern in the annual inspections of CCC camps about the sanitary conditions of the latrine and shower facilities. Peter Lutz remembered how enrollees used to take showers in winter: "And this is about when it's real cold, we're talking about real cold right? So you would go to the shower with your ... big GI shoes on, no socks, a hat and just your heavy GI ... army overcoat. And [there] would be nothing underneath, okay? So you go to the shower, this is like ten below zero! ... You'd slop through maybe a foot of snow, you'd take your hot shower, it was good hot showers, get yourself nice and clean, dry yourself off the best you can. Then you'd make a mad dash from the shower room into ... your own barracks. That way you would dry yourself off a little more. These guys would come out, they'd be steaming! You'd see the steam coming off them!"[20]

Recreational Facilities & Activities

Enrollees were free to pursue their own activities after work and on weekends unless they had special duties. They were also given regular leave time including a six-day paid leave when they re-enlisted. They were allowed to take the following holidays: New Years Day, Lincoln's birthday, Memorial Day, Independence Day, Labor Day, Thanksgiving and Christmas as well as religious holidays.[21] For boys who were unable to get home during the holidays or simply wanted to stay, special meals were made by the cooking staff.

Any enrollee who was "absent without leave" was subject to reprimands, fines and even a dishonorable discharge. If an enrollee were absent for fourteen days without permission, he was considered a deserter. After an enrollee had been on the CCC payroll for six months, he was entitled to six paid days off. Emergency leave was also available. Time off was used for education, personal needs like doing laundry, cleaning the barracks and visiting local communities. However, all leave was with the permission of the camp commander. Enrollees were still bound by the rules governing life in camp when they were out of camp. Army trucks, with canvas tops and wooden benches along each side, were used to bring men into local communities, usually accompanied by a leader.

Hitch-hiking and riding on freight trains was prohibited.

Albert Mastriani remembered that: "Enrollees were free to go home during the weekends and since most of them lived in the Newark and New York areas, many of them did just that. A local bus service for which they paid a small fare was available. There was a baseball team that I coached for two years. We practiced and played games in Port Jervis ... Many of the enrollees who were at High Point for years spent a lot of time in Port Jervis, dated, and a few even got married to local girls. One who comes to mind was Red Sisco who operated heavy equipment and was also a fine baseball pitcher."[22]

It must be remembered that most of the men were young and were living away from home for the first time. Some men went to great lengths to get home like enrollee Robert Wilbert who said: "We would hitchhike home once in awhile, me and my buddy ... We did have a man [an enrollee at High Point] that was from Trenton. And he would take us to Trenton. [Of] course we had to pay for gas, chip in you know, help him with the gas. He had a model A, and he kept the car in Port Jervis cause they weren't allowed to have cars ... and so he would take us to Trenton and then either my brother would take us on to Barnegat or we would hitchhike, because I had a brother who lived in Trenton. So that's how we got home."[23]

Neil Thiede lived within a short distance of High Point and he recalled:

"I went home quite often. I won't say every weekend, but I went home an awful lot of weekends. I mentioned to my wife this morning, I must have hitchhiked down and back from High Point to the city of Paterson and Hawthorne at least a hundred times in the period that I was up there. It was always very easy. You walk out to [Route] 23 from the barracks and start hitchhiking and almost everybody who went by would pick you up. A little different today I guess.

"... My mother had a car at that time, well it was her mother's car. Actually I lived with my mother and my grandmother, my grandfather. My mother would take me out to Wayne on [Route] 23 and drop me off, and I would hitchhike back. I never had any problems. It was very easy. Later on I did a little hitchhiking in the army from Delaware up to Hawthorne and Paterson, and that was a little harder.

"I did go out a lot of weekends and went home, and one thing I remember about the weekends in the warm weather, you'd walk through the park and you would see all the visitors having picnics ... they might offer us [food] and then fall would come, it would get a little sadder or drearier because the people weren't coming anymore and the first thing you are there all alone. Nobody came you know."[24]

Peter Lutz remembered forms of entertainment common at the time:

"In the evening, well, we played a lot of games. We had musical instruments or we made musical instruments like the harmonica and some other crazy little things. And then we'd play certain games ... we had a little rec [sic] hall you know. So we would borrow things from the rec [sic] hall ... like checkers and all sorts of things like that. You'd be surprised, there was cards and stuff but there was nothing in there where there was violence involved, where somebody would get really angry and go to kill somebody; who really got up hyper and said 'I'm gonna,' you know, cuss words or whatever. We didn't, in our barracks there was little or no cuss words ... we'd hear a group down that end with a harmonica and harmonizing so we'd leave the card game, we'd go down there and join them in the fun. See that's the way the fun was then; we made our own.

"One Thanksgiving ... we decided to go visit some old buddies in Branchville on Skellinger Road from High Point. So we dressed up in galoshes and everything else [and walked] through the Appalachian Trail. Well it was so darn cold our legs felt like stumps, at least mine did. And we come out at probably [Route] 206, Culver Lake there. And there was a little bit of ... a road stand. He had a pot bellied stove going. We all got in there and warmed up our legs 'cause we were walking like we were zombies.

Then he was nice enough, people in them days was very nice! You know, they didn't ask us money for it.

"They called up the camp [at High Point] and then ... a truck [came] for us. Pick us up and bring us to [back to] the camp. So we showered up and everything else and they had a nice Thanksgiving dinner for us. We were a little late, but they saved some for us ... That's a ... beautiful view from High Point on the [Appalachian Trail.]"[25]

The men often availed themselves of the park's facilities. A float and dock were placed in Lake Marcia for enrollees to use, separate from public facilities. C boys often hiked on the Appalachian Trail and visited High Point monument.

There were more than fourteen hundred C-boys in the area and there was interest in the surrounding communities to provide entertainment programs. While it is not mentioned in any source, there must have also been some concern about so many young men having moved to the area from the urban areas in such a short period of time.

The American Legion organizations in the county and the Sussex County Association of Patriotic Order of Sons had committees to undertake this entertainment and regularly sponsored programs. Typical was the "C.C.C. Nite" sponsored December 14, 1933, by the Patriotic Order. Another group that sponsored programs included the Everyman's Club of the

Sussex Baptist Church where they provided refreshments.[26] The Sussex County branch of the Red Cross provided a "smoker" program for Company 1280.[27]

In return, enrollees and army officers gave programs for civic organizations describing what was being done in local camps and across the state. The C boys even brought a bit of Broadway to the local community by performing plays in area theaters.[28] Army officer Wilfred Baetz, who was active in the affairs of Company 216, was also a playwright. He wrote a play in two acts in 1933 called "Murder in Night Court" and it was presented at camp later in the year. Baetz, who had a beautiful baritone voice, also gave a recital with pianist Helen Wilson at Sussex during the Christmas holiday in 1933.[29]

Company 1280 had a Dramatics Club which performed regularly and its director was Lt. Frederick Udall, one of the army officers. Other programs were provided by the Drama Department funded by the Emergency Relief Act of 1935 and the Federal Theater Group, another of FDR's programs to put unemployed actors to work. A motion picture unit traveled around the district showing movies for which enrollees paid a small admission. Company 1280 was a member of the district's moving picture circuit. For a small fee, men could see the latest movies in camp. Each week the camp was provided with a new movie and a 35 mm projector with good sound equipment.

We Can Take It!

Dances took place and invitations were sent out to local young ladies of surrounding communities. Women were allowed in the Recreation Hall where the dances were normally held, but they were not allowed to wander through the camp. Some functions took place in the Kuser Mansion, particularly events that involved the higher echelon of the administration of the camp and army officers. Refreshments were provided by staff cooks.

The army offered to provide transportation to dances at camp if potential participants wrote the Dance Committee in advance.[30] The dances were not always a great success and, in fact, some girls refused to come back after negative comments were made about their dancing ability.[31] Local bands like the Mulvaney Band from Port Jervis came to the camp and performed along with a program provided by CCC men. The Mack Dance Studio of Port Jervis supervised a September 13, 1940, dance with musicians coming from Paterson, New Jersey.

There were frequent social functions at the camp including open houses for the public to see what was being done in the park and to promote continuance of the CCC program in general. Many of these programs were tied to the anniversary of the creation of the CCC on April 7, 1933. This anniversary was celebrated nationally every year and had a special place in the affections of those associated with the CCC.

The camp was opened for inspection and the administrative personnel would discuss their various projects. Meals were served in the mess hall along with informational talks given for groups that wanted to see what was going on.[32] In 1939, three hundred visitors came to the park and sixty-two had dinner at the camp.[33] Army officers guided visitors within the camp while NPS and park officials gave a tour of work done. The education advisor provided a program that reviewed his vocational and educational programs.

One of the most popular activities among C-boys was visiting one of Port Jervis's many "Foam Emporiums," or bars and taverns. Ads for local bars appeared occasionally in newsletters. In 1937, after a long quarantine by the camp was lifted, many of the men came into Port Jervis to go to places like "Fay's Café" and the "New Yorker" or "Oasis." There the boys were described as being literally "afloat in beer suds."[34]

Drinking alcoholic beverages as well as the sale of them was prohibited in the camp. Violations of this rule could end an enrollee's enlistment in the CCC. While the camp could not forbid the drinking of alcoholic beverages outside the camp, the handbook given to CCC enrollees suggested they wait until they were twenty-five and more mature. That idea was obviously not popular with enrollees, and newsletters frequently contained descriptions of the drinking habits of various men.

Enrollee Robert Wilbert was typical of the under-aged enrollee who wanted to have a beer and he remembered: "Of course the ones that could drink, they'd have a few beers ... If the bartender would serve them ... Some were twenty-one, some passed for twenty-one ... I remember ... the little bar room going down towards Sussex on [Route] 23 ... It's just a little old place ... Me and my buddy stopped there one day ... and we walked in there, 'Have a beer?,' and the guy looked at us, and says, 'Well I tell you what fellas,' he says, he looks out the door, he says, 'I'm gonna give you each a beer, drink it up' he says, 'and get out of here because' he says, 'I know your not of age!' - that's the first and the last time we went ... But he was nice. He give us the one beer ... because he would have lost his license."[35]

Another forbidden activity was playing dice or shooting craps. Robert Wilbert remembered the special precautions taken after payday to prevent such activity: "Some would shoot craps in the latrine. No, that wasn't allowed and the funny part about it, the sergeant, he was an older man, and when the boys would get paid he would have the boys in there and he would have somebody keeping watch for the commander ... They were shooting in there because if they got caught they'd be discharged."[36]

A favorite pastime of many enrollees was to listen to the radio on their time off. Radio was the major entertainment of the era. There were a number of efforts to extend time in the evening when radios could be listened to in the barracks and they could be found all around camp. Men listened to their favorite music, commentators and programs including Lowell Thomas, Amos and Andy and the Shadow. They also listened to news broadcasts and as things worsened in Europe, President Roosevelt's fireside chats.

Neil Theide, remembered his favorite radio program: "There was a program from New York, I cannot remember the name of the station, but they had this program called "The Milkman's Matinee" and that would start us off every morning. He must have came on at 6 a.m. and he would come down the Milky Way ... I'll never forget that."[37]

One of the most memorable events of the decade on the radio was the broadcast by Orson Welles on the evening of Sunday, October 30, 1938, called "The War of the Worlds." That night there were a number of small groups of men around camp at High Point taking advantage of their free time. Others were in the library, some were working on correspondence courses and others were studying for First Aid classes.

The Welles program began with a disclaimer that it was fiction, then there was a steady stream of news bulletins announcing the landing of Martians and the destruction of the metropolitan New York area. Welles relayed to millions of listeners the defeat of the New Jersey State Militia and the complete annihilation of New York City and the surrounding areas where many of the C boys lived.

The program transfixed the men and as they listened there was, according to one company newsletter, many who actually believed the country was being destroyed. At the end of the broadcast, army officer Lt. Louis Ebert and Project Superintendent Melvin Gemmill toured the camp and tried to put the boys' minds at ease.

The next company newsletter poked fun at the reaction of some to the Orson Welles broadcast:

"Three Enrollees were kneeling down beside their beds and they weren't fixing them either.

"Baldauf was seen running down Company Street with a mattress under one arm and a bank book under the other.

"Lisowski the sandwich man, ran into the icebox and ate one of his sandwiches - he felt that it was better to die by his own hand.

"Zoeller queried 'Keep drinking, everything will be OK.'"[38]

They reacted as E.B. White described the general populace in 1940 when he wrote: "Hitherto they had believed everything they heard on the air, and now their confidence was shaken. They resented this and felt a sense of loss. One of them stuck to his religion to the bitter end. He said 'Even after this I still will believe what I hear on the radio."[39]

Another major social event of the decade was the 1939 New York World's Fair. One hundred and five C boys from High Point went to visit the exposition in New York City. Six army trucks drove 3 ½ hours to the event which was described as "the world of tomorrow."

Sports In The CCC

Sports activities of all kinds played a major role in the leisure time of the C boys. Ping Pong and pool were popular in the camp and there were regular competitions between the two companies, intra-barracks and between the camps at Stokes State Forest including boxing and wrestling matches and baseball games.[40] Also popular were card games, basketball, horseshoes, volleyball, soccer and swimming. Winter activities included ice skating, sleigh riding and skiing.

In February 1937 the following appeared in a newsletter: "One of the other feature attractions were the two boxing bouts put on by 1280. The first fight resulted in a technical K.O. in the first minute and twenty seconds with a victory for Walker over Shaurger. The second bout was hotly contested and went the limit of the scheduled three rounds with Tange winning by a decision over Kaberter."[41]

In 1936 there was a pool tournament at High Point with thirty-two contestants. Company 216 took first and third place and Company 1280 took second place. As the company newsletter described it, the contest had "many moments of excitement and suspense."⁴² A basketball game on January 12, 1938, between Company 1280 and Company 1266 from Stokes State Forest was considered a thriller right up to the last minute. The final score was 48-24 in High Point's favor. Education Advisor David Traub was the coach of the High Point team. A company-wide ping pong tournament was held in 1936 and "Mickey" Markovich came in first; "Stumpy" DeVaul, second and "Eddie" Manning, third.

At least one Company 1280 member, Alex Nester, who wore a size thirteen shoe much to the good natured ribbing of his fellow enrollees, signed a minor league baseball contract with the Trenton Senators in 1938 at a wage of $125 per month, a far cry from the $30 per month he made at the CCC camp.⁴³ He was on the baseball team that placed second in the district finals and was seen in a playoff game by a baseball scout.

The companies at High Point participated in regional sports tournaments wearing their own uniforms. In 1938, the 1280 basketball team placed seventh in the area tournament. In 1939, they won the championship of the Northern Section of Subdistrict #8. The 1280 ping pong team went to the state championships. Company 1280's baseball team won the CCC Division

Championship in October 1936.⁴⁴ The 1938 baseball team from Company 1280 got to second place in the finals for the state championship and the following year, the 1939 team won the championship. The basketball team received national attention when it was mentioned in the national CCC "Happy Days" newsletter. A track team and swimming team also competed around the region.

Teams from High Point competed against teams from local leagues including the City of Port Jervis. Names like the Port Jervis "Y" team, the Sussex Farmers, the West End Club, the Port Jervis Kings, the Teddy Moeller Association and the Newton Collegians were all formidable opponents.

Teams were drawn from enrollees although occasionally a foremen participated. Coaches were drawn from the camp's administration and were recruited by education advisors. Enrollees even coached occasionally. Larry Jones, Albert Mastriani and Oliver Wells served as baseball coaches and Superintendent Howard Platt served as a swimming coach. Melvin Gemmell and Lt. Samuel Loyd served as boxing coaches. Other enrollees went to the games to cheer their friends and barracks mates on to victory. A baseball field was built along Company Street where oats had been previously grown.⁴⁵

At least one sports banquet was held at High Point for 120 members of the Twi-League. Among the program's participants were the mayor of

Port Jervis, Wendell Phillips; the city's chief of police, the editor of the local newspaper and park superintendent John Gibbons. One of the most positive interactions between the camp and the community was through sports competitions, particularly the baseball leagues.⁴⁶

Religious Accommodations In The CCC

There were no religious facilities at the camp and rarely a mention of religious services in company newsletters, but enrollees had access to them. Catholic services were conducted by a priest from Newton every Sunday at the assembly hall. Jewish boys went to services in Port Jervis. For Protestants, services were held in camp on Sunday afternoon or army trucks took the men to Port Jervis. However, they do not seem to have been held regularly because there was not as much interest.

A 1934 inspection report said an average of eighteen men went by army truck on Sunday and about forty attended services at the camp.⁴⁷ Albert Mastriani remembered: "There were also religious services in the movie barracks. One of our foremen, Frank Clark, with the help of some enrollees, designed and built a beautiful altar for Catholic services. Although I don't specifically remember, there may have been transportation provided to Port Jervis for those of other religions."⁴⁸

After Frank Clark built the altar, Patrick B. Fay, Trenton District chaplain, said, "I have not seen an altar, which for usefulness and beauty could outdo the one in Company 1280."[49]

Enrollee Turnover

There was a continual turnover of enrollees when they found jobs, completed their time of service, were occasionally sent to other camps to assist in a particular operation or to help set a camp up, moved on to other camps or joined the military. Enrollment periods brought new groups of men into the camp and as companies elsewhere were broken up, men were sent to High Point. For example, Company 216 took in a number of enrollees from Company 1217, Camp S-71 at Branchville, New Jersey, in February 1936. And, when Company 216 folded up in June 1937, some enrollees moved across the street to Company 1280.

In April 1938, the former barracks of Company 216 was used as a way station for CCC men from other places who were being transferred west and passing through the area. Two different groups of men, each staying for about two weeks and numbering about five hundred, passed through Camp Kuser. Men from Company 1280 were occasionally shipped to other corps areas as well.[50]

A number of enrollees were associated with the camp for many years including Robert Drimmer and Edward Doyle who became fixtures. Some enrollees served beyond their two-year limit, particularly if they were part of the administration.

Enrollee Paperwork

Each enrollee was given a serial number that stayed with him until discharge and after 1940, enrollees were fingerprinted because of war department regulations. Fingerprinting, a relatively new form of identification, also became common practice across the nation at this time. One enrollee at High Point, Frank Klymer, garnered media attention as "one in a million" when it was found he had no fingerprints.[51]

Extensive records were kept on each enrollee including dates of service, place of service, work performed and how it had been performed. Promising enrollees were sent to special schools to improve or learn new skills and upon completion, were presented with certificates of proficiency.

Any disciplinary actions were recorded and any kind of advancement for an enrollee was contingent on having a clean record. Because records were filed with the federal government, if an enrollee chose to enlist in the military,

Peter Osborne

records would be consulted before he could be inducted into the service.

The final and most important piece of paperwork was an honorable discharge and a letter of recommendation. With those two items, enrollees could re-enter the work force with a significant advantage over other men.

CHAPTER 5

The Golden Age Of Parks And Forests

That the President of the United States may, from time to time, set apart and reserve in any State or Territory having public lands bearing forests, any part of the public lands wholly or in part covered with timber or undergrowth, whether of commercial value or not, as public reservations, and the President shall, by public proclamation, declare the establishment of such reservations and the limits thereof.
-Park Protection Act of 1891, United States Congress

Theodore Roosevelt: The Naturalist

I cannot too often repeat that the essential feature in the present management of the Yellowstone Park, as in all similar places, is its essential democracy - it is the preservation of the scenery, of the forests, of the wilderness life and the wilderness game for the people as a whole, instead of leaving the enjoyment thereof to be confined to the very rich who can control the private reserves.
-President Theodore Roosevelt
Laying of the Cornerstone of the Gateway at Yellowstone Park,
April 23, 1904

Theodore Roosevelt: The Naturalist

From the 1910s until 1941, our nation celebrated a "Golden Age of the Parks and Forests." The first phase of this three-decade period was a development that was national in scope and included the creation of a large number of state parks and forests across the nation during the 1910s and 1920s. This happened at the same time as the creation of millions of acres of national forest reserves, later to be known as the national forests, under the leadership of the first chief of the United States Forest Service, Gifford Pinchot. The National Park Service, a relatively new federal agency, was also developing a series of national parks, monuments and historic sites. It can be argued it was the single most important era in our nation's conservation history and all of these events are part of the High Point story.

The second development in this process was the enormous amount of work undertaken by the CCC across the country at newly created state parks and forests, national parks and forests and historic sites which gave the public accessibility to these lands. For the first time in history, there was adequate funding to undertake a large number of projects on both the federal and state level. Prior to the creation of the CCC some states actually had no state park systems. During the nine years of the CCC's existence, the number of state park lands across the country doubled as the CCC improved existing facilities and provided a stimulus to create new parks in many states. Many of the buildings and infrastructure in our parks today are a direct result of this effort as well as the millions of acres that were set aside by the government.

When the CCC was voted out of existence in 1942, a great era came to an end. This four-decade long effort was begun by President Theodore Roosevelt and reached its climax with a second Roosevelt, President Franklin Delano Roosevelt. Their ideals represent the feelings of many of their generation, in that government could do good things, particularly in the field of conservation and the environment.

A third development was the popularity of the growing number of state and national parks and the ability to get to them by automobile. The capability of a growing middle class to purchase automobiles and the development of an extensive system of paved roads in the 1920s, including New Jersey State Route 23, led huge numbers of visitors to the few existing state parks and the growing system of national parks and forests. FDR's Secretary of Interior, Harold Ickes, declared 1934 would be "National Parks Year" and, following that pronouncement, there was a marked increase in national park visitation.[1] In addition, there was a belief that the outdoors was a tonic to the ills of the urban, industrial life in the early decades of the twentieth century. This development allowed for the lower and middle classes to enjoy the outdoors as the wealthier classes had been doing for decades on large estates.[2]

George Warren, president of the New Jersey Fish and Game Commission in 1933, said it best at a meeting of conservation officials: "With the rapid changes we are facing in industrial and social conditions, it is imperative that we be prepared to meet the fast-growing demand for additional recreation grounds. Shorter working hours will further increase this demand. Hiking, camping and fishing are recreations that appeal to old and young and then can be enjoyed at a minimum cost. The beauty of the valleys of our woodlands and mountain streams in New Jersey forms one of our state's greatest assets."[3]

High Point Park's popularity extended far beyond the immediate vicinity and by 1933 it was being used far beyond its capacity. The peak for which it was named was at the highest altitude in the state of New Jersey, 1,803 feet above sea level. After 1930, it had the attraction of having a beautiful 220-foot tall obelisk constructed and dedicated to the memory of New Jersey's veterans. The obelisk could be seen for miles around. It was a gift of Colonel and Mrs. Anthony Kuser, the donors of High Point State Park.

A Port Jervis newspaper reported in June 1933: "The roads to High Point are in good condition and the crowds already started going to the Park by the hundreds on Sundays,

Saturdays and holidays, but on the other days, there will be large crowds too."[4]

High Point was soon a destination for many visitors from the East Coast and its facilities were being overwhelmed.[5] A 1933 report by the High Point Park Commission, the agency created to manage the affairs of the park in 1923, said: "The season of 1933 has been the most successful since the inception of the park. The attendance has more than doubled on weekdays, Sundays and holidays. The attendance has severely taxed the present facilities and employees to meet this inroad of visitors and tourists."[6]

It was estimated by the park commission that four hundred thousand came in 1934 and five hundred and fifty thousand in 1938. By the late 1930s, more than one hundred and fifty thousand people were coming each summer.[7] On a single weekend in May 1937, twelve thousand motorists visited the park and two thousand individuals climbed to the top of the monument. By fall of 1937, this intense use of the small area around the monument and Lake Marcia had damaged to some degree the quality of the experience at the park. A number of people wrote letters to the editor of the *Newark Sunday Call* relating the shortcomings of the park including the condition of the first floor of the Kuser Mansion and the campsites, particularly those built by the CCC.[8]

Park officials responded by pointing out the many new features that had been constructed and how much of the park was still maintained at its previous levels in spite of budgets that had dropped precipitously from $187,000 in 1922 to $35,000 in 1937.[9]

A final development in the nation's love affair with the parks and forests was the rapid rise of the newly created Boy Scout and Girl Scout movements. These organizations required places for summer camps that could accommodate large numbers of young people.[10] There were both Boy Scout and Girl Scout camps at High Point.

The Olmsted Brothers Plan

All four developments previously mentioned came together with the arrival of the CCC at High Point. The park was acquired by the state in 1923 when a 10,600-acre parcel of mountaintop land was donated by Anthony and Susan Dryden Kuser to the people of New Jersey. In the months that followed the 1923 Memorial Day grand opening, the Olmsted Brothers firm of Brookline, Massachusetts, was engaged to draw up a master plan for the new park. The firm was probably the largest landscape firm in the country at the time and perhaps in the world.[11] In a High Point Park Commission Report in 1934, the Olmsteds are called "National Park Engineers noted the world over."[12]

John and Frederick Olmsted Jr. were the sons of Frederick Law Olmsted, (1822-1903) one of the most important landscape architects of the 19th century. He, along with Calvert Vaux, designed Central Park in New York City (1858-1876). In other collaborations, he designed the 1893 World's Columbian Exposition in Chicago (1888-1893) and the U.S. Capitol grounds in Washington, D.C.(1875-1894). He also designed numerous parks across the country including Prospect Park in Brooklyn, the (New York) State Reservation at Niagara Falls, Riverside Park in New York City and the Seattle, Washington parks. Between 1857 and 1950 the Olmsted firm participated in some 5,500 projects, many of which were regional parks.[13]

At the time the firm worked at High Point, only the namesake brother was still alive, but the firm was engaged in a number of park and housing projects spread across the country which included the Rancho Palos Verdes residential community in Palos Verdes, California and the Forest Hills Gardens residential community in Queens, New York.[14] The firm would design, after its contract with High Point, the prestigious California state park system.[15]

It is not known if Frederick Olmsted Jr. came to High Point, although it seems likely he did. The firm's representative, Percy Gallagher, came to commission meetings. After site visits and research, a large map with existing and proposed features was created and an 18-page report filled with analysis and suggestions was submitted to the park commission. Commissioner Felix Fuld personally paid for the effort.[16] In early 1924, the plan was presented to the public and the *Sussex Independent* printed the whole report. The newspaper was then owned by John Stanton, secretary for the park commission. Fuld also paid for an initial run of five hundred copies of the report, and when those were distributed across the state to many government officials and agencies, he printed another three hundred.[17]

```
STATE OF NEW JERSEY
HIGH POINT PARK
SUSSEX COUNTY
MAP TO ACCOMPANY REPORT OF
OLMSTED BROTHERS - LANDSCAPE ARCHITECTS-
BROOKLINE, MASS.   OCTOBER 1923
SCALE 1760' = 1"

                    LEGEND
PARK BOUNDARY (approximate)
OPENINGS IN FOREST
BUILDINGS (existing) ............... ■ (black)
PARK ROADS & HIGHWAYS OF APPROACH
```

Courtesy High Point State Park
Legend from the drawing submitted to the High Point Park Commission.

The Olmsted plan was required to address some specific concerns the enabling legislation spelled out. The brothers, in a general way, called for major improvements to the road system in the park, the acquisition of additional lands, camping areas, the creation of new lakes and improving the existing lakes. Other projects included the creation of a golf course and the establishment of a fish hatchery. Interestingly, upon receipt of the report, Colonel Kuser disagreed with only one of the proposed uses for the park: the idea of building the golf course.[18] Other than that he was most approving of the report.

The plan divided the park into two parts that would be used in different ways. It would be bisected by Route 23. The eastern part of the park was dedicated to short-term visitors, particularly those wanting to visit the monument, and the western part for those who would be staying in the park for longer periods of time like campers and vacationers.[19]

The proposals were the result of a great interest and devotion shown by the American public to various parks and forests around the country and at High Point. In 1924, there were about one hundred and fifty state parks containing about two million acres in 23 states.[20] All of these parks, most of which were relatively new, were forced to deal with issues like adequate roads, restroom facilities, picnic and camping areas and parking just as the automobile was becoming a fixture on the

American landscape, and Americans flocked to these wild preserves.

Some of the Olmsted recommendations were carried out. Within weeks of the presentation of the plan, the state legislature appropriated $25,000 to undertake the work. Most of the appropriation went towards road work and the removal of dead trees. An amendment was also passed to allow the park to purchase and condemn land.[21] The Olmsteds maintained a relationship with the park commission from 1924 until 1931 through their representative Percy Gallagher.[22]

In the next few years, there was discussion of New York State creating a park that would contain 7,500 acres that abutted High Point. It was suggested an interstate commission be created similar to the Palisades Interstate Park Commission to manage the joint park system.

NPS Designers Arrive At High Point

With the passage of the Emergency Conservation Work law in 1933, a new avenue for developing the park became available to commissioners. After the passage of the act, the governors of each state were invited to participate in the program. Each governor reacted differently, some more willing than others to participate in this major new federal program. The reluctance was in some cases political and in other cases because of the uncertainty of the program. Pennsylvania's Governor Pinchot was the first to apply and New Jersey's Governor A. Harry Moore was not far behind. The governors of Idaho and Illinois lobbied FDR directly and a group of governors from the middle and western parts of the country signed a joint letter that was presented to the president.[23]

By May of 1933, there were three CCC camps proposed for New Jersey to be posted in Sussex, Atlantic and Burlington counties. It is not known if the camp in Sussex was to be at High Point or Stokes. On May 27, 1933, Robert Fechner wrote to Louis Howe, the president's personal secretary, to tell him the state had accepted the federal government's terms covering state and private lands.[24]

High Point was the state's jewel in the crown so that Gov. Moore probably placed it at the top of his list of places where a camp could be housed and work accomplished. The Kusers, who still had a voice and political connections in state government in the form of their son Dryden Kuser, a state senator (1930-1934), certainly must have lobbied for a camp as soon as the program was announced. John Kuser, twin brother of the late Colonel Anthony Kuser and a one-time president of the state's Conservation and Development Commission, probably lobbied as well. John Kuser's fate turned decidedly downward during the depression as his fortune was lost and he died in 1937 financially ruined.

High Point Park Commission members, who were politically well connected, were probably another powerful lobby.[25]

Another important supporter of the park who probably lobbied for a CCC camp was a man of considerable influence in the northern part of the state, John J. Stanton. When the High Point Park Commission (HPPC) was established by the state's governor to manage the affairs of the park, among those first commissioners was Stanton. He stepped down as the secretary of the commission and was appointed its first executive secretary in 1924.[26] Until his retirement in 1934 from the affairs of the commission, High Point had been a major focus of his personal and professional life for fifty years.

Stanton (1857-1940) was the owner of the *Sussex Independent* newspaper, active in the affairs of the county and a prominent resident of Sussex, New Jersey. Stanton played an important role in county politics, was an outdoorsman and regularly promoted High Point in his newspaper. He was long associated with the Kuser family having acted as their real estate agent when they acquired the High Point property in 1909-1910.[27]

We Can Take It!

Reprinted from *Northwestern New Jersey: A History of Somerset, Morris, Hunterdon, Warren and Sussex Counties*

*John J. Stanton
First Executive Secretary
High Point Park Commission*

While he did not lobby for High Point State Park directly, Charles Lathrop Peck, president of the American Tree Association in Washington, D.C., is typical of the men who supported efforts to have CCC camps located in their target areas. Peck lobbied the president directly and urged him to act upon a recommendation by Robert Fechner to approve four camps, including the one at Stokes State Forest. He mentioned his friendship with the governor.[28]

Another person who may have had a hand in lobbying on behalf of the state was Owen Winston, a boyhood chum, classmate and usher at FDR's wedding. He was also vice president of Brooks Brothers. Winston had served for many years on the New Jersey State Board of Conservation which had direct supervision of the state's parks and forests.[29]

Each state had to agree to "share with the Federal government a portion of the increased value which would accrue to the state" because of the CCC.[30] It is believed each state provided some sort of match towards the camps but, apparently, it was not required. Each potential work site had to be inspected and approved by CCC officials before work could begin. The CCC was not allowed to build highways or work on private lands where individuals could cultivate more land. Approval for each project was given by CCC director Robert Fechner.

High Point was unique in that it was one of the earlier state parks created, but it was limited in the ways its resources had been developed. Fortunately for the state, this combination of factors, an established park, plans for creating access to large new tracts of acreage and the governor's quick application for CCC camps dovetailed nicely with FDR's plans to get the CCC camps up and running quickly and to create public access into new parklands that were inaccessible.

We Can Take It!

When National Park Service officials arrived at High Point early in the summer of 1933, there were numerous resources on hand to draw upon. Most importantly, NPS representatives found the Olmsted plan and map, which probably was a major factor in getting two CCC camps at High Point. There were also drawings from a recent effort to build a dam on the Steeny Brook, trail plans, and recent surveys undertaken by Sussex County engineers Clark and E. N. Millen and Roe, who had done work for the Kusers.

They also had access to design books and plans from the service itself so they could create features that would, in the words of the Olmsted firm, be: "The matter of good taste in what is done in the way of improvements and in all structural features. This is obviously true as to architectural character in buildings, but it is equally true of such simple matters as signboards and the lettering upon them. They should be simple and dignified in character without filigree and affectation. Thoroughness and substantiality should distinguish all work in public parks."[31]

From those resources they began to build a long-term vision to implement the features previously called for in addition to proposing new recreation facilities that would open up the park to more visitors than was ever contemplated. Their work would culminate with a new master plan announced to the public in 1938.

Another resource to draw upon was New Jersey State forester, Charles P. Wilber, Chief, Division of Forests and Parks of the Department of Conservation and Development. He served in that position from 1922 until 1953. Wilbur's role in the first year of the CCC's presence in New Jersey cannot be overstated. His tireless efforts provided the work projects for all forestry efforts across the state and early work reports filed from High Point carry his signature.

Through 1933, he created the plan for what forestry crews would do in the parks and forests across the state. He called for the thinning and cutting of sixteen thousand acres of woodland to improve the stand and to promote better tree growth. He also called for increased forestry nursery work, including the preparation of seed beds. He proposed thirty seven hundred acres of trees be planted in 1934 alone.

Wilber also proposed stream improvement work, construction of a lake, campsites, foot bridges, bridal paths and hiking trails. Two hundred and fifty miles of firebreaks were to be created along with the necessary clearing of underbrush along more than two hundred miles of roadway. Ninety miles of roads were proposed along with breeding ponds for fish, all to be carried out by twenty-two camps spread across the state. He also proposed experimental stream projects in Warren County.[32]

Wilber's efforts were so impressive, a CCC official, Herbert Evison, wrote the following on

We Can Take It!

December 28, 1933: "What I wanted to do was simply express to you in behalf of Mr. Wirth and myself our appreciation, not only of the way in which this was gotten up, but also of the perfectly splendid way in which you have worked with this office since the first state park camps of New Jersey were under consideration. We have had some very pleasant dealings indeed with state park authorities all over the country and none have been more pleasant nor freer from friction than have our relations with you and your office. You have appeared always to know where you were going and how you were going to get there, and this has made our task as well as that of Mr. Borgeson, as far as our dealings with New Jersey have been concerned, a very pleasant and easy one."[33]

Work projects proposed and completed at High Point from 1933-1941 were typical of work done by the CCC in parks and forests all across the country. The projects at High Point were done in a series of phases and NPS drawings that remain in the park's archives reveal the evolution of the park's development during the CCC era.

Company 216 was used for forestry projects in the park. Their projects included creating fire breaks, fire prevention, fire fighting, planting trees, thinning and trimming trees, clearing areas of forest waste, landscaping and assisting in building roads, constructing bridges, culverts and watershed protection. It is also believed they did some work outside the park in Montague Township, something common to those kinds of companies. Forestry companies tended to have shorter lives, between two and four years and such was the case with 216.

Company 1280 took on major construction projects such as road building, dam development, building construction and the creation of campsites. Typically, the construction companies were in existence for longer periods of time and by and large served for most or all of the nine years of the CCC's existence. Company 1280 went out of existence just months before the CCC was de-authorized in 1942.

When the CCC arrived at High Point, the state park's visitor facilities were located in the area immediately around Lake Marcia, the highest lake in New Jersey, and the High Point Monument.[34] The facilities around Lake Marcia were heavily used and included swimming, camping, hiking and picnicing. The park was then and is now divided into two parcels by New Jersey State Route 23. There was the twenty-two hundred acre tract on the northern side of Route 23 acquired by the Kusers. In addition, an eight thousand acre tract on the southern side of Route 23 was acquired by Susie Dryden's father, John F. Dryden.

National Park Service officials found a park that was rugged and rocky, made up of former small hardscrabble farms. Many old fields had grown up with pines and hardwoods. Ice storms, forest fires and the chestnut blight had badly damaged thousands of trees in the forest. Project Superintendent Oswald Brown described it as a "veritable fire trap" and said it looked like a cyclone had struck the park. Eighty-five percent of the trees in the area around Lake Marcia and the monument were in some way damaged. There was only one lake in use, Lake Marcia. Lake Rutherfurd at the southeastern end of the park was not accessible because it was the water source for Sussex Borough. It was estimated by one of the project superintendents that about ninety-five hundred acres were woodland and fifteen hundred acres, open fields.[35]

Contemporary newspaper articles estimated only two hundred of the 10,200 acres that made up High Point were accessible to the public. Estimates by one NPS official put the number even smaller at one hundred and fifty acres. The activities of the park were crowded into such a small space that Oswald Brown said proposed NPS projects would "eliminate the Coney Island effect that had been produced."[36] Most of the land lying west of Route 23 remained inaccessible or unusable because there were no passable roads. There were few recreational facilities aside from those around Lake Marcia.

One of the earliest surviving drawings done by NPS personnel was an inventory of park resources and it visually demonstrates how little of the park was being used. There was the Kuser Mansion, or as it was known in the CCC-era,

"The State Building" or "The Administration Building." This was, in terms of elevation, the highest building in the state.[37] There was a visitor's center, museum and restrooms on the first floor of the mansion and the Park Commission offices were on the second floor.[38] There was a cafeteria building or the Grey Rock Inn (the current Interpretive Center), several playgrounds and a series of buildings that made up the Experiment Station and maintenance buildings at the junction of Cedar Swamp Road and Administration and Monument drives.[39]

A Boy Scout camp located on the southern shore of Lake Marcia consisted of two buildings, a float and boat dock in the lake. On the western shore of Lake Marcia was the public bathing beach, bathhouses, a refreshment stand, ticket stand and a bear pen. In a northeasterly direction beyond Lake Marcia was the High Point Monument.

On the main road coming into the park were the Lodge House (also known as the Gate House), four stone picnic shelters that predated the CCC's arrival and a maintenance area just before the entrance to the park. To the east was Scenic Drive with its wide vistas of Sussex, Orange and Pike counties. To the west was a vast void, aside from the old Fuller homestead which was later used as a Girl Scout camp and then for the New Jersey's Commission for the Blind's camp for children.[40]

We Can Take It!

Courtesy The Center For Research Libraries Collection

The view of High Point Monument looking across Lake Marcia. The monument was designed by architects M.S.Wyeth and F.R. King, the same men who designed the Grey Rock Inn (current Interpretive enter). The CCC camp was to the left, on Laurel Drive.

Peter Osborne

Evolution Of The Work Projects

During the early years of the CCC's existence, there was constant uncertainty as to whether the CCC would continue as a national relief and conservation program. Camps were opened and closed regularly as both politics and budgetary concerns influenced the process. Project superintendents note in their reports that because approvals were not always forthcoming for new projects or the continuation of old projects, periods of uncertainty and "lost motion" were common. Delayed budget approvals slowed progress on work projects. It was not until 1937 that the CCC became a permanent agency allowing for more long-range planning.

The initial project at High Point was getting a tent-camp set up for Company 216 in the summer of 1933. In the early months, trees were planted near Lusscroft farm, fire hazards were removed and forest stand improvements were made around Lake Marcia and the monument.

With the arrival of resident designers in the fall of 1933, a more detailed construction work project could be developed. Soon, additional forestry projects were called for to improve the park's unhealthy forests. The next set of projects included opening up the vast interior of the park on the western side of Route 23.

What roads did exist in that part of the park were old wood roads, some without culverts or bridges and none of them having been used as major byways in the years immediately preceding the CCC. The building of an improved network of roads within the park was critical to making the park's resources accessible. This followed the general trend of what happened elsewhere across the country. In all, more than twenty miles of roads were built or reconstructed in the park.

The final set of projects were much more complex and would fundamentally change the way the park would be used in the future. They centered around what became Steenykill Lake, Sawmill Lake and a proposed Shale Lake. One of the most extensive construction projects undertaken was the work done at Sawmill Lake. When the C boys arrived, there was only a large swampy area. An old dam, previously used by a local sawmill, had fallen into disrepair.

The plan at Sawmill called for the removal of the old dam and creation of a new recreational facility with camping, hiking, boating and swimming. It also included building roads leading into the area and clearing of woodland. The entire facility was built from the ground up by the CCC.

Another major project was the building of Steenykill Dam and a colony of twelve cabins along the eastern shore of the lake. In the end, only the dam and two cabins were built. Other projects planned were a recreational complex at another artificially created lake, Shale Lake, and two other camping facilities at what would have been Mashipacong Lake and Lake Montague.

The Shale Lake facility was started but has not been accessible in recent years because it was within the Mountainview Correctional Facility, just off of Route 23 and south of the Visitor Center. Additional picnic and camping areas were proposed along the present-day Park Ridge and Sawmill roads. Had all the projects been built, it would have taken several more years to complete.

Implementation Of Work Projects

The process for developing and implementing projects at High Point was similar at all CCC facilities. Because High Point was a state park, the United States Department of Interior's National Park Service State Park Division, which had full-time representatives in the camp, created the project's design drawings and supervised the work. Those designers were temporary employees of the NPS and in some cases also served as foremen.

There was usually one designer in the Technical Services office assigned to Company 1280 at High Point unless there were larger projects going on. Because of the nature of Company 216's work, they apparently did not require the services of a full time designer.

In each case, NPS designers would create plans and drawings which had to be approved and signed by the camp superintendent, the executive secretary of the High Point Park Commission, the procurement officer, an inspector and the district officer. Later, the process was more formalized and the plans were reviewed by the Branch of Planning in the State Park Division.

The plans and drawings bear the title of the NPS and, in early years, were labeled "Emergency Conservation Work" as the original legislation creating the CCC was called. The initials "ECW" are also found on the back of many photographs in the High Point State Park collection. An index numbering system was used so projects could be quantified on monthly progress reports. For example, in the early years, road work, categorized as Category Number 7 on the report, was divided into truck trails or standard. Later, classifications for roads came into use and roads were given a "202" designation for truck trails and "205" for park roads.

Upon approval, work projects were undertaken by the CCC under the supervision of the NPS's Technical Services. NPS was provided with work details by the army. Smaller work groups sometimes had their own nicknames. For example, men who worked on the roads were called the "road gang."

Howard Platt, project superintendent, regularly reported on how well the work projects were going. As he pointed out in the following report, young men, most of whom had no previous construction experience, developed into a fine labor force once trained: "The work of the Camp NJSP 8 is progressing at a rate of speed comparable to that of the work done by the average contractor under similar circumstances, that of doing ninety percent of the operation by hand.

"The first enrollment of boys, not only knew little or nothing of the project at hand, but were very reticent about working at it. This attitude changed noticeably as the boys became accustomed to and familiar with the work. A greater interest was taken in the work and pride shown in its accomplishment with the least amount of time lost.

"An active interest being displayed by the supervisory personnel on the job, a willingness to teach the boys anything they express a desire to learn, has brought an enthusiasm to the project that has gradually increased the quantity as well as the quality of the work accomplished."[41]

By the late fall of 1941, work gangs, along with the NPS and army personnel, had accomplished much of the original 1924 Olmsted vision and their own plans. Access had been created to the park's interior and the public could make use of the Kuser's wonderful donation, and the forest's health was in good order.

Relationship Between The Park And The CCC

The relationship between the High Point Park Commission and the CCC was an enormously productive one for eight years. Over the last sixty-five years hundreds of thousands of visitors have enjoyed the results of that partnership that opened up so much of the park.

Although John Stanton's relationship with the CCC lasted for less than a year, it was a cooperative one. One newspaper clipping stated the progress made at High Point was better than at any other camp in the 2nd Corps area.[42] In February 1934, John Stanton retired as executive secretary of the park commission. At the time he was seventy-seven years old and ailing. It is believed he may have been encouraged to resign because of the massive undertaking that was about to be started.[43]

Immediately after the resignation became known, a number of men applied for the job. Among them were Captain Clarke Millen, commander of CCC Company 1220 in Scottsburg, Virginia; Charles Schwartz, project superintendent of the ECW Camp No.5 at Voorhees State Park in High Bridge, New Jersey, and Charles Henkel of Ridgewood, New Jersey.

Millen may have been the engineer who did work for the Kusers, including the original design of Steenykill Lake. Henkel was the NPS foreman then working for Company 216. Other applicants sent in resumes, and in the end, eleven applications were reviewed.

On February 6, 1934, Stanton's resignation was read at the park commission's meeting. The commission already had the final three resumes in hand and were ready to make a decision. However, just before the meeting, the commission received a telegram from Dryden Kuser. In his telegram he urged commissioners to refrain from making a final decision because there was a vast pool of resources they could draw upon in getting the best man for the job.[44]

In 1960, Kuser recalled one of the most important things the commission's new secretary was to deal with was the management of the park's construction projects undertaken by the CCC. He wrote: "The Commission's president [Gouverneur Carnochan] was to fulfill what he realized was of great importance - the selection of a qualified engineer to fill Mr. Stanton's place as Executive Secretary - important, because he was to plan, work with and approve the projects of the US Department of Interior for the CCC. Through the efforts of Frederick C. Sutro, Executive Director of the Palisades Interstate Park Commission, an Assistant of their superintendent, John F. Gibbons, was interested in accepting the appointment at High Point."[45]

We Can Take It!

At the next meeting on March 6, 1934, John Gibbons was interviewed by the commissioners. Born in Brooklyn, New York in 1895, he was a licensed civil engineer and had been assistant superintendent at Palisades Interstate Park since 1930 under the highly respected Major William A. Welch. Welch was one of the nation's leading figures in park management and also the park's general manager. High Point was in many ways equal in stature to the Bear Mountain and Harriman state park facilities in New York and which were managed by the Palisades Interstate Park Commission. There had also been some correspondence between Stanton and William Welch, the chief engineer and general manager of the park.

Courtesy Jane Gibbons Proctor
John Gibbons
Executive Secretary
High Point Park Commission
Superintendent
High Point State Park

Prior to his work with the Palisade Interstate Park Commission Gibbons worked in the Bergen County, New Jersey engineer's office and served in the army in 1918 during World War I.[46] Gibbons was married to the former Grace Egglesfield and had three children, John, Jr., Jane and Joan.[47] The park's commissioners had a sense of accomplishment in having lured away an important official from a park that was to some degree in competition with High Point. Bear Mountain and Harriman state parks provided much inspiration to the development of High Point.[48]

In the final vote, taken March 6, 1934, John Gibbons received three votes and Captain Millen, two. On April 1, 1934, Gibbons began work at the park, and one of his first acts was to move the secretary's office from Sussex Borough to the Administration Building in the park. Gibbons and his family moved into the Gate House at the main entrance to the park where he and his wife lived until 1956.[49] The hiring of Gibbons began the most cooperative intergovernmental partnership in the park's history, a relationship which was productive and harmonious. John Gibbons along with Melvin Gemmill were two of the major figures in the park during the CCC era.

The relationship between Gibbons and the CCC was a compatible one and those who had recollections of the era could not recall any major problems. Whatever problems did arise, Gibbons must have taken care of them because they are not to be found in the park commission minutes. His cooperative nature was shown repeatedly. For instance, he provided a darkroom in the mansion for the CCC and also loaned them his mimeograph machine when theirs broke.

Albert Mastriani recalled: "He was a fine gentleman who was very cooperative in all the work we did and was our only contact with the High Point State Park Commission to my knowledge ... I think Mr. Gibbons was vitally interested in our work and rode out to the sites to look, not really to inspect, but I am sure he knew what was going on at all times. In addition, he had his own people for routine maintenance and policing. My favorite memory of him is that he took a lot of interest in the CCC, and Melvin Gemmill and I talked with him frequently about how things were going when Melvin was appointed project superintendent about 1938."[50]

While the CCC occasionally is mentioned in the minutes of the park commission, Gibbons tended to consolidate the projects of the CCC and park staff together into one listing. The record of the interaction between the two groups over the next nine years in the minutes is, for the most part, largely silent.

The commission met several times a year in various locations around the state. Members were generally prominent people from the metropolitan New York area. In late June 1933, they met at the Newark Athletic Club in Newark, New Jersey and while the CCC had already arrived and set up a tent camp at the Lusscroft farm, they did not merit any mention in the minutes of the meeting. Much of the meeting focused on internal matters including a discussion on pay toilets and an employee in the museum who was subsequently fired.

It was not until the October 8, 1933 commission meeting that the CCC was mentioned when John Stanton reported on the activities of Company 216 during the previous summer which included forest and road work in the park. He told commissioners the federal government was planning to build a camp to accommodate four hundred men for the winter months. The secretary was directed to: "Communicate with the CCC authorities regarding keeping peace and order within the confines of the Park during the occupancy."[51]

Stanton was authorized to let one CCC officer stay in the Administration Building until he could find living quarters for himself and his family. It is curious there was no recorded debate at board meetings or even any discussion concerning how projects at the park would be authorized or what the relationship would be between the park and the CCC. With those two resolutions, the CCC era had begun.

There was also no discussion, at least as evidenced in the minutes, as to where the camp location would be because perhaps no one could foresee how long the work projects would last and commissioners were just delighted to get free manpower to do the job.

There can be no doubt the commissioners wanted the CCC at High Point because it was the first state park camp in New Jersey. Company

216 was on location in early June, a little less than two months after legislation was passed in Washington and only days after almost three hundred work projects were approved by the CCC's Advisory Council.[52]

There were only two times when tensions between the two organizations were publicly recorded in the minutes of the park commission. Both of these events occurred just as Gibbons was coming on board and demonstrate how the relationship between the CCC and commission had not yet been sorted out. The events took place in the interim between the arrival of Gibbons and the departure of Stanton. At the March 1934 meeting of the commissioners, member Seeley Frank Quince said: "that in his opinion considerable damage had been done to the natural beauties of Cedar Swamp Drive by the CCC forces, in that they had needlessly removed a number of trees in widening the road and destroyed quantities of rhododendron and laurel, and that those in charge of the CCC work apparently did not consult with Park authorities in regard to what should and should not be done."[53]

The issue was resolved when, "Mr. Quince was instructed to advise those in charge of CCC work to consult him before undertaking any new projects."[54] Quince was also empowered by commissioners to take charge of the park's affairs until a new secretary was found. Albert Mastriani remembered the incident and said:

"Mr. Quince was entirely correct in his assessment about Cedar Swamp Drive. We were sent down to clear for a road without any instructions about the environmental sensitivity of the area, and we handled it like any other road job. At this late date I would lay the blame at the hands of our superiors for not sending down an expert to mark the trees and shrubs that were to come down. Even after more than sixty five years, I shudder at the damage that we did. Of course, I guess I'm a lot smarter now, I hope!"[55]

In spite of the criticism that Howard Platt did not have a sense of the importance of the Cedar Swamp, the project superintendent wrote in his report to his superiors that: "Cedar Drive an old and impassable logging trail runs along the valley nearly northeast from Lake Marcia to and around a swamp at the upper end of the park. The swamp being a depression, at one end of the mountain valley, filled with a luxuriant growth of rare white cedars, spruce, hemlock, and masses of rhododendron, winter berry, etcetera, is of considerably more than casual interest from the conservation point of view ... At the fork of the trail on that section known as Cedar Drive it was found that a corner of the Cedar Swamp had been denuded of its natural flora by reason of an old quarry track terminating at this point. The planting project for this camp consisted of refurnishing this eye-sore in the otherwise very interesting plant colony."[56]

Another problem occurred at the same time as the Cedar Swamp controversy when the park commission gave CCC officials a bill for $1,480 to cover the cost of bringing shale to grade the area around Camp Kuser. CCC officials refused to pay the bill and the president of the commission, Dr. John F. Hagerty, was authorized to take the matter up with the state's attorney general. The issue continued to play out over the next few meetings until in October 1934, army officers gave affidavits as did John Stanton to find out how the work had come to be authorized. The park commission, agreeing with CCC officials in their assessment of the situation, disposed of the bill at no cost to the federal government.

When park issues impacted the CCC or a project they were working on needed assistance, Gibbons consulted with NPS and army officials. For example, in the fall of 1934, road work was being done on Deckertown Turnpike on the section west of the junction with Sawmill Road to connect the park with Stokes State Forest. Because some of the turnpike was not then within park boundaries, work was ordered stopped. If work had continued, it would have connected the Mashipacong Pond property to a usable road. This would have made it worth considerably more to the private owner who was then trying to sell it to someone other than the park.[57]

We Can Take It!

It is believed Gibbons brought projects sponsored by NPS designers to the commissioners for their approval. In the October 1934 commission meeting, discussion on two new proposed lakes, presumably Sawmill and Steenykill, was tabled apparently because of planning being done by the NPS. In May 1935, when names were needed for the new lakes at Sawmill and Steenykill and for the central truck trail, the task was left to commissioners. After 1935, Gibbons prepared a list of projects for approval. Some were CCC projects and others were to be done by park staff.

Park commissioners did not reduce their own load of projects however. From 1923-1933 the park's staff built and added many new features to the park.[58] Major projects were not undertaken from 1930 until 1933 because of the deepening depression and cutbacks in the state budget. Even the monument was closed to save money.

Once the CCC arrived and the economy began to recover, the state once again began to invest in its largest park. For example, in the 1935-1936 budget, the commission proposed spending $17,500 for resurfacing five miles of park roads. In 1937, the Kuser mansion was converted into a modern hotel that could accommodate fifty guests with meals to be served at the Grey Rock Inn.[59] The park's staff took care of regular maintenance needs along with new construction of public facilities. In many ways, the two organizations were distinct, working on their own priorities and operating under the umbrella of the park.

The CCC also assisted with a number of projects that promoted the park's public image and interpretation. In the spring of 1937, the National Park Service's laboratories at Fort Hunt, Virginia created four geographic relief models of the park's landscape and the CCC boys installed them at the base of the High Point Monument.[60] NPS foreman Albert Mastriani provided at least one photograph for what may be the earliest park brochure (c. 1940-1941) that shows two hikers on the Monument Trail. It is believed NPS designer Melvin Gemmill provided the handsome drawing of the map of the park (c. 1940-1941) that was altered slightly over the years but used in park brochures until fairly recent times.

In the first four to six years of joint efforts, the budgets of the HPPC and the CCC were separate from each other. The park essentially paid for its own maintenance and for the construction of new projects, particularly those on the eastern side of the park and those at the blind children's camp along the Park Ridge Road. The CCC paid for its own operations, supplies and payroll without any help from the state. To save money, the ECW was not to purchase new supplies if they were available on site or in a government inventory.[61]

We Can Take It!

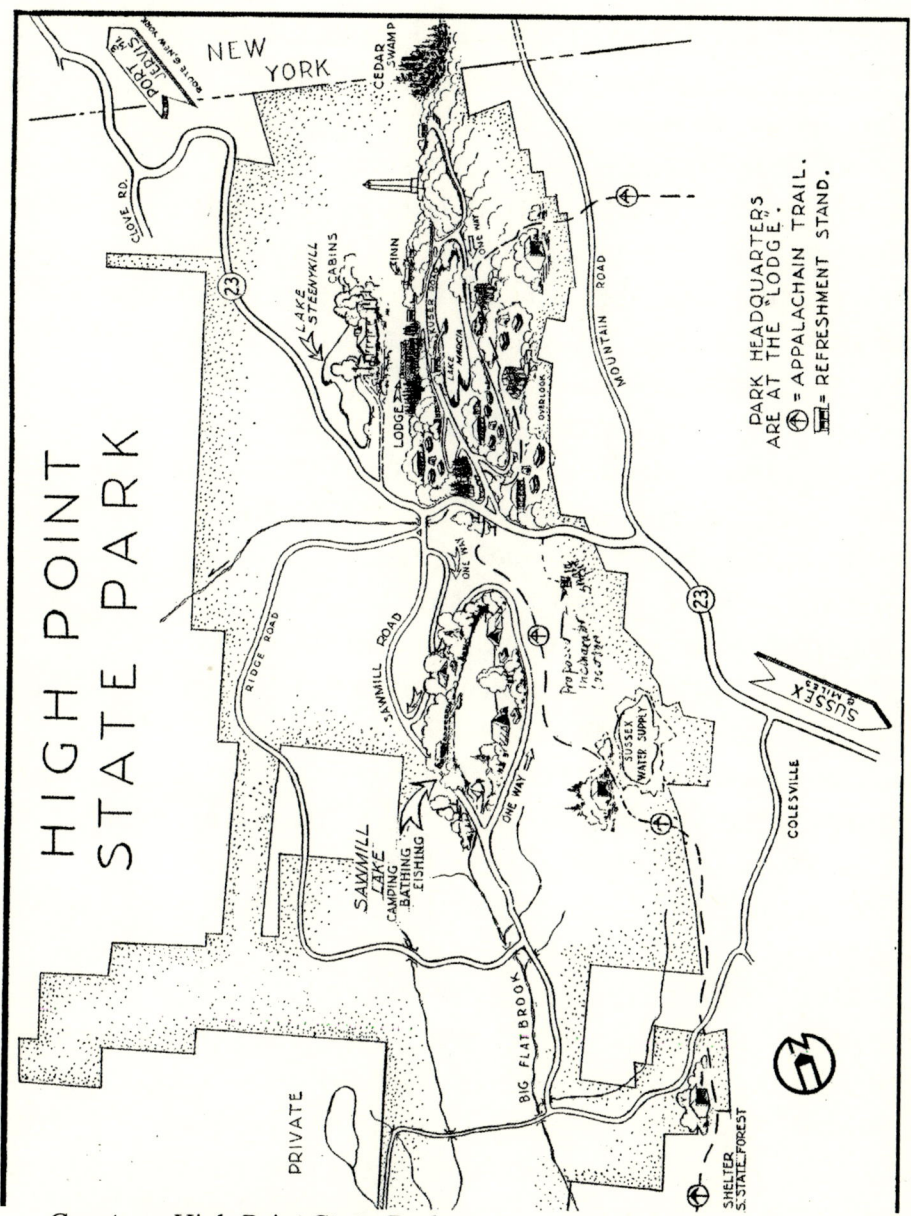

Courtesy High Point State Park
This drawing of High Point State Park is believed to have been by Melvin Gemmill and probably dates from 1940 or 1941.

In 1937, FDR proposed the CCC become a permanent agency of the federal government and during the course of creating the new legislation, there was internal discussion about what the states had committed to the projects financially. That particular issue was left unresolved during the initial legislation creating the organization. As discussions moved forward, it was agreed the states must maintain CCC projects that had been built. Until 1936, only Connecticut reimbursed the federal government for sales of lands or products from those lands which was part of the original agreement.[62]

After 1937, and certainly after 1939, that financial relationship was somewhat altered. The CCC asked the park commission for funding to cover some of the costs of its projects both at Sawmill Lake and the proposed Shale Lake. The costs were only for materials and the amounts vary from $700-$1,500, however, materials for the grandstand at Shale Lake complex were $3,000.

The only number ever suggested for federal funding that the CCC put into the park is the hundreds of thousands of dollars cited in a resolution commending John Gibbons for his work.[63] Based on the average cost of running a camp, it can be estimated the CCC contributed about $720,000 (1930s dollars) worth of labor and materials to High Point Park, not including materials obtained on site.

The relationship between the C boys and the park staff is a curious one in that they were quite distinct and separate from each other. Editorials in the newsletter reminded the CCC boys that they should be on best behavior when visitors were in the park because they were conceivably a large and supportive constituency.

During the early 1930s, with as many as one hundred and fifty thousand people visiting High Point Park each year, the C boys were encouraged to make a positive impression upon them.[64] Enrollees worked in some of the park's facilities on weekends and an occasional weekday. Some worked at part time jobs, doing laundry for other enrollees, cutting hair, working at the Grey Rock Inn as waiters or dishwashers and even cooking for political functions and parties at the Kuser Mansion. Some served as guides and escorts.

The park tried to make the quality of life for the C boys a little better. The park's management made special arrangements for enrollees to go swimming in Lake Marcia in an area directly across from the public area below the Kuser Mansion. They were given their own pier and diving board. Trained lifeguards, from the ranks of the CCC men, were on hand to oversee their fellow enrollees.

In the final analysis, the relationship between the park and CCC is best described in the 1934 annual report which said: "Two forest fires broke out in the Park area this summer during one of the hot spells, but with the aid of the Park force and boys from the Civilian Conservation Camp the fires were put out before making much headway. The one fire burned twenty-five acres of grass and the other burned sixty acres of forest. The Civilian Conservation Camp, which consists of Company No.1 and Company No.8 is located on Cedar Drive. They have been a great benefactor to the Park, cleaning up, clearing truck trails, widening roads, paths, etc."[65]

The High Point Park Commission was deauthorized in 1945 as the state created a new Department of Conservation headed by Morgan Larson, a former governor of the state. The commission voted against disbanding itself, but in the end, the Department of Conservation took over the operations of the park. John Gibbons continued to serve as superintendent until he was killed when the light truck he was driving along Park Ridge Road swayed off the road and hit a tree on January 11, 1956. Found by a passing driver, he was taken to St. Francis Hospital in Port Jervis where he died. He and some of his family members are buried in St. Mary's Cemetery in Port Jervis.[66]

CHAPTER 6

The Roosevelt Tree Army

They had people ... that knew the difference of what kind of tree it was ... [if it] was diseased ... it would be marked ... the leader, the ranger would get a map and ... he would stake it out and say, 'this is what I want cleaned out.' And then we'd clean [it] out and get it all into the center of the area and ... burn it.
-Michael Sagursky, Company 1280 Enrollee

We Can Take It: The Roosevelt Tree Army at High Point State Park 1933-1941: Interviews With Former Civilian Conservation Corps Enrollees, Camp Kuser, Companies 216 & 1280. vol. 1.

I had sore legs ... fighting in the brush. We used to have these five gallon cans filled with water and go in and fight the forest fire. We fought it for two weeks. I remember that one.
-Carl LoGrand, Company 1280 Enrollee

We Can Take It: The Roosevelt Tree Army at High Point State Park 1933-1941: Interviews With Former Civilian Conservation Corps Enrollees, Camp Kuser, Companies 216 & 1280. vol. 1.

When Company 216 arrived at the Lusscroft farm the surrounding forests were in trouble. Fires regularly swept through the area and severe ice storms had damaged thousands of trees in both High Point State Park and Stokes State Forest. The undergrowth was thick, and there were fire hazards all around the park. Company 216's main focus was to repair the forests, clear them of hazards and to improve the stand of timber in the park.

Hundreds of CCC companies around the country did work like this on private, state and national forests. Company 1280's first assignment, prior to its being stationed at High Point, was blister control work in a private forest in Idaho, probably adjacent to a national forest. Unfortunately, there is not much archival material on the forestry projects remaining at High Point. Only general work project reports survive. Some interviews with enrollees remain to tell the story of 216's work, but in the end, most of its trimming and clearing has long been overgrown and taken over by the forest's natural progression. As a result, the work of 216 is not as well remembered as are the efforts of 1280.

Forestry Projects Completed By The CCC

By and large forestry work at High Point was done by Company 216 although Company 1280 undertook some of it. They cleared thousands of acres of dead fall improving the timber stand, controlled White Pine Blister Rust by destroying alternatives hosts, eliminated fire hazards and removed trees and stumps from areas where new lakes were to be constructed. They also performed salvage cutting of trees killed by chestnut blight and Dutch elm disease. Company 216 also helped build roads in the western part of the park, created campsites and improved the trail system.

Michael Sagursky remembered the battle waged against Dutch elm disease which struck down millions of trees across America. He said: "This is one of our big projects here [at High Point] too. And we had certain areas where we had to cut the trees and then put them on a pile and burn them. And this is the way we ... protected the elm itself."[1]

One of the earliest surviving NPS drawings in the park's archives (1934) shows miles of fire breaks, varying in width from one hundred to two hundred feet, being created along the Appalachian Trail which ran along the Kittatinny ridge line. Also, along the route of the present-day Deckertown Turnpike from a point just west of Mashipacong Pond to the park's boundary on the east, along the southern section of Sawmill Road, Park Ridge Road, the wood road now known as the Ayers Trail and a portion of Route 23 near the park's northern border.

The entire park boundary along the border with New York was cleared because a number of fires arose on the New York side. Campgrounds were cleared around Sawmill Lake and a large area to the south and east of what would become the lake was to have forest improvements made and forest hazards removed. The area around Lake Marcia was generally cleaned up.

Projects called for removal of dead wood and trimming and thinning of existing trees, but not to damage the crown cover. A 1936 news article said three hundred and fifty acres were trimmed after significant damage caused by an ice storm. An additional seven hundred and fifty acres were given fire prevention treatment. About twenty-five miles of fire breaks were created, probably done by Company 216. Finally, five miles of fencing from the Kuser's original enclosed elk park was removed.[2]

Enormous numbers of brush piles were created by the acres of trimming, repairing damaged trees and clearing underbrush. Peter Lutz remembered what was done with the brush piles. He said: "The winter time was very severe and ... we would go back to where these brush piles were. This was in the dead of winter. And then we would ... set these brush piles afire you know, to burn them so they wouldn't be so obnoxious to look at ...

"We wouldn't use rubber tires or anything. Everything was more or less natural. [We] just used a couple of oil rags ... to start the fire and stuck it under these brush piles and then ... it would take them almost all day to burn some of these brush piles, they were so high ... [when] we were planning to quit, we would completely douse them out because we didn't want to fight these forest fires."[3]

One of the results of the extensive forestry program was the removal of thousands of chestnut trees struck with the blight. Thousands of feet of guard rail that lined the parks roads were made from these trees. Peter Lutz was on a crew that harvested chestnut logs from Cedar Swamp using both mules and "donkeys" and remembered: "Well, with the tree stumps, we would pull them aside you know, some of those stumps we had to blast ... There was a lot of dead chestnut trees which had been killed by the blight and they were big ... like telephone poles ... We would cut them and then we would take them out of the swamp. It'd be maybe ten men on one side [and] ten men on the other. They would have a pole underneath as thick as a baseball bat and all of us were like prisoners you know down in the South America ... through the swamps. We'd haul them out and then we ... made a fence ..."[4]

On the subject of mules, Lutz reflected that: "We had problems with them. They're pretty hard to [deal with], you got to be an experienced mule man, not a donkey man ... a mule man. You had to know how to handle those donkeys, mules rather. But we had them for about two days and ... you can't make them move you know! ... So we used the donkeys, that was the CC boys!

"We would all lift up together and then take it out to where we would get to dry land to put them on the truck or have the truck drag them around Lake Marcia here to make a fence so the automobiles wouldn't go over. We creosote[d] them, and we draw shaved them... We enjoyed it."[5]

Forestry officials from the state and federal level were on site inspecting the work and proposing projects, especially in the first year of the CCC's involvement at High Point. Oswald Brown proposed and supervised projects at High Point and Stokes.[6] New Jersey State Forester Charles P. Wilber and his assistants also inspected the work and made proposals.

Courtesy The Center for Research Library Collections

Tree Planting And Landscaping

The forestry company did not plant large numbers of tree seedlings at High Point although there are places where they transplanted trees including the entrance to Cedar Swamp, at the main entrance along Route 23 and along some of the roads that were constructed or upgraded. There were no major tree plantations created at High Point unlike those at Stokes.

There are several patches of red pines at Steenykill Lake and also along Park Ridge Road near the gas line which were probably planted by the CCC. Red pines were widely used by the CCC in northern New Jersey because of their hardiness. Nelson Kessler, the state's forester who was in charge of the nurseries, said "it was ordinarily a healthy, thrifty growing tree"[7]

Tree seedlings were grown by the state's Department of Conservation and Development and numbered in the millions. During the course of one year, four million seedlings were made available to the public, the majority of which were used by CCC camps. Seedlings cost between $4 and $7 per thousand. Purchasers of the trees could not use them for commercial or ornamental purposes.[8]

Landscape work done by the C boys included finish work along new roads, moving and planting trees and shrubs, lake bank protection and clearing stream beds. The health of forests was given priority and when trees were near recently constructed roads, tree pits were created so they would not be damaged by new road contours. Several tree pits can still be seen along roads built by the CCC. In the spring of 1936 Company 216 moved over four hundred trees and shrubs to new locations, particularly along culvert crossings, barren areas along roads and to the park's main entrance.

Enrollees were taught how to trim trees without hurting themselves or the trees, how to climb trees with ropes, how to recognize diseases and how to develop confidence when working up in a tree. Oswald Brown estimated it took about a month to gain the necessary skills to undertake the work. By the end of the training, enrollees were considered to be the equal of commercial tree trimmers.[9]

Courtesy High Point State Park
Enrollees from Company 216 plant trees at the main entrance to the park along State Route 23.

We Can Take It!

Forest Fire Suppression And Prevention

One of the most important functions of the CCC was the prevention and suppression of forest fires. The 1930s witnessed large numbers of raging fires as forests across the country were tinder boxes waiting to explode, filled with dead fall and thick brush. The situation was no different at High Point State Park.

In 1934, the C boys put out seven forest fires ranging from two to three hundred acres and in 1936, Company 216 spent 228 man-days fighting forest fires. By the end of the 1930s, forest fire damage was cut dramatically across the country because of the CCC's efforts. Among the first projects completed by Company 216 were miles of roadside and trailside clearing of fire hazards.[10] Hundreds of acres of forest fire hazard reduction projects were completed by 216 and the removal of hazardous materials continued until the end of the company's existence. With removal of those materials, fires remained close to the ground and were more easily suppressed. Because of their training, many acres of woodland were saved in the years that the CCC served at High Point.

C boys were called upon to fight forest fires in New York, New Jersey and Pennsylvania. A camp fire chief was appointed and in charge of enrollees when fires broke out. Training conducted by NPS foremen was given to enrollees and the camp's management attended schools on firefighting techniques. If enrollees did not take the course, they could not fight fires. This skill was one of the most important C boys learned for they stood shoulder to shoulder with state forest fire officials as they battled blazes. C boys were rarely called out on fire duty, perhaps once or twice a year.[11]

Major fires were fought by the High Point companies in Sparrowbush and Wurtsboro, New York. The fire at Sparrowbush was remembered by Carl LoGrand when he said: "I had sore legs ... fighting in the brush. We used to have these five gallon cans filled with water and go in and fight the forest fire. We fought it for two weeks. I remember that one."[12] He also remembered the cause of the fire: "[It was] in a wooded area ... I think [somebody] cooking out there didn't put the fire out right or something and that got out of control ... it was a dry season then."[13] Peter Lutz remembered a firefighting detail he was on: "We'd be trucked over there ... The technique ... used ... was very primitive. I used to carry a first aid kit. All the little guys are carrying these sacks ... full of water. Up these inclines, I'll tell you, we had to climb up some of these cliffs, it was something else ... I was the first aider ... There were some injuries.

"You would have to wear a special type clothing which was, even though it was hot, you'd have to wear like a GI wool shirt and GI wool pants, because if you wore cotton and the sparks happen to hit you, the spark would ignite on your clothing, your cotton garments. They would burn a hole and continue on! See where you had, if you had a woolen shirt, it was damp, probably from your own sweat, it [the fire] wouldn't ... penetrate it."[14]

In May 1935, a major fire occurred along Scenic Drive, started by an ember from a picnic gathering. Because it was on the eastern slope of the ridge, strong winds fanned the flames and destroyed about one hundred and twenty-five acres of forest near Lake Marcia, around the monument and across Scenic Drive. Sixty C boys and park employees fought the fire after coming back from a fire in Otisville, New York, some twenty miles north of the park.[15]

Another blaze occurred in the park in July 1936 when an old barn caught fire. The family of Louis Jacobus, a park employee, lived nearby and C boys who were among the first to arrive, formed a bucket brigade in a effort to protect the residence and stable building. CCC trucks were used to bring in barrels of water. Unfortunately, personal items, farm equipment and park equipment were lost in the blaze. C boys even helped to rescue some of the livestock.[16]

The most damaging fire occurred November 24, 1936, when a large garage that housed thirteen trucks, a new car and a sizable amount of the camp's equipment was burned to the ground. The trucks of Company 1280 and one truck from Company 216 were destroyed in the garage which measured 20' x 140'. Fire departments from Port Jervis and Sussex were called but the fire had completely engulfed the building by the time they arrived. Over three hundred men formed a bucket brigade to fight the fire. Earlier that evening, about three hundred enrollees had used the same trucks to go to lectures on forestry at the Sussex High School.[17]

Neil Thiede, an enrollee, remembered: "This was down in the far end of the camp towards the swamp, the Cedar, and incidentally we called it, if I remember correctly, the Cypress Swamp, I understand that they call it the Cedar Swamp now. But we had a string of garages where they serviced, we had a lot of dump trucks you know in addition to the rack trucks. This garage caught fire and it was in the wee small hours and what could we do [but] carry water in a pail? Get a fire engine from Port Jervis or Sussex? And it was burning for a couple of hours and you'd hear these gas tanks go every once in a while, gasoline and a little explosion, you must of heard about ten or fifteen of them. It was an awful mess the next morning, all these trucks burned and everything. I don't know what they did for a while after that for equipment. It was a big event."[18]

Another major fire occurred in March 1938 that destroyed the education building of Company 1280. It was discovered by a C boy who was serving as a night watchman. Water was pumped from Lake Marcia to extinguish the blaze and to prevent it from destroying other nearby buildings.[19]

Frank Seddio remembered the event and the coincidence that the fire occurred on a night the men were at a class on fire prevention when he said:

"I remember ... one night they took us, the whole camp down to Sussex, New Jersey for fire prevention week ... they took us down there to orientate us on fire prevention. And I distinctly remember coming back and our building was on fire! That was really something! I mean that, well the personnel that was left behind they [had] already tried [to start] putting it out.

"Naturally we had our work putting it out and also it got to the fire department ... from, I don't know if Colesville had a fire department then or not. And from Sussex, New Jersey they all came up."[20] To the great humor of the C boys, the Port Jervis Fire Department did not arrive until the building was completely burned to the ground.

A fire in Monticello, New York in October 1938 saw fifty members of Company 1280 called into service over a twenty-four hour period. Under the direction of Messers. Parry, Platt, Turner and Mastriani, the fire was contained. Another fire in Barryville in 1939 brought twenty men from High Point into service and eighty men were called to a fire in Ellenville, New York a few days later.

Peter Osborne

A forest fire protection plan, drawn up in 1940 by Albert Mastriani, shows the fire detail district that included much of Sussex County, western Orange and southern Sullivan counties in New York and the eastern half of Pike County, Pennsylvania. Both companies participated in these duties and were usually joined by other firefighters from the region.

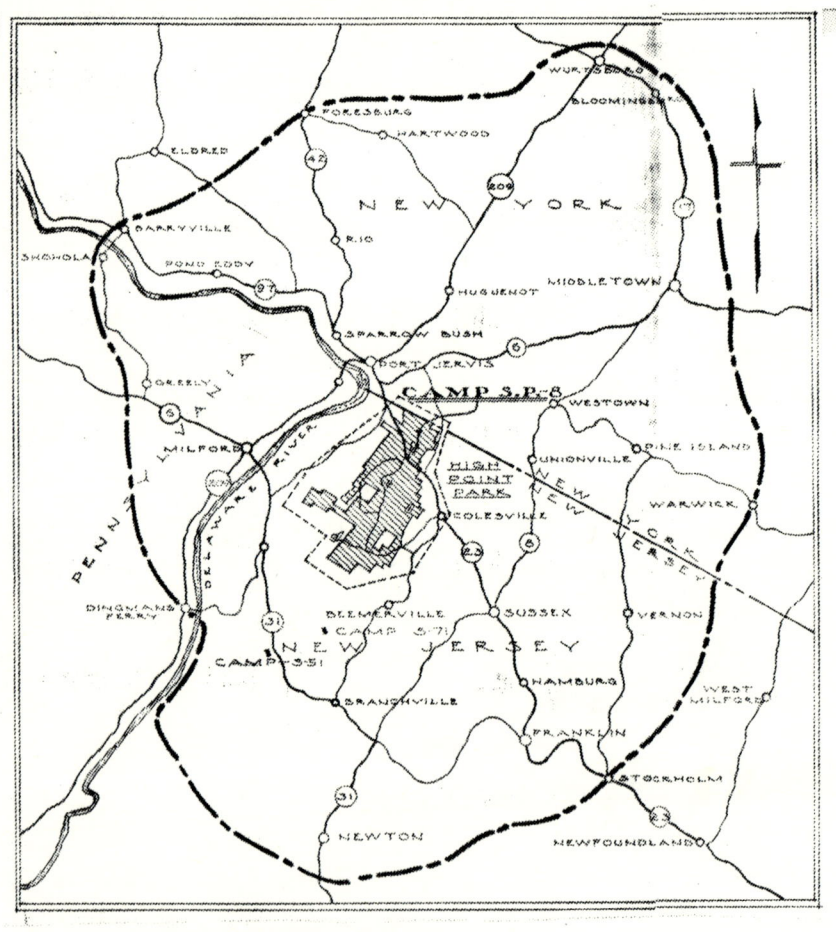

Courtesy High Point State Park
CCC Fire Protection Plan for High Point State Park.

We Can Take It!

The CCC was responsible for fighting any fires inside the protection zone marked off by the dotted line near the park boundaries. Within the local zone, park authorities would request the assistance of C boys. If a fire occurred in the cooperation zone outside the park, which is shown on the map as a large circle extending beyond the camp, enrollees and foremen were under the jurisdiction of NPS rangers if it were on federal property. Under all other conditions, C boys were under the jurisdiction of local authorities.

In June 1937, Company 216, the forestry company, was closed down. The closure probably came about because a large number of CCC camps were shuttered for budgetary reasons. However, at High Point, most of the conservation and forestry projects were completed and with that, its mission accomplished and the forests within the park boundaries in good health again. The success of companies like 216 earned the CCC one of its most well known nicknames, the *"Roosevelt Tree Army."*

CHAPTER 7

We Can Take It!

I was on the dynamite crew. Used to blast these mud packs, these big rocks and blast them ... You see the high hill ... [the one going] down below going towards Sussex. There's a hill there. And the police chief's house ... was a little ways, like a couple hundred feet down. And we put eighty-one pounds of dynamite into this road and I pulled the switch. And you see rocks flying all over and we broke every window in the police chief's house, you know, the vibration and all ...
-Carl LoGrand, Company 1280 Enrollee, Road Gang

We Can Take It: The Roosevelt Tree Army at High Point State Park 1933-1941: Interviews With Former Civilian Conservation Corps Enrollees, Camp Kuser, Companies 216 & 1280. vol. 1.

We had to go out there, and we had to get stone. A certain size, it'd be two men, we had a litter, a regular carrier ... Two men picked up a stone, put it on this litter and brought it out to the road. And then we loaded it on the truck, and the truck brought it over to this other park that they were building.
-Robert Wilber, Company 1280 Enrollee, Road Gang

We Can Take It: The Roosevelt Tree Army at High Point State Park 1933-1941: Interviews With Former Civilian Conservation Corps Enrollees, Camp Kuser, Companies 216 & 1280. vol. 1.

The first big projects undertaken at High Point were the construction of Camp Kuser and the creation of a road network in the western section of the park. The design of the CCC camp at High Point was typical of camps across the country. The army created a series of layouts that suited the landscapes where they might be located. In getting the camp at High Point constructed before the winter of 1933, private contractors were used with some assistance from enrollees.

Camp Kuser

Camp Kuser lined both sides of Laurel Drive (currently Cedar Swamp Drive) with a company on each side. It included twenty-six wood frame buildings that housed both companies and the supervisory personnel. After the camp was erected, the road dividing the companies was called Company Street. There are no known drawings that show the original layout.

Unfortunately, none of the original 1933 construction drawings remain; however, three drawings survive of additions to buildings at Camp Kuser. Camp Kuser can best be described as a work in progress. After it was built, changes were made regularly. Additions were made to buildings, fire destroyed several others and buildings were taken down after Company 216 was disbanded.

Peter Osborne

Courtesy High Point State Park

The CCC camp was located at the base of the hill on which the High Point Monument stands. It can be seen from this postcard view and was a large operation. Company 216 was located on the lower half of the rows of buildings and Company 1280 was located on the other side of the street. This particular view was reproduced as a postcard enrollees could use for writing home.

The original foremen's and officers' quarters for Company 1280 was destroyed by fire about 1939, and they moved across the street into a former Company 216 building. After Company 216 was disbanded, its recreation hall was turned into a motion picture house and a former barracks building was turned into an education building. This change was necessary after a fire destroyed Company 1280's facility in 1938 along with a former barracks building.

The concrete pad on which the 216 latrine was placed was kept for use as a handball court. In the early summer of 1938, all the remaining 216 buildings were torn down by the wrecking crew of the Trenton District, part of a larger effort to dismantle other abandoned camps.[1]

Because of constant use, the buildings began to show signs of wear and tear. In 1938, almost five years after the construction of the camp, major renovations took place. New floors were laid and electrical fixtures replaced, a new schoolhouse was built and repairs made in the kitchen and canteen. Walkways were beautified and a new floor and equipment were installed in the scullery.[2]

By 1940 the camp included the barracks, parade ground, flagpole, a latrine, a recreation hall, camp meeting hall, technical service garages and offices, supply house, oil house, chlorinator, officers' and foremen's quarters, first aid building, army administration buildings, the NPS administration building that housed designers and the project superintendent, warehouse and blacksmith shop.

At least one enrollee interviewed by William Wurst remembered what the camp looked like in 1940. Robert Wilbert said:

"There was barracks and, of course, the commander of the company. His was just a little office right at the head, right when you first come in. Then we had two barracks on the street, and then the mess hall was on the street.

Along the street going towards the swamp, and then below the mess hall was [what] we call it [a] canteen or P.X. [post exchange] ... And then as you went over the other way, in toward the woodside ... there was a big long building, it was a latrine. [Of] course we had another barrack[s]. It was one, two and three and four.

"And then in the back there was a big building for the maintenance men, truck drivers and like that. And the cook and the mess sergeant, they had their building by their selves. And when you first come in, mine was the first barrack, and on the opposite side of the street you went up a little hill and there was a big long barrack that the Department of the Interior [used] ... the foremen and all, they lived in that.

"And they ... had great big dining room like where they brought their wives up you know, and the commander ... And they had their, their little get togethers. And they had ... bedrooms on one side ... we had hot, showers, everything. Toilets, everything ... And then, right alongside the latrine, each barrack had four stoves in it. And ... we were assigned different ones to keep coal in at night ... Course we banked them down ... and they burned soft coal."[3]

Access To The Hinterlands
Road Work Projects

After the camp was built, road construction projects were given the highest priority. Through the 1920s and 1930s the conditions of the roads leading into the park were of ongoing concern. The steepness of the road leading up to High Point caused many maintenance problems. Many roads that the CCC built were formerly public roads but fell into disuse and became impassable.

Road building opened much of the park for access and development. It was believed in 1933 that only about 15 percent of the park was accessible by the existing road network. By late 1934, 45 percent of the total acreage was accessible. Project superintendent Howard Platt noted in a report that with the construction of Cedar Swamp Drive and Sawmill Road, both of which ran down the center of the valley, access to the entire park's resources as well as Stokes State Forest from its northern end had been created.[4]

At most CCC camps, either United States Forest Service road building standards were used or the NPS Forest Truck Trail Handbook to design roads. For example, specifications called for a maximum load on a bridge of ten tons. Deckings of bridges were to be painted with asphalt paint while the wood frame and members were to be painted with creosote. Estimates for road construction at High Point show project designers thought each mile of road construction required about 1,000 man-days of work.[5] Superintendent Oswald Brown reported during two months in the winter of 1933-34 that .3 of a mile of the surface of the truck trail (Sawmill Road) had been completed and that .4 of a mile had to be cut out, sub-base laid and rough surfaced.[6]

At one point, Colonel Kuser, in corresponding with the High Point Park Commission estimated it cost $3,000 a mile to grade a road and $3,000 a mile for hauling and distributing shale. Those numbers are from the late 1920s but give a sense of what it would cost for the CCC to build the roads.

Building roads was probably the most physically demanding of the projects undertaken by the CCC although most former enrollees and NPS foremen would probably argue that all of the tasks were difficult. Initially, survey teams led by a foreman determined the proposed route, most of which were either unused old woods roads or old public roads. The boys then repaired eroded parts of the road or where necessary created a new road entirely. Peter Lutz described the process: "We followed the surveyors making roads. The surveyor would survey the area out with different little symbols ... left turn, right turn, whatever. And then we would use a two-man saw and an ax to cut the big trees down ...

and then they had what they called the trimmers, would trim it, cut the logs into four foot lengths and set them on the side. And then we would keep proceeding further and further towards the surveyors ... they were building legitimate roads through as you see in the area now."7

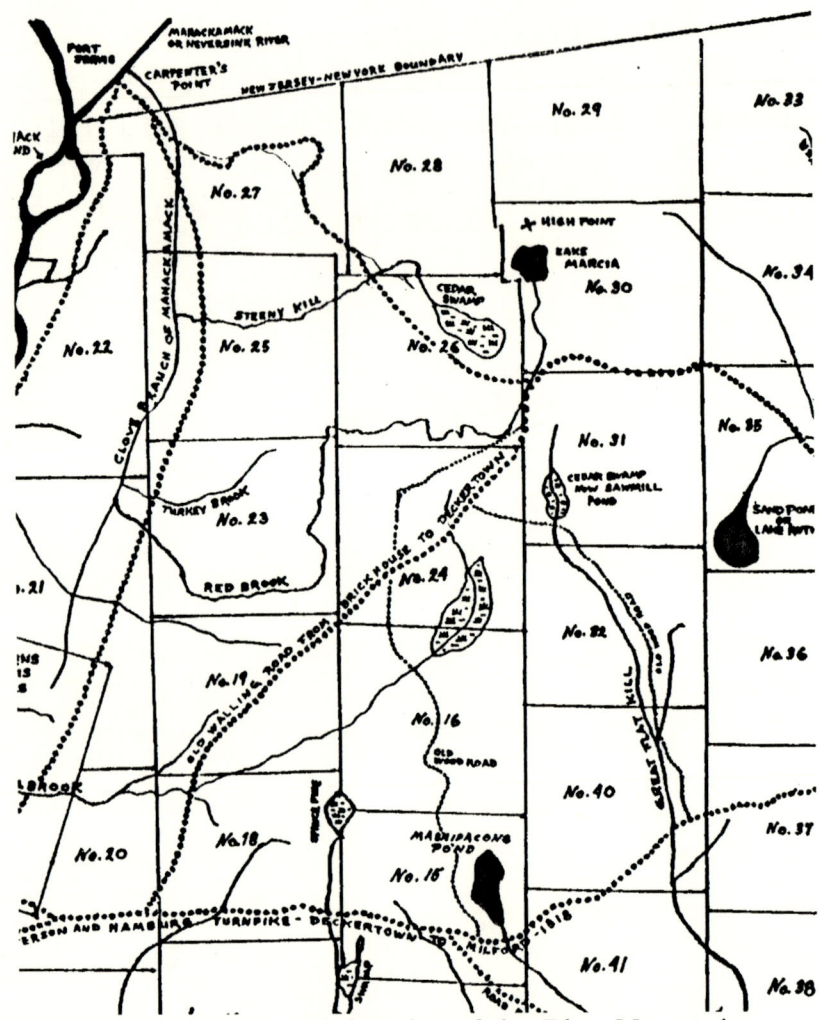

*Reprinted from High Point of the Blue Mountains
Drawn by Kevin Wright*

This circa 1845 map of the Sussex Allotments, as they were known, shows the road system at High Point before the arrival of Colonel Anthony Kuser and the CCC. The park is within Lots 16, 24-34, 36-37 and 40. Steenykill Lake is shown as a cedar swamp as is Sawmill Lake. The Park Ridge Road and Sawmill Road are both shown as wood roads.

We Can Take It!

The road gangs of companies 216 and 1280 cut down most of the trees along the proposed route, trimmed those trees that were to remain, and removed and burned the brush. The next step was to get the road bed to an acceptable grade which often required drilling and blasting of stone. Enrollee William DeGhetto remembered the process: "But we laid [them, the roads] ... Oh, there's a lotta shale under there, big stones, everything. All hand work too. No shovels you know, backhoes and all that. We didn't have that. And then you know when they did the blasting, we didn't have none of this stuff - jackhammers. One guy will hold the chisel, a star chisel, to drill the holes into stone, to put the dynamite in there. And one guy will stand here, and one guy there with a sledge hammer - boom bang! If they ever missed it, they would have broke your arm! But those guys were good boys; they had a good eye. It was mostly all hand work. It was, it was tough work!"[8]

Peter Lutz also remembered the process of drilling rock and how roads had to be cleared of protruding ledges before the finish surface could be made. He said:

"There was the areas where there was slab rock, which ... would run maybe twenty or thirty feet across that road at an angle, so we had to hand drill holes down about two, three foot deep. And then put dynamite in and blast it. It was considered all road work.

"... We used to hand drill. We had different lengths of drills and you'd start off with a small drill and different spots of this rock like this here. And a man would start, a man would sit down on an old blanket or something and we would drill a hole with the starter drill, which is bigger. And there'd be three men ... it was done where I would hit the drill ... with the hammer, [and] when the hammer would bounce back to my shoulder, the other man would hit the drill and then when it'd bounce back to his shoulder. The third man would hit the drill. And it went around like you say, a clock.

"And that's how we, instead of a jack hammer which I don't know whether the government ever supplied us with jack hammers ... we had to do it real primitive ... the man who was sitting down for about an hour, he had goggles on and a respirator. He would pour water in the hole as the hole would be drilled then he would scoop the mud out of it, because, the stone as you know, it sticks ... it's like a marble. It's very hard."[9]

Road gang member Edwin Jackobowski remembered his experiences with the use of dynamite: "Well, I worked on the road gang first you know ... I was in charge one time of the dynamite, blasting out trees, and I used the galvanometer you know and I checked that we got the dynamite in right ... Then you check it and put the thing on and blow the thing up."[10]

Enrollee Carl LoGrande described the process for blasting: "We had long ... drills. We'd drill holes and we pack it [dynamite] in. And we had big rocks. We'd mud pack it ... We put the dynamite on top of the rock and we put the cap in and then we put mud over it, pack it with mud, and that would blast the rock open."[11]

Sometimes dynamiting created problems such as when the CCC helped the state's highway department on work it was doing on Route 23. Carl LoGrande remembered the following experience. He said: "I was on [a] dynamite crew. Used to blast these mud packs, these big rocks and blast them ... The hill got cut to High Point ... going towards Sussex ...So we flattened that hill down. We did that ... Yeah, used to be a steep hill. People would come up and they'd overheat you know, the steep going up, so we took it down quite a bit."[12]

As roads were being graded, enrollees from Company 1280 would build culverts so that roads could pass over streams. Culverts were of a simple beam construction with rough flooring and stone abutments. Road gang member Jackobowski remembered the next step: "Wherever we needed a bridge, we put a bridge in. You know, a wooden bridge ... you get the logs and cut them with that knife, drill holes and peg them."[13]

The boys gathered or "harvested" random stones from adjacent woods and laid them on the road sub-grade to form a tight sub-base. The stones were eight to ten inches in diameter except for fillings, which were smaller. Enrollee Robert Wilbert remembered gathering rocks by hand for use on the roads: "We had to go out there and we had to get stone. A certain size ... we had a litter, a regular carrier ... two men picked up a stone, put it on this litter and brought it out to the road. And then we loaded it on the truck, and the truck brought it over to this other park that they were building across ... [Route 23]."[14]

Then shale was brought in by the dump trucks and spread by hand or by a bulldozer, forming a five or six inch layer. As the shale was crushed by traffic, it gradually sifted down between the voids in the rock making it suitable for a bituminous material topping course at some later time. After road construction was completed, shoulders and slopes were graded, filled in and landscaped. Thousands of feet of guardrail were built by members of both companies, some replacing rails installed by the park in the 1920s. Unsightly areas were repaired and replanted as necessary creating a natural appearance.

After roads were completed, the state highway department was responsible for them. In 1938, a prime oil treatment was given to Sawmill Road and some time later, a surface treatment of asphalt and crushed stone was laid. Park Ridge Road was also given a similar treatment and in

1941, the roads were resurfaced with sheet asphalt.¹⁵

Cedar Swamp Drive

Cedar Swamp Drive was originally built by the Kuser family in 1910 as a narrow access into the cedar swamp at the northern boundary of the park. It was opened to park patrons in 1927. The road currently follows the outside perimeter of the only cedar swamp to survive commercial timbering.¹⁶

The southern section was upgraded and improved by the CCC, and the loop around the swamp was completed, upgraded and surfaced with shale by both companies and finished in the spring of 1935. Most of the road, which is now a pedestrian trail, is one of the few projects both companies worked on at the same time. It was quickly completed in an effort to meet a deadline for a special event or inspection by CCC officials.

Cedar Swamp Drive has had various names including Laurel Drive, Cedar Park Drive, Cedar Prospect and Sprucevale Drive. During the CCC-era, it was also known as Company Street and Platt's Boulevard. It is about 1.5 miles in length and the southern section, where the camp was located, remains open to vehicular traffic. Evidence of camp facilities and foundations can still be seen on each side of the road among the picnic tables and playground equipment. The more northern section of the road, now known as

Cedar Swamp Trail, still encircles the swamp and is open to pedestrian traffic only. That part of the park is known as the Dryden Kuser Natural Area.

Steenykill Boat Launch Road
Steenykill Cabins Access Road

These old road fragments were once part of the Colesville and Carpenter's Point Turnpike, a public highway connecting Port Jervis, New York to Colesville, New Jersey that predates the CCC. When the CCC arrived, it was State Highway Route 23. After plans for the construction of Steenykill Lake were announced, Route 23 was rerouted to its current location.

Its original route passed in front of the Steenykill Cabins, proceeded north directly through the middle of the current Steenykill Lake, and then along the section now used for launching boats. Most relocation work was already done when the CCC arrived, and it completed whatever repair work remained on the old road on either side of Steenykill Lake to bring the road up to NPS standards.

The road on both sides of Steenykill Lake is still in use. Standing on either side of the lake, you can see the former route of the highway. The design work was finished in 1935 and construction was completed by 1937.

We Can Take It!

New Jersey State Route 23

New Jersey State Route 23, formerly the Colesville-Carpenter's Point Turnpike, provided the main access into the park both from Port Jervis, New York and Sussex, New Jersey. The road was never in good condition, particularly at the top of the mountain where the grade was very steep. State work crews regularly worked on the roadway as reflected in the minutes of the High Point Park Commission. As early as 1924, the Olmsted firm noted the road needed improvement. In 1935, Company 216 cleaned up the shoulders and slopes in an effort to improve its appearance.[17]

Road gangs from Company 1280 reduced the considerable incline on the southeastern side of the park. While the CCC did not have the capability to blacktop roads and CCC regulations did not allow for the construction of highways, apparently this work was done because it was within the park's boundaries. C boys probably did some of the preparation work and then the state highway department surfaced the road. In at least one winter storm, C boys shoveled snow off Route 23 by hand part of the way to Port Jervis and along the steep incline going towards Sussex.

If NPS planners had been able to carry through with their plans, Route 23 would have been totally eliminated and through traffic would have been rerouted to Federal Route 6 in New

York. The road remains the main entrance into the park and while the steep grades have been cut considerably, cars and trucks are still slow to climb the ascent.

Courtesy High Point State Park
CCC boys widen a road by filling in the right side with newly harvested stone.

Sawmill Road

The history of Sawmill Road is murky. The "old wood road," drawn on a circa 1845 map, branched off the Old Walling Road that went from the Brick House (Montague) to Deckertown (Sussex), and ended at Deckertown Turnpike. Other maps add to the confusion. The 1924 Olmsted map has a faint line indicating Sawmill Road as an existing road as does a 1931 map in the High Point archives. It is generally agreed the road went from Route 23 to a cedar swamp (present-day Sawmill Lake), which served as a water source for a sawmill operated by the Fuller family, and this would predate the arrival of the CCC.

However, there is some question as to whether the road actually existed south of Sawmill Lake when the CCC boys began their efforts. Both Albert Mastriani and Ronald J. Dupont, Jr. believe there was no road there when company 1280 started working on it in 1933.[18]

It was rebuilt in sections by both companies and was one of the earliest projects undertaken. The section between Route 23 to a location about fifteen hundred feet south of Sawmill Lake, was finished in 1935. The road, which was broken up into projects No. 107 and 108, was completed in 1936. Once the section to the cedar swamp which became Sawmill Lake was opened, work began on the dam and camping facilities around the lake. The road was initially known as Flat

Brook Drive and in the CCC-era, was called the Central Truck Trail. After its completion it became known as the Sawmill Road by a vote of the High Point Park Commission.

The road, which is about 4.5 miles in length, is still in use and is a major thoroughfare north and south through the park. Evidence of the CCC's culverts can still be found along it and an occasional rock with drill holes. In places, the nicely sloped banks demonstrate the great pride the CCC and NPS took in constructing their projects and in the finish work.

Service Drive

Service Drive eventually came to be called the Sawmill Lake Entrance Road. It was created as an alternative drive into the Sawmill Lake campsites and served the early campsites located along it. It also was used by the public until the permanent facilities on Sawmill Lake were completed. Additional campsites were proposed for much of the length of the road. The road was about one mile long, designated as Project Number 205, and built by Company 216 in 1935. It is currently closed to vehicles and is in poor condition.

Sawmill Lake Service Drive

We Can Take It!

This road was built around Sawmill Lake to get to the campsites that ringed the lake. It was designated Project Number 202 and completed by Company 216 in 1935 or 1936. Built in the same fashion as other roads around the park, it has since been blacktopped. At each parking area, a curb of cut stone was laid, slightly raised from ground level and some of them can still be seen. The road is still used and is 1.2 miles long.

Courtesy High Point State Park
This bridge passes over the Flatbrook on either Park Ridge or Sawmill road.

Park Ridge Road

Prior to the reconstruction of the Park Ridge Road by the CCC, it was an old wood road that proceeded in a southerly direction and passed Mashipacong Pond on the west to Deckertown Turnpike. The Olmsted plan called for this road to be part of a "perimeter road" which would loop around the outside boundary of the park. It was also known as Westerly Drive and Ridge Road. Most recently, the more historically accurate name has come into use again.

The CCC built the road, which is 5.2 miles long, beginning in 1935 and completing it in 1939. Much of the clearing of the road was undertaken by Company 216.[19] NPS plans proposed keeping the road's general course in place but, ultimately, that was not possible because park officials were unable to acquire the Mashipacong property. Instead, the road was rerouted, in an easterly direction, to the Sawmill Road near the southern boundary of the park.

The road served several purposes including opening previously inaccessible areas including what the Olmsted plan describes as the "Summit Area." This road would have also created access to the site for the proposed golf course and could be used for fire fighting purposes. It remains open and is the longest stretch of road the CCC built at High Point and one of the most beautiful, passing by several large swamps.

Lake Rutherfurd Road

A bridal path, beginning near the AT&T towers and going along what is now the Iris Trail, was to have broken off and passed around Lake Rutherfurd, the municipal water supply for the Borough of Sussex. It is unclear if the current road is the work of the CCC. It is now a limited access road.

Deckertown Turnpike

By the time the CCC arrived Deckertown Turnpike was badly overgrown but still passable, according to long-time residents, and was initially cleared as a fire break. The section of Deckertown Road east from Sawmill Road to the junction of Brink and File roads was rebuilt by both companies in 1934-1935. This part of the road was 1.95 miles long. Vista cuttings of both the Delaware and Wallkill river valleys were made near the peak of Deckertown Turnpike as it heads eastward and some 2,150 feet of guardrail was installed along the road on the eastward, and downward slope by Company 216.

The section of the turnpike from the junction with Sawmill Road going west towards Mashipacong Lake was also in poor condition and reconstructed based on the drawings at the HP archives and the recollections of Albert Mastriani. One progress plan shows that the road was to be reconstructed all the way to Clove Road, and it is believed that the project was done with help from CCC boys stationed at Stokes State Forest.

The road now serves as a major east-west route between Milford, Pennsylvania and Route 23. During the 19th century, the road was known as Paterson-Hamburg Turnpike and considered to be one of the county's better roads. By the 1880s, the road had fallen into disrepair.[20] At the time of the CCC involvement at High Point, it was known as the Old Scranton-Hoboken Turnpike according to one CCC report and as the Paterson and Hamburg Turnpike to most local historians.

Scenic Drive

The drive was designed in 1920 and constructed in 1927. It has been suggested the CCC may have built the boulder guard rails and rock work retaining walls along the drive or helped to build them in 1935-1936.

Access Roads

The CCC probably built several access roads including two that access the Appalachian Trail shelters, one on Deckertown Turnpike and the High Point Monument shelter just below the monument. Project superintendents probably had the roads built to access job sites.

CHAPTER 8

The Splendor Of Our Lakes

A little stream [was] running through there [future site of Sawmill Lake], and it was like a big gully. But you had to pick trees the heck outta there and pull the stumps. You can't leave them in there. They cleaned ... that whole gully out ... Before we could dig [out the tree stumps in the winter], you know we didn't have no machines in them days, we had to build a fire to thaw the ground out so you could pick it and pick at the soft ground ... chop the trees down. Then you'd have trucks, dump trucks, Chevy dump trucks, and a couple of rack body trucks, but most of them were all dump trucks. You'd tie a rope on it, dug around the stumps ... because in them days you didn't have the equipment like you got now. Oh, it was a lot of work!

-William DeGhetto, Enrollee, Company 1280

We Can Take It: The Roosevelt Tree Army at High Point State Park 1933-1941: Interviews With Former Civilian Conservation Corps Enrollees, Camp Kuser, Companies 216 & 1280. vol. 1.

The solitude and beauty of our woods and mountains ... the splendor of our lakes ... the comfort and convenience of our facilities ... the hospitality and cooperation of our entire staff await you.

-High Point Park brochure, circa 1940

The most enduring legacy of the CCC at High Point State Park after the construction of the road network is the two lakes they constructed, Sawmill and Steenykill. They were the most complex projects undertaken. After almost seventy years, the lakes remain one of the park's great attractions for fishermen, boaters and those seeking solitude.

It is a curious piece of the CCC's history that Harold Ickes, the U.S. Secretary of Interior, viewed the state parks as a "buffer deflecting rabid recreation-seekers from the more tranquil and inviolate reaches of its territory," or the national parks. Because of this attitude, Ickes did not allow new lakes to be built in national parks, only in the state parks.[1] Therefore, to deflect those "rabid visitors," High Point ultimately received two new lakes, and if plans had come to fruition, there would have been six lakes.

One of the most influential factors in the creation and location of lakes, campgrounds and cabin colonies proposed for High Point State Park by both the Olmsted plan and the National Park Service, concerns a body of water never owned by the park. In 1924, the Olmsted firm recommended purchasing the tract of land that encompassed Lake Mashipacong (or Mashipacong Pond as described on a 1907 USGS map) and an area known as the "Pine Swamp."

We Can Take It!

The plan suggested the Pine Swamp be converted to a two hundred and seventy acre lake. An enlargement proposed for Lake Mashipacong would have doubled its size to approximately one hundred and thirty acres. The strip of land between these two lakes was to serve as the major camping center and would have added considerable acreage to the southwestern corner of the park.

By 1927, park commissioners had budgeted funds for three lakes, presumably for the "Pine Swamp" lake, the Lake Mashipacong expansion and Steenykill Lake. However, the owner of the Mashipacong land, meeting with park officials in the late 1920s, was not willing to negotiate on his price, and the state, which was already heavily indebted, was reluctant to take the property by eminent domain.[2]

With the state unable to acquire the Mashipacong tract, park officials considered other alternatives. The first was to dam Steeny Brook and create Steenykill Lake. The project was begun in 1931 by a private contractor, although it was completed by the CCC. A second lake site was chosen, and it became Sawmill Lake. Two other lakes were proposed, Shale Lake and Lake Montague, but neither was built. In the end, the total acreage of the four proposed lakes would not have equaled that of Mashipacong Lake and the Pine Swamp lake.

Peter Osborne

Sawmill Lake Dam

It is not entirely clear when it was decided to build a lake at the cedar swamp that is now Sawmill Lake. On the Olmsted plan, there appears to be a penciled in lake, and it may have been the third lake park commissioners budgeted for in 1927. This change may be a later addition to the drawing, perhaps by NPS designers. The planning began for the first phase of the Sawmill Lake complex in the summer of 1934.

NPS designers Emmett L. Paige and Edward Taubert created a plan, drawn by Taubert and D. W. McNulty, that called for the removal of an earthen dam that stood about seventy-five to one hundred feet downstream from the current dam.[3] The new concrete gravity and core dam, flooding over a cedar swamp and fed by the Big Flatbrook, was to be given a handsome hand-cut stone face. The plan for a "Reconstructed Dam" was submitted on Dam Application Number 244 to the State Water Policy Commission in December 1934 and was approved.

The original design called for a flattened "V-shape' with the bottom of the "V" at about thirty-six feet from the sluice gate. One attractive feature not used in the final plan was for a log-rail walkway over the spillway. The final design by Edward Taubert utilized a straight concrete wall that extended two hundred and ten feet and was given NPS project number 50. It is not

We Can Take It!

known why the plan was revised and the latter design used. The design of Sawmill dam probably differs substantially from Steenykill dam because of the composition of the soils on which each was built and the shorter length of the structure.[4]

Company 216 cleared the lake site area, twenty acres in all, in 1934 and prepared for it to be flooded. Dredging of the swamp to create the lake was completed by a power shovel rented by the NPS. The material excavated was taken to the Steenykill dam site to be used for fill.

Company 1280 constructed the dam which included a core wall and a gravity section eighteen feet high at its deepest point and stepping up as it extended outward. The core wall used forty-six barrels of cement, fourteen cubic yards of sand and twenty-seven cubic yards of stone, and it took four pourings of concrete to create it. There were hundreds of reinforcing rods implanted in the cement. A flood gate conduit was installed at the very bottom of the dam, and below the dam, a large circular pool of water was created.

Peter Osborne

Courtesy High Point State Park

Among the most complicated projects at High Point was the building of dams that impounded the Big Flatbrook and Steenykill. Large forms had to be constructed that allowed for the pouring of the gravity section that was angled so cut stone could be laid on the downstream side. The pipe pictured in the center of the form is the relief valve and just behind the form is the sluiceway that allowed the Big Flatbrook to run unobstructed while construction of the Sawmill Lake dam was completed.

The construction of Sawmill dam brought with it a whole set of problems. In the fall of 1935, with work not yet complete, a torrential rain storm filled the lake with water damaging the work in progress. Because much of the excavation work was done in the winter of 1934-35, the ground had to be kept warm by constantly burning fires, using brush and old stumps pulled during road and dam construction. For much of the winter, two enrollees stayed overnight to watch the fires and equipment on the site.

The facade of the downstream side of the dam was lined with stones found along Sawmill Road, from the lake bed and around the park. They were placed on top of each other using a stiff-leg derrick constructed on the south side of the dam.

The lake was flooded in the spring of 1936 although it could not be used by the public because of the accumulation of silt and debris.[5] The dam created a lake that measured 19.5 acres and had a capacity of 24 million gallons. During the course of construction of both Sawmill and Steenykill dams, inspections were made by officials from the state's geology office and Water Policy Commission.

One of the stories regarding the Sawmill dam is that some local enrollees were concerned the large boulders in place on the dam would be heaved loose because of thaw and freeze cycles, well known in Sussex County. But the stones remain in place to this day and only a few of them have cracked vertically.

The lake is called Sawmill Pond on all NPS drawings and in contemporary accounts, but it has come to be known as Sawmill Lake. The lake is still open to the public and used by fisherman, boaters, campers and visitors, and the dam retains its natural features. The concrete core dam is now partially exposed on the western side due to erosion effects by the lake.

Sawmill Lake Dam Plantings

A landscaping plan for the Sawmill dam was created by Melvin Gemmill and it called for extensive plantings. In the area surrounding the dam, almost one hundred birch trees, thirty maples, one hundred and twenty mountain laurel, azalea and witch hazel shrubs were planted. Older trees were left in place. Goldenrod and autumn aster were planted on the banks. There is some disagreement whether this part of the project was carried out, but the design drawings show it was laid out in 1935 and completed in 1937.

Most of the area is now covered with grass and the few trees that remain, including some birches, may be descendants of the original trees that were planted more than sixty years ago. The extensive plantings created a very different appearance than it has today which is more spartan. The footbridge that now spans the Flatbrook was built in 1999. There was no bridge at this site during the CCC era.

We Can Take It!

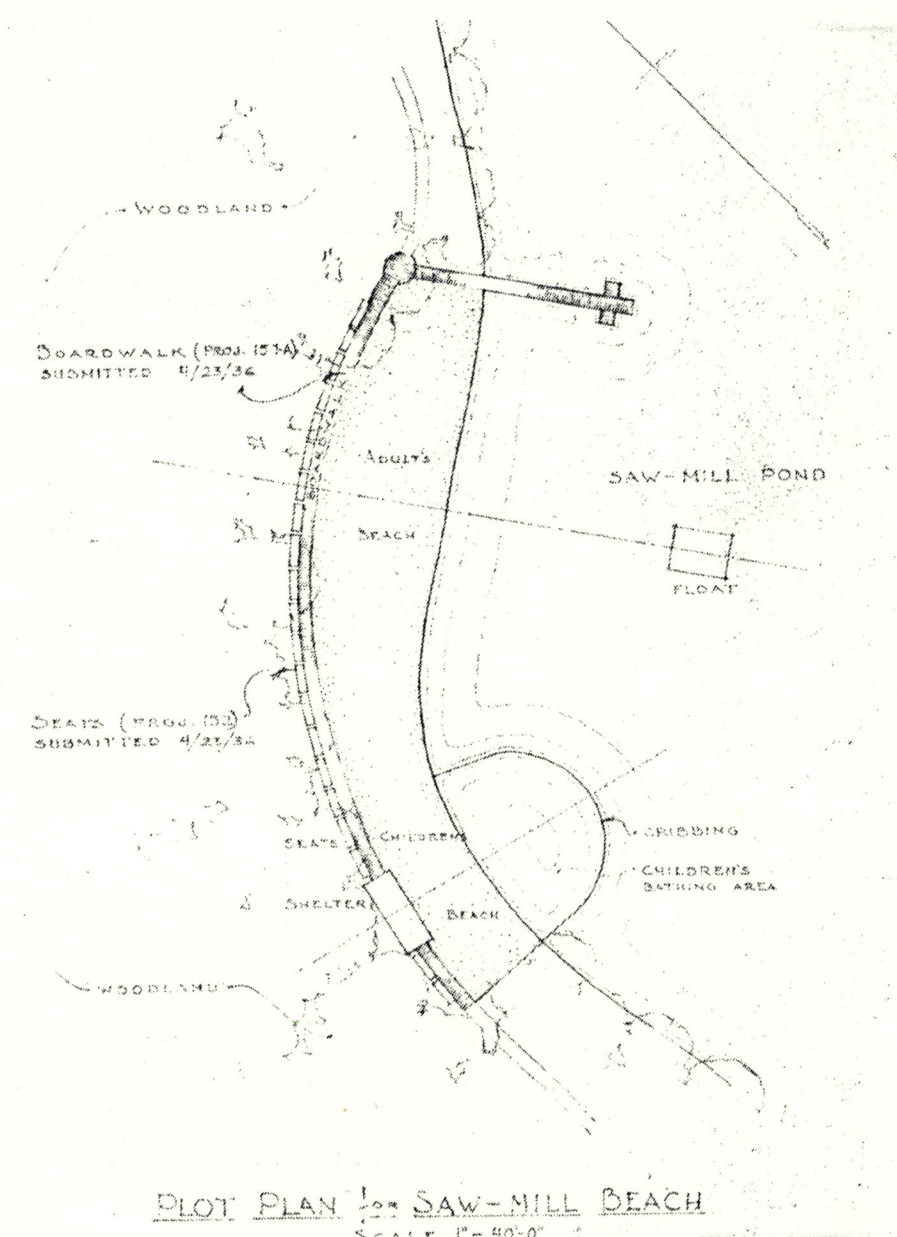

Courtesy High Point State Park
Plot plan for Sawmill Beach

Peter Osborne

Sawmill Lake Beach Improvements

This project was one of the most impressive visitor accommodations designed for the park by the NPS. It included a long boardwalk (Project 157A), ten handsome benches (Project 152), a dock, lifeguard chair, diving board, swimming float, boat dock and shelter. The dock extended forty feet into the lake and a boat landing was incorporated into it. The children's beach, enclosed by cribbing that went into the lake, occupied the area directly in front of the shelter. To keep the pontoons from rotting, they were coated with pitch.

The plans created by Melvin Gemmill in 1935-1936 represent an optimistic time in the park's history when anything seemed possible. The beach opened to campers who were using the Sawmill campsites in 1936. Sadly, the beach development is completely gone today and only a set of hand-cut stone stairs and a foundation for the shelter remain. "No Swimming" signs line the beach. Ironically, some of the facilities, after they were not maintained for years, were demolished by the Young Adult Conservation Corp in the late 1970s, a federal agency with its roots in the CCC.[6]

Steenykill Lake

The Steenykill Lake project has a history that predates the CCC era. The Olmsted plan notes the large swamp at that location in its map of the property although it is not listed as a potential lake. It was probably one of the places described as follows: "There are other opportunities to impound water, but they would not produce areas of usable size for campers. They would be valuable, however as brightening the scenery of the park and should be considered."[7]

It was such a place commissioners planned for when they budgeted for three lakes in 1927. An appropriation was made by the state legislature in the spring of 1931 to create Steenykill Lake which would provide recreational facilities and a view of two lakes from the Grey Rock Inn on top of the ridge. This new effort presumably came about after attempts to obtain the Mashipacong property failed, and there was no hope for the immediate future in creating a lake there.

Design work by a private engineering firm was completed and construction was started in 1931 by the contractor who was also the builder of the High Point Monument, Hoffman Construction Company of Bernardsville, New Jersey.[8] New Jersey Water Policy Commission approvals note that a set of 1931 drawings created by Sussex engineers Clarke Millen and James Roe were approved. Hoffman completed some of the lake bed clearing and excavation work at the dam site. The company also built the deepest footings for the concrete core dam. Work was halted in 1932 because of the Depression and lack of funding, and twenty-four men were let go as work was suspended.[9]

It was not until the CCC arrived that the project began in earnest again. In 1935, NPS planners created new drawings (Project #122, Job #704A) using data and the design from the original Millen and Roe drawing which showed Route 23 being rerouted and the old road, at least the section under the lake, being eliminated.

In May 1935, NPS designers Emmett L. Paige and Edward Taubut submitted Dam Application No. 190 to the State Water Policy Commission. The plans were approved in July. Soon after, five test borings were done to ascertain what the depth of dam would be. Additional planning for the lake itself continued through late 1936, and final approval for other parts of the Steenykill project was given in November 1936. This endeavor would be the last major project Company 216 would undertake.

We Can Take It!

Courtesy High Point State Park

The progression of necessary forms, including footers and forms for the core wall that was required for pouring cement is seen here.

The clearing of trees and stumps from the lake bed and cutting of stumps to ground level was undertaken by enrollees from both company 216 and 1280. In the shallow sections of the lake, stumps of trees were completely removed and in deeper sections, they were left at twelve inches in height. The lake bed at the southern end where stumps were cut flush to the ground has now eroded to such a degree that the stumps rise above the level of the lake during the driest part of the summer. Stumps were removed completely in the area west of the boat launch. Estimates called for two thousand man-days to clear the site.[10]

The construction of the dam and lake bed excavations were undertaken by enrollees from Company 1280 and supervised by NPS foremen Albert Mastriani and Lawrence Jones. At times, between sixteen and fifty men were assigned to the project.[11] When the concrete was being poured, all the men were on site, sometimes in twenty-four hour shifts.

Construction of the twelve hundred foot dam commenced with a concrete core wall being constructed that was anywhere from ten to forty-five feet high and contained five thousand cubic yards of fill. Steel sheath piling was used for about two hundred feet of the dam.[12] A five hundred foot channel was cut into the Mill Brook to divert the overflow from Lake Marcia into Steenykill Lake.

The dam was lined with a stone rip rap on the lake side and graded with top soil on the opposite side. The spillway was lined with boulders to create a natural effect and to blend into the surrounding landscape. Aside from the blow-off manhole cover, it is difficult to tell a dam had been created. That effect is even more pronounced as years have gone by and trees planted by the C boys took hold and grew.

The construction of the dam also had its problems. In the fall of 1935 a heavy rainfall that lasted three days flooded the partially completed lake and destroyed tools and cement and other supplies in two construction buildings on the lake bed. Also flooded was part of the stone crusher installed at the site.

After the completion of the dam in the summer of 1938, the lake was filled with water and by September of 1939, opened to the public.[13] The lake was stocked with at least one thousand black bass but fishing was restricted for two years to allow fish to develop.[14] A beach and diving board was considered for the lake but never constructed. This project was one of the largest undertaken by the CCC in the state of New Jersey and was one of the highest bodies of water in the state.[15]

The lake is still popular with fishermen and boaters and is as pretty today as it was when it was built. The lake's shoreline is 1.6 miles long, forty acres in size with an average depth of 5.75 feet. It holds 73 million gallons of water.

Peter Osborne

Stream Improvements

The C boys undertook about five miles of trout stream improvements, mainly along the Flat Brook, beginning in 1939.

CHAPTER 9

Conveniences To Make A Return to Nature Easier

On Sawmill Lake ... an area has been developed for the use of campers. Here, away from the daily used sections of the park, the camper may find privacy and quiet.
-High Point Park brochure, circa 1940

The Park is traversed by roads and trails which take the hiker over mountains, through woods, and along the lakes and streams. The roads and trails are plainly marked. The most famous of them is a section of the Appalachian Trail ... At intervals along this trail are shelters where hikers may rest or stop overnight. For those who enjoy solitude and seclusion many of the trails pass through the forest and along mountain ridges.
-High Point Park brochure, circa 1940

With roadwork complete, a host of new options for long-term use of the park became available. After construction of the roads was underway, work on the recreation facilities began. It was these facilities, the camping areas, cabin colonies, trails, trail shelters and winter sports areas at High Point that had the greatest impact and ultimately endeared the public to the CCC. As soon as the facilities opened, thousands of people flocked to the park to use them. Metropolitan newspapers featured stories extolling the virtues of the new park facilities.

Most of what the CCC built at High Point is still being used. It is a bargain when one considers that hundreds of thousands of dollars were spent over sixty-five years ago and probably millions of people have used them.

Sawmill Lake Recreational Facility

It was clear the Mashipacong tract could never be acquired so the NPS proceeded to develop different campgrounds and cabin colonies that would offer a degree of privacy away from tourists and day-use visitors. Contemporary planners thought of visitors in two distinct groups, tourists and day visitors (short-term) and campers (long-term). Tourists were people who were passing through, perhaps visiting the monument or Kuser Mansion, taking a meal at the Grey Rock Inn or swimming at Lake Marcia.

We Can Take It!

Campers would be in the park for longer periods and hence needed sleeping, restroom and water recreation facilities.

One major difference between what the Olmsted plan recommended and what the NPS called for in its plan related to the camping facilities. The former plan envisioned group camping similar to what was being done at Bear Mountain State Park at the time. This included a mess or dining hall serving meals to campers. The Olmsted firm did not think individual campsites would be popular with the public, yet the NPS designed exactly those kinds of sites which during the summer are still in high demand.

The development of the facility at Sawmill Lake was probably the most significant individual contribution the CCC made to High Point Park.[1] It created a park within the park and helped to alleviate overcrowding occurring at Lake Marcia. It was hoped the camping facilities would allow for removal of the Boy Scout camp from Lake Marcia to the western portion of the park.

If the final 1938 master plan prepared by NPS designers had been carried out, the Sawmill Lake site would have been the first major step in a series of picnic and camping areas constructed further south and west along Sawmill and Park Ridge roads. Documentation of this effort is the best preserved of all the remaining documents in the park's archives.

Peter Osborne

Sawmill Lake Campsite Development

With completion of the dam at Sawmill, the next phase of work was the creation of a series of individual campsites, or a "tent colony." The park's camping facilities had been located along Lake Marcia, and news of the camp sites being moved to the other side of the park caused some distress to long-time campers. In February 1936, a petition with hundreds of signatures was presented to park commissioners protesting the new camping area for the following reasons: "the lower altitude [of the camping facilities], mosquitoes, snakes and other biting insects, which will be a menace to the health benefits of our families."[2]

Commissioners voted to proceed with work at Sawmill and in the end the campsites were heavily used. In 1934, and again in 1935, planners called for most of the campsites to be on the eastern side of the lake with a small group of sites on the western side near where the point (Campsite 25) is now. By 1936, twenty-three campsites were planned along with five wooden framed pit latrines around the lake. Additional campsites were proposed along Park Ridge Road and a new road was suggested for the eastern side of the lake, further up on the ridge, that would have added even more campsites. For unknown reasons, that service road was not built nor were the campsites along Park Ridge Road.

In 1936, tent platforms, fireplaces, a bathing beach, rustic benches and a rustic beach shelter were constructed, and the first official camping season in the western part of the park was underway. By 1937, all the campsites around Sawmill were ready for use, and during that summer, lifeguards were on duty and the boat dock was available for use.

In 1938, a plan to more than double the number of campsites was approved. There were also plans for additional campsites along the service road that led back to the junction of Sawmill and Park Ridge roads. Eight chemical latrines were also proposed including one directly behind the dock at the beach. Each site was to have access to a well pump, placed within a short walking distance.

Peter Osborne

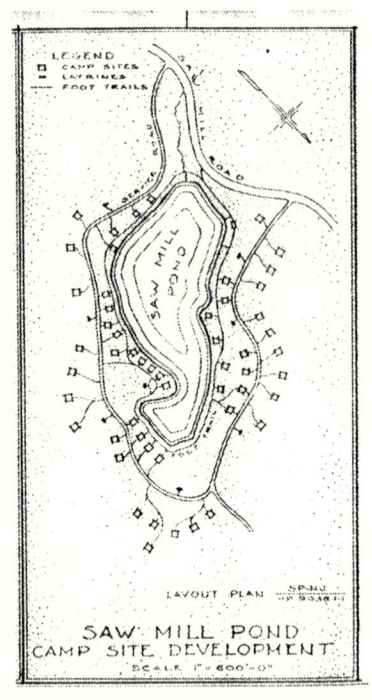

Courtesy High Point State Park
This site plan shows the layout for Sawmill Lake Campsite Development which is essentially what it looks like today except for the beach facilities which are now gone.

Again, for unknown reasons, the plans were changed. Only three latrines were built, but they were constructed of local cut stone and designed in a rustic manner. By 1939, the stone latrines were finished and the campsite development completed.

A typical campsite included a tent platform with outriggers, table and bench and a cut-stone fireplace along with an individual parking spur. The stone fireplaces, which included a cooking grate, were made with hand-cut quartz quarried at the local Pochuck quarry in New Jersey. Some of the stone used was left over from the High Point Monument construction.[3] Company 216 did the clearing work for Sawmill Lake Service

We Can Take It!

Drive, individual campsites and parking areas, while Company 1280 did most construction work including building the handsome latrines.

The original configurations remain although the quarried stone fireplaces were removed in the 1980s. Pieces of quarried stone with drill holes can be seen scattered about the camping areas. The wells were capped although a number of foundations for them still survive. Some of the stone curbing for the parking areas remain buried under shale. The CCC designers planned for campsites along the service road and they were finally built in the 1960s or early 1970s. The overflow sites were closed sometime before 1978 and all that remains is a single pit toilet.[4]

It is worth noting the names of the designers who were involved because the campsites are some of the most beautiful in the state park system. The original design and layout of the campsites in 1934 was completed by Edward Taubert. When additional design work called for more campsites in 1936, George Schmierer completed the drawings. When the final round of designs were required including the comfort stations in 1938, Melvin Gemmill completed the work.

Peter Osborne

A New Trail System

The NPS called for an extensive series of trails and paths that would have made all of the park, particularly the western part, completely accessible by foot. A plan for new trails was approved by the park commission in July 1939, and work was finished by the summer of 1940. The network included not only pedestrian paths but mixed-use paths for horses. It is believed that the iron pipe markers at the various trail heads may be from the CCC-era but it is not certain.[5] While the Appalachian Trail already wound through the park and there were other trails in the park particularly around Lake Marcia, there were no park trails that showcased the magnificent scenery of the ridge lines.

We Can Take It!

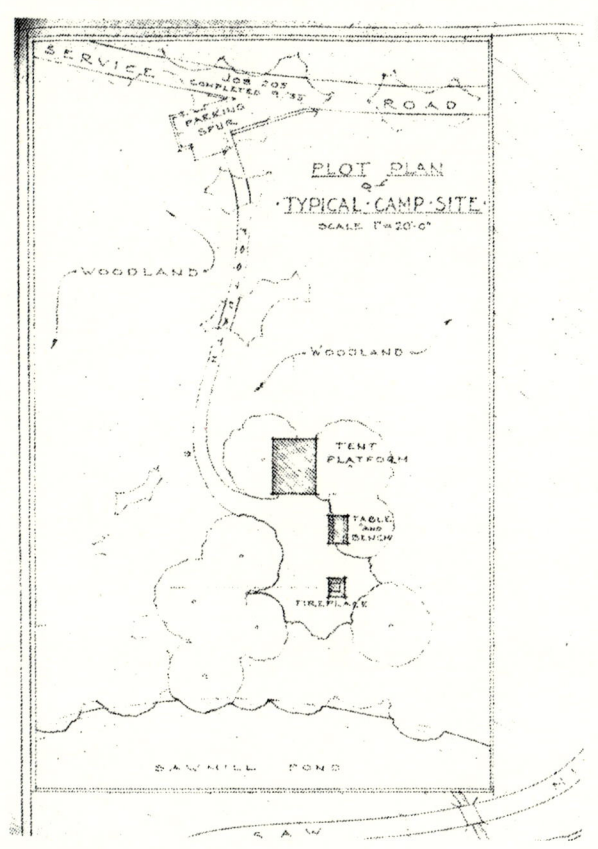

Courtesy High Point State Park
Designs used at High Point were generated internally although some designs came from the NPS Branch of Plans and Design.

Appalachian Trail

The Appalachian Trail (AT), designed and constructed by the Appalachian Trail Conference, was already built in the late 1920s or early 1930s before the CCC arrived. The trail was being used in the park by 1934.

The C boys undertook additional trail construction, maintenance and repair work and built the Adirondack-type shelters used by AT hikers. A fifty to one hundred foot swath on either side of the trail was cleared of inflammable stubs, brush, scrub oak and debris. The boys from 216 also cleared a number of view sheds overlooking the Wallkill and Delaware river valleys. Prior to this, hikers walked through a tunnel of scrub oak. A number of enrollees remembered hiking on the trail on their time off.

The Appalachian Trail is still used by hikers although on several occasions over the decades it has been rerouted within the park.

Sawmill Lake Circular Path

This hiking path, also known as the Lakeside Walk, was constructed in 1939 and created for campers who were at Sawmill Lake. It almost encircles the lake. A sub-base layer was laid first with a shale finish surface. Stone borders can be seen today that were used as edging to prevent erosion. This path remains open for public use.

Monument Trail

This trail was surveyed and designed in 1939 by NPS foreman Oliver Wells and built under the oversight of NPS foreman Larry Jones. It begins at the Grey Rock Inn (Nature Interpretive Center) and continues 3.5 miles to the High Point Monument. Bridges were built along with stone walls, and there are impressive stone steps leading up the ridge below the monument. Construction of the trail was completed in 1940 and opened the same year. It is still used, and both of the ridge lines it passes along offer outstanding views.

Steenykill Trail

This trail was designed in 1940 by NPS Foreman Raymond Evans and winds its way from Route 23 to Steenykill Lake and then to the Monument Trail. Construction was completed in 1940 and it is seven-tenths of a mile long. The most notable feature is the beautiful stone staircase up the mountainside. It is still in use by hikers.

Bridal Path-Iris Trail
Kittatinny Road

This section of old road, trail and bridal path, now known as the Iris Trail, has an interesting history and to some degree incorporates ideas from both the Olmsted and National Park Service plans. It is believed the present-day Iris Trail is, in part, the eastern section of what was the "perimeter road" in the Olmsted plan. The National Park Service, borrowing from the concept, designed a bridal path for horses that in 1935 originally began on what would become the northern side of the visitor's center on Route 23.

It passed where the ATT towers are now located and met what is now the Iris Trail a short distance to the south. It continued to the southern end of Lake Rutherfurd where it looped around to the road that borders the lake on the east. The original Olmsted plan called for it to wind back towards the park, as a horse trail and a fire break. During the winter it was used for skiing.

The road was constructed ten feet wide and parts of the Iris Trail at least to Lake Rutherfurd are wide enough to have served as a road at one time. The C boys built about four miles of the "Bridal Path" which is now part of the Iris Trail. Unfortunately, the records are not clear about the path, trail and perimeter road so that it seems safe to assume the current trail is a compilation of all of the ideas.

The Iris Trail is still in use although the bridal path, which at one time served as the treadway for the Appalachian Trail, was rerouted to the south. The Iris Trail is 4.3 miles long and passes the western shore of Lake Rutherfurd and then continues south to Deckertown Turnpike. The road that now runs on the eastern shore at Lake Rutherfurd is closed.

Trailside Shelters

All the trailside shelters at High Point were designed in the rustic style by Melvin Gemmill in 1935 and the original plans remain. All were built in 1936. The shelters had laid stone walls with a lean-to roof covered with cedar shakes. The original design called for dirt floors. Fireplaces and log benches were also built. At the time the original design drawings were completed, only two shelters were planned, one at Lake Marcia and another at Lake Rutherfurd. The final locations were suggested by Charles Hobein, the Green Mountain Club and Raymond Torrey.

In the end, four shelters were built, three on the Appalachian Trail including the Mashipacong Shelter near the juncture of Deckertown Turnpike and the AT; the High Point Trailside Shelter located east of and below the monument on the AT and the Lake Rutherfurd Shelter located at the southern end of the reservoir. The last shelter, located near the Iris Trail, was destroyed by fire sometime between 1947 and 1958. Remnants are still visible. A replacement shelter was built by inmates of the Annandale Youth Correctional Institute and made of logs, unlike the CCC shelter which was built of stone.[6]

A fourth shelter, the Sawmill Lake Trailside Shelter, was built about the same time along the eastern shore of the lake. It was demolished at an unknown date. Contemporary newspaper accounts do not count this as an Appalachian Trail shelter, probably because the trail did not come down from the ridge and pass along Sawmill Lake. The exact location of the shelter is not known.[7]

Two of the shelters are still in use by Appalachian Trail hikers, the Mashipacong and the High Point shelters. The shelters were built under the direction of Oswald Brown, superintendent of SP-1, by members of Company 216 and were called "one of the outstanding projects in the park." John Gibbons supervised the work because the park had responsibility for the trail within the park.[8] The design and beautiful construction techniques used for the AT shelters attracted the attention of widely-known trails promoter Raymond Torrey and the New York-New Jersey Trail Conference. In August 1936, he described them in his well-read column called *The Long Brown Path*.[9]

Winter Sports Facilities

Winter outdoor sports, particularly skiing and tobogganing, grew in popularity in the park in the 1930s. In the winter of 1936, the CCC's survey gang at High Point laid out a number of lines for various jumps, trails and elevation profiles. They included a main ski jump across from the current Visitor Center and several small ski jumps near the mansion. The proposal prepared by John Gibbons was to focus skiing activities around the mansion and skating around Lake Marcia. It is believed Company 216 did a lot of this work. Because of the proximity of the new Steenykill Lake, it was also proposed that a number of small cabins be erected there.[10]

During the course of the next year, many facilities were built including 20 miles of ski trails (many of those existing today in the form of hiking trails), a ski jump at the southern end of Scenic Drive and the use of Scenic Drive and Monument Road as ski trails. The governor of the state came to inspect the facilities in December 1936.

CHAPTER 10

The High Water Mark

plan (plan) n. a drawing representing a thing's horizontal section; a diagram; a map: a project; a design; a scheme
-Webster's Dictionary

I think I went out a couple times on the surveying crew ... surveyed the monuments ... for High Point Park. They put a monument in on top [of the concrete marker] ... if you go in the woods you'll see them around.
-Edwin Jakowbowski, Enrollee Company 1280

We Can Take It: The Roosevelt Tree Army at High Point State Park 1933-1941: Interviews With Former Civilian Conservation Corps Enrollees, Camp Kuser, Companies 216 & 1280. vol. 1.

The CCC is usually thought of in the context of forestry and construction projects and young men in the woods doing heavy labor. However, an equally important component in the success of the CCC was the planning efforts of the National Park Service project superintendents, designers and foremen including those at High Point. Without them, the CCC would not have been so successful or safe because of the practices put into place.

When the CCC was created, there were only ten landscape architects on the NPS payroll.[1] There was suddenly a great need for professional designers who were trained to create gardens and beautiful landscapes, mainly in the eastern and northeastern United States. When the NPS instituted a policy to have a designer for each camp, prospects changed dramatically for the landscaping profession.

By 1936, there were two hundred and twenty architects working full time for the park service. One estimate put the number at four hundred.[2] Herbert Evison, the NPS state park planning official, estimated that in 1934, seven hundred landscape architects, architects and engineers were working in state parks with the CCC.[3] By 1934, virtually every landscape architect in the country was hired to work in one of the New Deal programs.[4] In all, they would design five hundred and sixty non-federal park areas in forty-seven states.[5]

The NPS promoted the rustic architectural styles, and the architect for the state park program Albert Good assembled a pattern book of designs that became the basic model for wilderness design. Other updated versions of his book followed and were available to designers at High Point.

The most significant NPS employee at High Point during the CCC-era was Melvin Gemmill. Many of his drawings, done in a beautiful hand, remain in the park's archives. His most significant contribution was the design of the master plan for the park. While he had a number of designers who worked for him over the years, it was his vision that created High Point as we know it.

About one hundred drawings survive in the park archives and from them, most of the history of the projects can be recreated. One of the more interesting aspects of the CCC efforts was the ability of supervisors to quantify the work planned and completed and then report the data to higher levels of administration. Administrators shared that information with the public, mainly through the newspapers and programs at the camps. Because of that public relations effort, the CCC was more popular than most New Deal programs.

The planning process began in the fall of 1933 with an inventory of existing resources, and then a general plan for development was made. Topographic base maps were created and used in future planning efforts. Special projects were then designed, and by 1938, the NPS had developed a master plan for the park. The NPS developed a list of projects to be completed in a certain period of time called Period Progress Plans. The periods were six months long, January to June and July to August. For example, the third period at High Point was from July-December 1934. Only five of these drawings still exist, but they provide much information about work done in a typical period. These reports were forwarded to regional, state and national officials. From these, annual reports were distributed to the public.

Initial Inventory Of Existing Park Resources

From that first inventory drawing, completed in October 1933 by Eric Flemming prior to the building of permanent winter headquarters it can be determined surveyors and designers had been on the property for several months inventorying existing structures, roads and the Appalachian Trail. The large vellum inked drawing is important because it shows how the CCC transformed the park from a wilderness area to a public facility. The future Camp Kuser is not shown on the drawing even though it was probably being built at that time.

Peter Osborne

Existing Period Progress Plans
Project Location Plan

This plan is the earliest of the surviving conceptual drawings proposed for the park. Completed by Edward Taubert in 1934, it demonstrates how much work was originally considered and how the final plans were altered. There was to have been a larger network of truck trails. Several were built, but not completed, including one that follows the eastern boundary of the park and begins at the Bridal Path and passes by Lake Rutherfurd on the eastern side. It comes out at Deckertown Turnpike and this may have become a portion of the Iris Trail. Another trail began at Cedar Swamp (Dyrden Kuser Natural Area), crossed Route 23 and looped around to Park Ridge Road. The southerly termination point of the Park Ridge Road was not at Sawmill Road as it is now but continued southwest into the Mashipacong Pond area.

The development at Steenykill Lake was to have two large comfort stations and one shelter, neither of which were built. At Sawmill Lake, forty-five cabin camps were called for along with one comfort station and one shelter. Along the Bridal Path, there were to be forty campsites, and at the southern end of the Iris Trail near the junction at Deckertown Turnpike, there were to be an additional thirty-five cabin camps and seven comfort stations. At Mashipacong Lake, plans called for fifty campsites and fifteen comfort stations.

Along Parker Brook, at the southwestern corner of the park, there were to be fifty campsites and fifteen comfort stations and along the Central Truck Drive, now Sawmill Road, there were to be several large picnic areas. A large camp of twenty cabins and five comfort stations were also proposed in the far northeastern corner of the park, not far from the present-day High Point Shelter on the Appalachian Trail.

Finally, a large athletic field and play area was proposed for Shale Lake. Near the dam for the lake would have been one shelter and two comfort stations along with forty campsites.

The trail system would have been more extensive than what was finally built, although the Iris (or at least a portion of it), the Steenykill and the Monument trails are shown and were ultimately built. Forest stand improvement cuttings were to be conducted on a wide swath of property to the south, west and north of Lake Marcia, which were ultimately accomplished.

Fifth Period Progress Plan – Sawmill Lake Complex

This progress plan for the fifth period in 1934 shows the work progressing at Sawmill Lake. The work schedule of Company 1280 shows work was well underway for Sawmill Road and that the dam was 80 percent complete. Other roadwork along Sawmill Road was being done in addition to the filling in of borrow pits adjacent to the proposed Shale Lake complex. Borrow pits were areas where fill was used for projects like road and campsite construction. The designer was Edward Taubert, and the plan was approved in 1934.

Fifth Period Progress Plan - Parkwide Projects

This plan, designed by Edward Taubert in 1935, shows the scope of forest work completed and underway. The biggest project completed was the creation of fire stops around the entire boundary of the park. From the drawing, it can be seen that fire stops were already created along the Appalachian Trail, Cedar Swamp Drive, Sawmill Road, Deckertown Turnpike, Route 23 and portions of the park's northern boundary.

Extensive forest stand improvements and lakeside clearing were done in the area around Lake Marcia. The Central Truck Trail, now known as Sawmill Road, was completed as well as a section of Deckertown Turnpike from Sawmill Road west to the park boundary at Mashipacong Lake. A half mile of guardrail was constructed on Deckertown Turnpike as it comes over the mountain towards Colesville. Forest stand improvements were to be made along Route 23 toward Port Jervis as well as clearing

We Can Take It!

the area that was to be flooded by Steenykill Lake.

Projects for the coming period included constructing five lean-tos; three shelters - at Sawmill, Shale and Steenykill - well pits and pumps for Sawmill Lake and additional comfort stations. Because of the lack of continuity in the drawings, it cannot be determined if those projects were built. If they were, few have survived. New picnic areas along Sawmill Road were proposed as well as locating the northern boundary of the park where it met the New York state line.

Ninth Period Progress Plan - Parkwide Projects

This drawing, completed by George Schmierer, illustrates the anticipated closing of Company 216 in June 1937 as its number SP-1 is scratched off the legend. The drawing was done in March 1937. It shows the park's boundary, with permanent markers for the first time, and it appears the effort to accomplish this task was a major one. The work at Sawmill Lake continued with the boardwalk, benches, float, shelter and seats being built by Company 1280. The channel to bring additional water into Steenykill Lake was to be built, and the dam was to be finished.

Peter Osborne

Eleventh and Twelfth Period Progress Plans

These two plans were created by Melvin Gemmill in 1938 and approved in the same year. During this period, the marking of the boundary continued as a carry over project from the previous year. In addition, the final leg of Park Ridge Road was being rebuilt including a bridge over the Flatbrook near the juncture with Sawmill Road. The Monument Trail and the trail around Sawmill Lake were built, and a campground at Sawmill was continued including the construction of tent platforms, fireplaces, parking areas and beach improvements. Landscaping of the previously built section of Park Ridge Road was being undertaken and finally, Steenykill Lake dam was being finished.

High Point State Park Master Plan
General Development Plan

The general development plan or master plan was typical of those done for every park developed by the CCC. The process began with the creation of a "base map" as NPS specifications called them. This showed the physical and topographic features of the park. The development plan was then created in layers on top of the base map. The plan was reviewed on a regional basis and by Washington officials.

They were as one author described them, "miniature versions of national park master plans." State park plans tended to propose more activities than national parks, and lakes were often centerpieces of the developments.[6] This feature of the plan to create high density use areas in state parks rather than the national parks created friction among the more active environmental groups including the Wilderness Society. The final stage of planning drawings came in the form of individual project plans. The procedures, size and content were all specified by the NPS State Park Division.

From 1933 to 1938, NPS designers inventoried the park's resources, created work projects and oversaw the CCC's operation and created a new master plan for the High Point Park Commission. The plan was unveiled to the public in April of 1938. It was an expansive document reflecting the vision of the 1924 Olmsted plan in many ways but also called for major changes from that original plan. The new plan omitted the golf course, a fish hatchery and the suggestion that hospitals or sanatoria be built. It also altered some of the improvements that had been proposed.

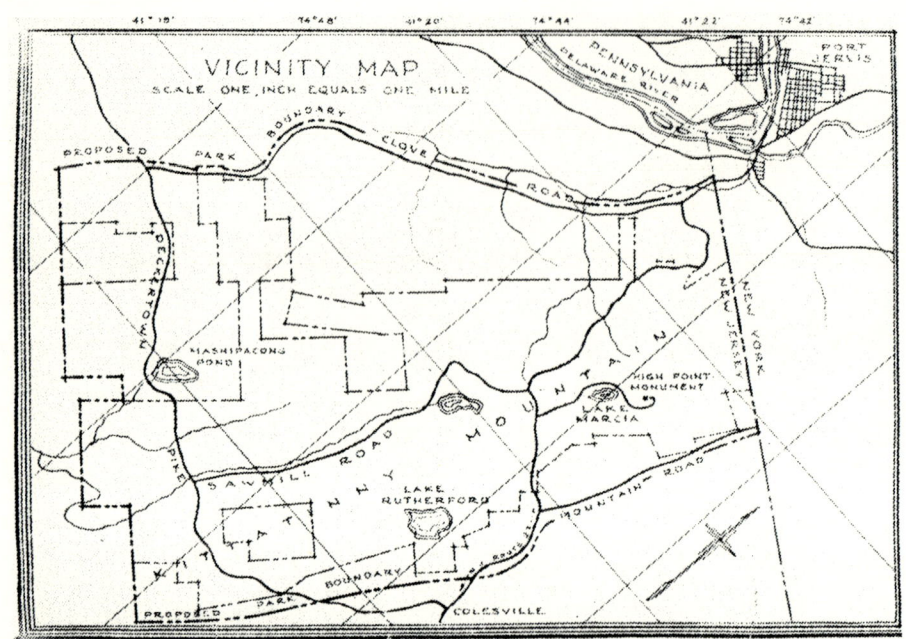

Courtesy High Point State Park

This map illustrates what the park boundary would have been if the master plan was implemented. The boundaries would have followed the natural lay of the land and not artificially drawn lines.

As the master plan was being developed, special consideration had to be given to the original law creating the park in 1923. One feature of the act was that improvements must be in keeping with a natural reservation. NPS designers saw as did the Olmsted firm the need to showcase panoramic views to the east and west of the ridge line. They called for continued land acquisitions by the state that would bring the park's total acreage to twenty thousand acres from twelve thousand acres.

We Can Take It!

The Kuser property acquisitions, prior to 1923, had not been done with any regard to the topography. The NPS plan looked to acquire an additional eight thousand acres that would bring the entire ridge line within the park and control the view shed and forests below it. The boundaries would have followed the natural lay of the land and not artificially drawn lines. The park's boundaries if the acquisitions had proceeded would have been the state boundary line to the north, Deckertown Turnpike to the south, Clove Road on the west and Mountain Road on the east. This aspect of the NPS plan continues at High Point, although not in the comprehensive way contemplated. Additions of small tracts have been made since the CCC-era and continue to be acquired.

One of the most interesting facets of the plan is the number of campsites, cabins and facilities contemplated. There would have been hundreds of additional campsites constructed in the western half of the park, a recreational facility around Shale Lake, a cabin colony around Steenykill Lake and another new lake - Lake Montague. Lake Montague, which would have been about forty-four acres, would have been located across from the southern edge of Sawmill Road at the junction with Deckertown Turnpike. Additional shelters would have been built as well.

There was even a proposal for a museum at the southern end of the CCC camp, perhaps using one of the C buildings. A new lookout would have been constructed near the middle of the parking lot at the base of the monument, and an inn was proposed on the site of the present-day Visitors Center on Route 23.

In some ways, this plan represents the high water mark of the NPS and CCC involvement at High Point. It is a grand vision that was never fully attained. If the plan had been carried to fruition, the park would have been able to accommodate many more thousands of people or those "rabid recreation seekers" as Harold Ickes called them.

Today, during summer months, the park is extremely busy, and visitation culminates with the fall foliage season when tens of thousands of people visit the park in a matter of weeks. Then, the wilderness experience, evident during the rest of the year, is greatly diminished as currently much of the park's acreage is undeveloped. An interesting question to consider is what the park might look like today if World War II had not interceded, and the CCC continued for a few more years. It probably would have looked more like Bear Mountain and Harriman state parks.

The NPS document contains a general development plan, a roads and trails plan and utilities plan creating a rather grand park in the vision of a blossoming national park system. The final master plan was presented at a well-attended open house in April 1938 when the public inspected the camp and property and was able to view drawings created by the NPS. It was reported in local newspapers that the plan would be complete in several more years. An entire set of these drawings remain in the park archives along with a large color-shaded topographic map.

Roads & Trails Plan

This part of the master plan, created by Gemmill (1937-1941), relied heavily upon the Olmsted plan which called for a system of roads and paths that would connect to roads inside and outside the park and adjacent to it. The Olmsted firm proposed "the importance of easy grades."[7] They suggested grades of 5 percent wherever possible and a maximum of 10 percent. A ride along Park Ridge Road or Sawmill Road demonstrates how that specification was followed by NPS designers. The grading was important because it created a more pleasant drive but also because maintenance expenses would be cheaper.[8]

An interesting facet of the master plan was the proposal to reroute Route 23 out of the park completely. This idea was in the original Olmsted plan when it suggested "the park be kept free of ordinary through traffic" although it did not call for the elimination of Route 23 but rerouting parts of it including a new section above Steenykill Lake to the east.[9] NPS designers took this step even farther as approaches on each side of the main entrance were to be obliterated.

The new road would have turned north onto Mountain Road and continued into New York State where it would have joined US Route 6. This is particularly remarkable because the state had just rerouted Route 23 a few years before around Steenykill Lake. It was lobbied, several years before that, to finish Route 23 to the city of Port Jervis. At the time, in the summer of 1933, New York State was considering creating a game preserve on the New York side of the border and this proposal was considered an enticement for New Jersey to complete the road into Port Jervis.[10]

The rerouting of Route 23 would have had a major impact on the park. This development would have impacted beneficially upon visitors at both Shale and Steenykill lakes as the sight and sound of traffic would have been eliminated. This proposal would have also had a major impact on housing and commercial development along Mountain Road, continuing into New York along the Greenville Mountain Road.

Other roads contemplated were a perimeter road of thirteen miles suggested by the Olmsteds. The route of this road called the Kittatinny Road would have approximately followed what is now the route of the Iris Trail to Deckertown Turnpike, to Sawmill Road to Park Ridge Road and along Park Ridge Road and back to the Kuser mansion. While the perimeter road was not built in its final form, it was to a large degree created.

In 1938, this road was considered to be a proposed route so that it is not clear if the CCC built it or if it was an old woods road that was cleared and renovated by the CCC. Another road planned but not built was to the east of Scenic Drive on the other side of the ridge. It was along this road, almost in a northeast line from the Shale Lake Play Area that a new Administration and Service Group area would have been built. A new road connecting Clove Road with Park Ridge Road was proposed as another point of entry into the park.

The bridal path, which began where the Iris Inn or Visitor Center and Park Office is now located, continued along Kittatinny Mountain Road and looped around Lake Rutherfurd to the base of the Shale Lake. A final segment was proposed from Shale Lake across Route 23 past the proposed administration building and back to the main entrance to Lake Marcia. Additional trails and trailside shelters were proposed that would have made most of the park accessible and usable by hikers.

Utilities Plan

A drawing, created by Melvin H. Gemmill from 1937-1941, contains utility information for the proposed and as-built structures in the park.

Peter Osborne

Working Drawings

A number of the working drawings survive in the collection at High Point and they give precise directions to foremen working in the field. They include specifications for materials to be used, design and elevations. Many drawings are inscribed with field notes made by foremen as work was being done.

Surveying Projects

A survey crew was made up of enrollees and overseen by a foreman. On average, the crew members selected were more adept at mathematical computations. They were involved with major work projects including the roads, lake construction, camping facilities, skiing facilities, boundary survey and master plan design. They also took measurements for the larger projects that were in progress.

In the early years, they were mainly involved with making surveys that allowed for the major projects to proceed. After that, they were occupied with the boundary line survey project. Neil Theide, an enrollee who served on the boundary crew, remembered: "Occasionally, we would leave the boundary survey and do a little work all through the park. Levels. What they called levels. They had to know how high this was or how low that was. We surveyed [Route]

23. It was a little narrow road then, from the park to Port Jervis. I guess we did all the surveying associated with the work ... we did all the survey related to all the construction. Mostly, we were on boundary survey, but we would spend a day at Sawmill or a day here or there doing other work."[11]

Another major survey project completed by Company 216 was of a topographic nature that provided NPS designers with data for the master plan. Other topographic surveys were of eighty-five acres and two hundred acres, parcels for tree trimming projects in the central part of the park.

Boundary Line Survey Of Park And Monument Placement

In one of the earliest lists of projects compiled for the CCC, the survey of a park or forest's boundary was given priority in every project across the country.[12] Because the federal government did not want to spend public monies on private lands, it was important to know exactly where a boundary was. For many states, the creation of a current boundary map in newly acquired park land was not a major priority.

The marking of the park's boundary took a sustained effort because boundaries were not always certain and there were private parcels within the park. While property acquisitions were minimal or non-existent in the CCC era, the map clearly delineated and marked the line. Deeds were initially researched by foreman Charles Henkel who gathered large quantities of material and notes.

Remembering the initial research, Neil Theide said: "As far as I know, Mr. Henkel had done it all before I got there [1936-1938]. He had volumes and volumes of notes ... I can't imagine the job he had to dig up all these deeds and get all of this information for us to go out in the woods and run these lines. The research he did must have been tremendous."[13]

CCC enrollees were given training and under supervision of a NPS foreman helped with some of the research at the Hall of Records at the county seat in Newton. Surveying classes were given in camp. When the research was complete, the survey of the forty-mile park boundary began.

Surveying the boundary took a great deal of effort because monuments were gone or had been disturbed. In some cases, deeds were not clear with regard to landmarks, and the most recent information available, mainly through surveys undertaken by Col. Kuser, were already at least ten years old.

Neil Theide, remembered not only how he got on the crew but how it went about its work on what was considered one of the largest and most complicated title searches and surveys ever conducted in the state of New Jersey:

"[Enrollee Allan Wilson] approached me and started talking to me, and it seemed that he was on the survey crew and he found out that I got out of high school, and part of my high school was algebra, geometry, trigonometry. I loved every bit of all of it, and they figured, here is the guy we need for the survey crew.

"So they took me on the survey crew, and at that time it was Mr. Henkel who was running it. Charles Henkel, I think his name was. He was from Ridgewood, New Jersey. He was either laid off or a former surveyor for the Erie Railroad. And he had been to Newton and dug up all these recordings of deeds from all the farmers all around and he had all this information. We were going out in the field and going from one corner so-called to the other ... I started out as a brush cutter, and we would go ahead and cut all the saplings for eleven hundred feet or two hundred feet ahead so that the surveyor [could see] with his instrument.

"I was only doing that for a little while, and then they made me the chain man and they had this one hundred foot steel tape and you'd drag it along and measure it from one stake to the other ... It was an accurate survey.

"There is something like 150 corners around the park. I don't know exactly but I say about. In other words, they would buy about one thousand feet from this farmer and over here maybe they'd buy a one thousand something, a couple of hundred this way and I think its something like forty miles around.

"It wasn't too long before they let me run the gun, the transit. I did pretty good at that. Then, for some reason or another, Mr. Henkel left us. I don't know what the reason was. I think that was about after the spring of '37 ... And we got Mr. Wells. Oliver W. Wells. He was very nice. He was a younger man. I guess he was an engineer, and maybe he couldn't find work at that time either, you know. I got along very good with him and one thing that I think impressed him very much, we'd completed the survey, this must be up in '38 now, and we're gonna make the map.

"He's got some system. I don't remember just what it was. It was something about going north and south or east and west so far and it all adds up to bring you back to the point where you started. We got maybe three-quarters of the way around and it looked like it was going the wrong way and my trigonometry is working again, you know; I figured out there has to be a mistake of about thirty some feet in order to do what's happening to our map. And I started going back over the notes and you know, this surveyor's chain, one hundred foot tape as you call it, has a 96 and down here some place 34, it has a 69. I says now there is the thirty foot error for that 69 to that 96, and sure enough, there was."[14]

A typical day on the survey crew is recalled by Neil Theide:

"The survey crew would get on the truck and they'd take us as near as they could by road to where we were working at that time ... We would walk the rest of the way. Sometime we had to walk in a mile or two to get where we were working. We would run the line for a day, and the interesting part of that was, let's say we are running a line a thousand feet, now this hasn't been surveyed in quite a few years probably ... and he has a bearing north by this and south by this, so we go and measure the distance as we go.

"But we know we are not going to land at that point so we come within twenty feet or ten feet or five feet of it, and then we scout around, and look, and we are either looking for a pipe or a stone, or a certain tree, or something like that and when we find one what we think is the point, possibly a pipe or iron pin, then we tie our line into that pin and that gives us a triangle and we can solve that triangle and find the true distance of the boundary itself. See we were off the boundary we came into that point.

"We'd ... have our lunch with us and we would be out there 'til 4:00 or something like that. Then the truck would come and he had notice, he had been told where to pick us up and we would get back in and have our supper."[15]

After the survey was complete, the marking of the boundary proceeded. About two hundred and fifty concrete monuments with a copper disc on top were placed around the forty mile boundary.

Peter Osborne

In some cases, High Point Park Commission monuments were already in place and in other cases, copper plugs were installed in boulders, such as around Lake Rutherfurd. In other places, stone piles, stakes, trees and iron pipes were used for monuments. A wide swath was cleared to delineate the boundary and served as a firebreak.

At the time of the final survey, the park encompassed 10,934 acres. Most of the original CCC-era monuments remain in place, but the park has acquired additional acreage outside those boundaries, and now they are within the current park. Some markers are probably gone because of road work including the widening of Route 23. The markers were originally placed twenty-five feet from the center of the road.

The next step was to complete a map of the boundary that would become part of the legal records for the park. Neil Theide remembered how that was done: "We did some survey work when the snow was on the ground. I can't remember how much ... We kept working most of the time indoors when the weather was bad. We always had a lot of work to do indoors. In those days there were no calculators, no scientific calculators ... computations were done with what they call logarithms and tables ... I remember I was familiar with that stuff because like I say in high school, algebra, plane geometry, trigonometry, I ate them up.

"I instructed the other guys in the crew how to solve these triangles that we had by looking up these sines and cosines and logarithms and so forth in these books so we could find the true line you know ... We did our work, our paperwork, for the map and all our survey work in what I guess was one of their [former Company 216] recreation rooms."[16]

A final copy of the boundary map was drawn by foremen Oliver Wells and then checked by Melvin Gemmill. Final approval was given by John J. Gibbons, the executive secretary of the High Point Park Commission. Because of the size of the map it could not be reproduced locally and was sent to New York City to have copies made. The map still remains on file in the archives of the park. Many of the monuments with a bronze dial inserted at the top remain in the park.

Peter Osborne

Courtesy High Point State Park
Enrollee Edmund Lauder works with a transit along a park road.

Safety Practices

Safety was an important issue for army officers, National Park Service superintendents and foremen particularly after 1934 when a CCC Safety Division was established. A manual was issued which included rules for equipment use, explosives and lifesaving techniques. Representatives from the division regularly visited the camps checking for safety hazards, and safety questionnaires were required to be filled out by camp officials. By 1936, death rates from disease and injury in the CCC were lower than the regular army and lower for the age group of enrollees.[17]

At High Point, a safety council was created that included NPS and army representatives. Some work gangs had meetings to discuss safety. Accidents caused by negligence subjected enrollees to disciplinary action. Columns in the company newsletter exhorted enrollees to work safely. The safety committee wrote in the 1939 newsletter: "The CCC safety program has two objectives: the elimination of physical hazards and the minimizing of human hazards. Accomplishment of these objectives results not only in individual safety benefit to each CCC boy but increases his efficiency and makes him more acceptable to an employer. The watchword 'Always Be Careful' has been called the ABC of the CCC."[18]

While no one was ever killed at High Point during the eight years the C boys were there, mishaps and injuries did occur. Albert Mastriani remembered one incident when an enrollee was chipping at a rock without wearing goggles. He was struck in the eye by a chip and lost his sight in that eye. He was given a glass eye and ultimately returned to work. There were occasional accidents involving army trucks which flipped over because drivers were traveling on narrow dirt roads at high speeds. If enrollees were involved in an accident that was their fault, they lost their jobs and ratings as drivers.[19]

One accident was remembered by Neil Theide as follows: "I don't remember how he happened to be doing it. I guess we were just hanging around or something, and we had this fellow who was like the camp electrician. I don't remember his name except that it was Ernie something and he was going to raise a flagpole out by the office at the entrance to the camp. He needs a little help, right, and there were three or four of us, and we're helping raise this, it was a metal flagpole ... and all of a sudden we're all knocked away from the flagpole. It hits a wire or something, and it was high voltage. It wasn't enough to do any serious damage, but it knocked us right away from the flagpole."[20]

It is surprising there were not more accidents given the number of men working around large equipment and with hand tools. Most of them did not have previous experience working with tools. Company 1280 won the Sub-District Safety Banner at least once for having gone the longest number of days without a lost-time accident.[21]

The most dangerous piece of equipment used at High Point was the stone crusher, and in March 1935, an enrollee was badly hurt in an accident. The *Sussex Independent* reported: "James Ripel, aged nineteen, of Rudeville, member of Company 1280, CCC, at High Point Park was rushed to Linn Hospital ... [he] suffered a fracture of two bones of the right leg that morning at the stone crusher used at a dam being constructed by CCC men at the state park. The trouser leg of Ripel's pants was caught in the machinery."[22]

Typical of safety instructions are the ones from Howard Platt. He wrote in one 1938 newsletter:

"Don't carry a heavy load unless your feet are firmly placed.

Don't walk in water when you don't have to. Colds are dangerous.

Don't move around while the truck is in motion.

Don't drive your truck carelessly over soft and slushy ground.

Don't drop heavy stone or rock(s) until you're sure your hands and feet are in the clear

Don't release your end of a load before the man you are working with lowers theirs.

Don't handle rock or carry heavy tools without using gloves.

Don't take unnecessary chances.

Don't forget the ABC's of safety. ALWAYS BE CAREFUL."[23]

Another comes from Melvin Gemmill, the safety engineer for the camp, who wrote in a March 1938 newsletter: "You fellows see the men that get the injured eyes and broken bones. What are you going to do about it. Keep on getting them? How about getting up on your hind legs and putting a stop to the many unnecessary accidents that occur so regularly in this camp.

"A close checkup on the accidents that have occurred in the past will reveal a startling lack of judgment and common sense on behalf of the victims. In many cases it is found that the victim had his mind in 'free wheeling' at the time of the accident. Accidents sometimes do occur because of unforeseen circumstances - but not often. We want a better safety record for company 1280, and you enrollees are the ones to get it."[24]

There were CCC enrollees who performed heroic deeds across the country and were given Certificates of Valor, the highest award given to an enrollee. Typical of these acts of heroism was the bravery of Michael Sagursky when he was called out to help fight a fire in Pennsylvania. In an interview he recounted the following: "Our company went out three days or so [on firefighting detail] and, of course, we got compensated ... I went out myself, volunteered and carried water on my back ... to help [fight the] fire, kill [the] fire. Of course, many of the youngsters wanted to drink the water, and I did save one of the guys' lives ... he was on his way out and I dragged him out of the fire and our first aid people took care of him ..."[25]

Miscellaneous Work Projects

Finally, there were miscellaneous work projects. For the most part, they were special requests by the park's secretary or surrounding communities. Enrollees from both companies spent almost two thousand man-days obliterating borrow pits and restoring them to a more natural appearance. Shale pits near the proposed Shale Lake were used for many years to provide materials for area roads. By 1936, some two thousand square yards of grading had been completed. In addition, Company 216 removed shale parking lots in the Lake Marcia area and replaced them with soil and shrubs and stones to give a more natural appearance.

CCC boys were sent to work in local communities on forests, graveyards and stone walls. This work appears to have been done by Company 216.[26] They also participated in search and rescue missions, razed old service buildings within the park, salvaged the lumber, and removed five miles of fencing that surrounded the Kuser's wildlife area.[27]

CHAPTER 11

What Might Have Been

Because the CCC helped the young men of the nation, and because the work they did held a deep and abiding interest for him [President Franklin D. Roosevelt], the CCC was one of the things he felt might well have become permanent.

-Eleanor Roosevelt

This I Remember

Since at least the 1880s, some form of "rustic" architecture had been deemed appropriate in larger scenic reservations of all types, including national parks. Virtually everyone involved in early national park management including army engineers, railroad executives and Forest Service supervisors, agreed that proposed architectural development should "blend" and "harmonize" with its surroundings ... naturalistic design had been applied in municipal and regional landscape parks not only in the design of buildings but in coordinated schemes of ... shelters, comfort stations and other buildings necessary for the convenience of park visitors.

Wilderness by Design: Landscape Architecture and the National Park Service

In history, there is always the question - what would have happened if ...? At High Point State Park, that question arises with the CCC work projects. When the master plan was finished in 1938, there were several more years of work left for the CCC, and there were reasons to be optimistic that it would be completed. In 1937, the CCC became a permanent agency, relieving its managers of the temporary nature of the organization. The work done by the CCC was well received by the public and politicians. Also, construction companies like 1280 tended to have a longer life span. Finally, there was a remarkably productive relationship between the park and the CCC.

The master plan called for the construction of at least two more lakes. Shale Lake was to be located just south of the Iris Inn near what became the Mountainview correctional facility. Lake Montague was to be located south of the junction of Sawmill Road and Deckertown Turnpike. In addition, a major recreation facility was to be built around Shale Lake along with a new administrative facility for the park's staff beneath the ridge where Scenic Drive is now located.

Seventy five percent of the Shale Lake Play Area was built but left uncompleted in November 1941 when 1280 was disbanded. The park never made an attempt to finish the project. The uncompleted facilities were far from public view and later replaced by a correctional facility. Most people forgot they had even been built.

If the CCC had been able to operate for another year or two, a whole new play facility might have been finished, and the controversial corrections facility never built. There might have been a major change in traffic flow in the park with the elimination of Route 23, and campers would have had a third lake to enjoy. The lakes were never created, the new service area never made it off the drawing board and the CCC faded from memory. Lake Montague remains a large wetland. As in all *what ifs*, the answers will always be elusive and unanswered.

Another issue raised by this question is the case of mistaken identities. A number of buildings and features at High Point have long been thought to have been constructed by the CCC. More recent research has either clearly shown otherwise or at least questions those earlier assumptions.

Shale Lake Recreational Facility

This was the next major project undertaken after completion of the Sawmill Lake facilities. As it turned out, it was the last major project the CCC would have built at High Point State Park had the war and the improving economy not interceded in the late fall of 1941. The setting for the proposed play area was magnificent with a commanding view of the valley looking to the south and east.

The construction of Shale Lake Play Area was considered by park planners as early as 1935. It is the type of facility purposely omitted from the Olmsted plan. The Olmsted firm felt the park was a scenic one and should have "higher aims ... conducive to quiet contemplation of nature."[1] In spite of that attitude, they did propose building a golf course midway between the campsites at Mashipacong Pond and the mansion.[2]

Whatever the feeling of the Olmsteds, the Shale Lake Play Area would have addressed a major need for the park, a place for sports. Included in the NPS plan was a tennis court, minor sports area and a baseball field. When finished, the project would have accommodated two hundred and fifty cars. The plan called for a new facility for "large outing groups" to "enjoy romping and playing about in a natural setting." The facility would have been separated from the lake by what was described as a "Natural Play Area."[3]

A 1940 news account anticipated the project would be finished in 1941. Through 1940 and 1941, it appears that most of the enrollees and NPS foremen were working solely on the project. Some of the work was completed or underway until the closure of the C camp in November. Most visitors to the park today do not realize the project was partially built because this area has been inaccessible to the public since the late 1960s. There is still a need for this type of facility in the park, and there is some consideration being given to one's being built.

Shale Lake Play Area

The Shale Lake Play Area, designed largely by Albert Mastriani, was well underway in 1940 with a crew of one hundred and five men working on a major drainage ditch consuming the bulk of their time that summer. Work was also being done on a minor sports area. Other drainage ditches and a ballfield were being constructed.

Only parts of this project were completed including the large baseball field, two-thirds of a large concrete bleacher behind the backstop, a parking area and the road into the facility. The bleacher was to have been given a stone facing for a more natural appearance and remains unfinished to this day.

Construction of the correctional facility may have changed, covered up or demolished facilities at Shale Lake but the ballfield was completed and used by inmates at the Mountainview Correctional Facility until 1999. An existing pond in the center of the present-day configuration was not part of the NPS plans and may have been the site for the recreation lodge. Parts of the sewerage disposal system were completed and may have been used by the correctional facility in the early years. The prison was created in 1954 and was supposed to accommodate twenty-five inmates. Near the end of its life, it was housing more than one hundred prisoners. It was closed in 1997 and demolished in 1999 because of intense local opposition.

Shale Lake

A new lake for the proposed recreation complex was considered early on by NPS planners and was to be called Shale Lake. The proposed lake was at a site Colonel Anthony Kuser also thought was a good spot because he built a dam there when it was part of his estate.[4] In the fall of 1935, it was called the Kuser Dam and Lake.[5]

Shale Lake would have been the third lake constructed by the CCC and much larger than Kuser envisioned. It would have covered fourteen acres and two earth-filled concrete core dams would have been built to impound water, similar in design to the Steenykill project. The explanatory statement says: "An irregular shoreline produced by bays and projecting shoreline will give the lake unusual interest."[6]

The name comes from extensive shale deposits in the area where it would have been built. There was a large borrow pit adjacent to the proposed lake, that was used frequently for road work. In preparation for the lake development, the pit was filled in and graded off.

The water source was to come from the spring fed streams running through the area. The average depth of the lake was to be 5.75 feet. Additional water sources considered included the drilling of a well or water being piped from Lake Marcia. A beautiful feature of the lake would have been a cascade of water created through a natural ravine just below the lake. Test borings were started in the spring of 1939 and completed. The outline of the lake can still be seen and the old Kuser dam is still on the site although it does not impound water any longer and has created a large swampy area. A trench for the dam was apparently begun and can still be seen.[7]

Recreation Lodge Entrance Building

The last major building project proposed by the NPS was never built. The conceptual drawings remain of this structure, created by Albert Mastriani in 1941. Part of the septic system was built and may have been used by the correctional facility after it was constructed. The design has features similar to the Franklin D. Roosevelt Museum building at Hyde Park, New York. It is also remarkably similar to the design used for the Iris Inn which was built by the state park work forces in 1941. In fact, the envelope the drawings are in at the park's archives are mistakenly labeled "Visitor Center - Iris Inn."

Mashipacong Pond

This property was never acquired by the state park and the extensive plans for it were never realized. As late as 1941, the park's master plan showed it as a possible acquisition, but today it remains outside the park's boundaries. It has been occupied by Trailblazer Camps since 1940 and is now owned by the Nature Conservancy.[8]

Lake Montague

In 1938, the master plan proposed an additional lake, to be called Lake Montague. It would have dammed up the Big Flatbrook and been about 44 acres in size and located at what was then a swamp along the Upper Flat Brook, directly across from the southern end of Sawmill Road. There would have been a beach facility and campsites ringing the lake, similar in design to Saw Mill Lake, however, no work was ever undertaken. This project would have followed the completion of Shale Lake.

Peter Osborne

Park Administration Service Group Buildings

While a whole new park administration area was proposed for the area near some of the present maintenance facilities on the eastern side of Route 23, the facilities were never built.

A Case Of Mistaken Identity

High Point State Park has a long and eventful history, but unfortunately, its archives do not reflect it. The park's main focus has been the management and interpretation of its natural resources rather than its historic resources. As such, the CCC-era until recently, was a neglected piece of the park's past. Initially, this author, like several who preceded him had to make assumptions about park buildings and structures. Many buildings and improvements in the park seemed to have the mark of the CCC, and many were built in the rustic style so popular from 1920-1945.

As it turns out, the state park also constructed a number of new buildings which are evocative of the designs used by the CCC. Some projects designated as being built by the CCC were not. Or, there is not enough evidence to list them in the final CCC project list. Most of the projects in question were built in 1933 and 1934, and if they were built by the CCC, they would have been built by Company 216. However in the final analysis this seems unlikely given that project designers were not on site until the late fall of 1933 and it took extensive planning to get these projects underway. In addition, during the early months of its time at High Point, the company did extensive forest work around Lake Marcia.

There are several projects the CCC has long been associated with including the laying of large boulders along roads in the eastern section of the park and lining of the stream that flows out of Lake Marcia with stone. There is no documentation to determine if this is true. Two of the most beautiful buildings at High Point, the Iris Inn (the current Visitor Center/Park Office) and Grey Rock Inn (the Interpretive Center), were not built by the CCC. The Grey Rock Inn was built by a private contractor prior to the arrival of the CCC. Not only can historians be wrong, but at least one enrollee thought the building did not exist when he was there in 1937. The Iris Inn was built in late 1941.

Grey Rock Inn
Cafeteria

The Grey Rock Inn or the Cafeteria as it was known during the CCC era was designed in 1930-31 by Marion Sims Wyeth and Frederic Rhinelander King whose office was at 52

Vanderbilt Avenue in New York City. Construction was completed in 1931-32.

The building was already in use as a restaurant for the public when the CCC arrived in 1933. The design and detailed construction drawings still remain in the High Point archives. The cafeteria became a popular place for meetings, dinners and reunions. The building, which could hold three hundred people, was closed as a cafeteria during the war, reopened in 1947 and closed again in 1959. It was reopened briefly in the 1960s and then renovated as an interpretive center which remains today.[9] The view, looking west is one of the most beautiful in the park especially if there is a lovely sunset. The building is listed on the State Register of Historic Places and the National Register of Historic Places.

Iris Inn
Visitor's Center/Park Office

This was the last major project built in the park during the CCC era. It was supposed to be used as a "on-the-highway restaurant and operated along the lines of a Howard Johnson."[10] The Iris Inn, shown as a proposed structure on the 1938 NPS master plan, was built in 1941 either by park employees or by a private contractor. Its designer is unknown. In November 1941, the shell of the building was complete and by 1942 construction was finished although the building was closed because of gas rationing. As late as 1958, the building was still unfinished. There was apparently no official opening ceremony, and it has been suggested that the park began to use the facility after 1958.

The design of the Iris Inn is typical of the "parkitecture" style. A more recent addition on the rear of the building was nicely incorporated into the original structure. This building is now used by the Division of Parks and Forestry as a visitor center and park office and has been since 1967.[11] In the 1970s, the park headquarters was moved here from the Kuser Mansion. The name comes from a circle of irises that were said to have existed naturally at the site.[12]

There are no surviving drawings of the Iris Inn in the park's archives, although a packet of drawings are mislabeled "Iris Inn" and are in an NPS envelope. These drawings were long considered to be conceptual drawings of the visitor center; however they are of the facility at Shale Lake which was never constructed. The building is listed on the State Register of Historic Places and the National Register of Historic Places.

Lake Rutherfurd

Lake Rutherfurd, formerly known as Sand Pond, predates the CCC era and remains the water source for Sussex Borough. It was a natural pond whose level had already been raised by the time the Olmsted firm was working on its plan. It was dammed to increase capacity in 1896 and became the borough's reservoir in 1897.[13] However, a number of NPS projects brought the CCC into contact with the lake including the building of the Iris Trail/Kittatinny Mountain Road, the bridal path, the Appalachian Trail shelter and survey crews marking the park's boundary.

Steenykill Cabins No. 1 & 2

A larger complex of twelve cabins or "cabin colony" as described in the 1938 master plan were first proposed in 1936. It was part of a larger effort to develop the park for multi-season use, particularly in the winter.[14] At one point, the park was described as having the "best physical basis for winter sport development of any public preserve in New Jersey."[15] The buildings were designed in the simple rustic style.

In the end, only two of the proposed cabins were built, Steenykill Cabins No. 1 & 2, although three were originally proposed in 1940. The design work and construction of the buildings was undertaken by the park in 1941. The rest of the complex was probably not built because World War II had begun. These buildings are often thought to be CCC-designed but the cabins were designed and built by the High Point Park

Commission. The cabins are still in use and can be rented.

Park Maintenance Yard Facilities On NJ Route 23

South of the park's entrance on Route 23, there is a maintenance yard still used by the park. In it are four buildings designed and constructed in 1939 and include the Repair Shop, Store Room, Oil House and Oil and Paint House. It has been long believed that the structures were built by the CCC and were moved from Camp Kuser to their current location. This is certainly a possibility since other buildings were moved after the camp closed.

However, like the Steenykill Cabins, the maintenance buildings have a rough-cut siding. Surviving drawings were done by the park commission and the work was completed by the park.

Viewing Towers & Observation Decks Scenic Overlooks

The observation deck, or overlook, on Scenic Drive may have been rebuilt or enhanced by the CCC in the 1930s. The two scenic overlooks, measuring 12' x 14' at the top, were built in 1928 by the park commission, one at or near the site of the current deck and the second near the first bend in the Scenic Drive as it comes up from Kuser Road. Unfortunately, no drawings survive of the decks. Both were still standing as late as 1941.

The remaining overlook has been rebuilt twice, once by the Young Adult Conservation Corps in the 1970s and more recently in 2000 by the park. The second did not survive.

Deer Run Picnic Shelter

Because of the style of construction, it has been suggested that the log Deer Run Picnic Shelter on Kuser Road may have been built by the CCC in the 1930s. It has shaved chestnut logs, similar to a CCC-built shelter at Stokes. This structure may have replaced the stone shelter shown on that location in October 1933.[16] There are no NPS drawings of the structure and a notation from a High Point Park Commission meeting states that a new shelter house was built in 1935 for $1,000. This suggests that park forces built it because of the way park projects were funded until 1937. It is still in use.

Lake Marcia Comfort Stations

It has been proposed that the CCC may have built the two restrooms facilities near Lake

Marcia in 1934. Because 216 was a forestry company, this seems unlikely, and the memories of 1280 personnel do not confirm that. No plans survive for the construction of these facilities and both reflect the architectural styles typical of the period. They are still used by the public.

High Point Monument Concession Stand

The southern section of this building still stands and is also typical of CCC-period construction. An addition was placed on this building that reflects the original design and the building is still used as a refreshment stand. A 1938 Company 1280 newsletter reports that the park commission opened the refreshment stand to the public; therefore, it probably was built by the park.[17]

High Point Monument Picnic Shelter

This building no longer stands and it has been suggested that it may have been built by the CCC in 1937. No records or drawings survive in the park's archives.[18]

Red Barn Pond

This small pond at the southern end of the park is not on the 1906 USGS map of the area or in the 1924 Olmsted plan. The CCC built a culvert for the stream that passes through the

Peter Osborne

area when it built Sawmill Road. This created a dam-like effect because water backed up to create a small pond shown on maps after 1947. It was never planned for by NPS designers but was probably the result of beavers whose descendants still block the culvert.[19]

CHAPTER 12

Memories

I personally believe that the CCC is a good organization. It occupies a fellow's mind and keeps him out of trouble he would get into if he were on the streets. It also benefits the government on the projects that have been completed. I hope it keeps going for others as well as myself.
-Enrollee Langridge, Company 1280 Enrollee, Barracks 2B

Company 1280 Newsletter

The food was good and the clothes were warm. I never had it so good!
-Edwin Jakobowski, Company 1280 Enrollee

We Can Take It: The Roosevelt Tree Army at High Point State Park 1933-1941: Interviews With Former Civilian Conservation Corps Enrollees, Camp Kuser, Companies 216 & 1280. vol. 1.

My least favorite memory is hopping out of bed in below zero weather and going out to work.
-Albert Mastriani, Foreman & Designer, NPS, Company 1280

What is most striking about the men who served in the CCC are the profoundly personal memories that remain from those years at High Point. They come to us via oral history tapes, letters, photographs and personal recollections. The effect the corps had on these young men remains with them. Some cry when they speak of the CCC and others remember events as if they happened yesterday. The effect the Depression and World War II had on this generation of Americans was profound and remains burned into their collective memories sixty-five years later.

The Great Depression

A common theme that runs through interviews with former CCC boys is the extraordinarily difficult times the "Dirty Thirties" were. Everyone knew someone who was out of a job or who lost his home due to unemployment. Images of a nation in a depression were everywhere. Thus it was with the C boys at High Point. They had first-hand knowledge of the difficulties caused by the depression.

Edwin F. Jakobowski was stationed at High Point and was from Paterson, New Jersey. He signed up for the CCC for the following reason:

"My mother was on welfare with five children, and if I didn't go in, they were gonna cut out the welfare. They were giving her five bucks a week and she said that if I don't go into the CCs, she'd lose her welfare. So I had to go ... I was in bad [physical] shape really to gain twenty pounds ... And most of the kids were in about the same shape. But, I met people here that shouldn't have been in there [the CCC] because they were just a fireman's son. They wanted to get rid of them you know from the city like Jersey City or Hoboken ... And those kind of people, I don't think they should have been here because their father was making enough money. My father wasn't making no money. He didn't even have a job you know. He worked on the WPA, five bucks a week. And when my mother said, 'Well how about father and mother for food?' And, the welfare people would say, 'Well usually children don't eat all their food so there should be some left over.' And now, how much do you get now on welfare? Now you get a fortune right?"[1]

The WPA was the Works Progress Administration, a federal agency that built many things in urban areas during the depression era including parks, streets, post offices and schools.

Remembering his time at High Point Frank Seddio said: "When I got to be second cook, I used to get $36 dollars a month. Then I got to be first cook, I was getting $45. And I think about $20 of that was going home, which my mother was putting away for me when she wasn't using it. When she had to use it, that was different ... I used to work eight hours a day for the NYA, the National Youth Administration, for the town of

Lyndhurst, New Jersey and my payment for the day was a load of firewood! Pay me in money."[2]

The National Youth Administration was considered a sister organization to the CCC and was created to help destitute young people. The original aim of the organization was to encourage young people to complete their education. It provided about 2.6 million people with work and had a much larger impact on both men and women in their home environments.[3] As the CCC struggled to survive in 1942, proposals were made to merge the two organizations into one.

Peter Lutz from Company 1280 remembered how he came to the CCC: "I had an uncle who had heard about it. He was working for the city of Jersey City and ... being I was an orphan, I had no mom and dad, I was with my grandma and my sister. So I had to get work somehow, instead of roaming the streets. So I quit Ferris High School ... reluctantly at first, to get some sort of job ... I was, I think seventeen at the time. I think you had to be eighteen, but I was kind of a big fellow ... I was unemployed ... At that time, there was no relief ... what we did is, I just quit school and I signed up with the CC camps ... I used to be quite an outdoors person. I loved the outdoors. I was in the Boy Scouts and I loved camping, and I was hoping to go to Wyoming or Colorado, someplace real woodsy (sic) ... and instead I wound up here in New Jersey."[4]

Carl LoGrand, remembered the pay and what he did with his allowance each month and also how he earned extra money while in the CCC: "We used to get $30 a month. Twenty five dollars went home and $5 lasted us a month ... You could buy an ice cream pop for a nickel ... everything was real cheap ... And I cut hair. I was the camp barber ... I used to get $.25 a head ... That was extra money for me. But I was always on the go there. I always did something."5

The camp at High Point gave many enrollees a new outlook and hope for the future. A question was put to the men in the December 1935 camp newsletter - "Do you think the CCC is a good organization? Reasons why and do you think it will continue?" Here are some responses:

Enrollee Langridge of Barracks 2B, Company 1280

I personally believe that the CCC is a good organization. It occupies a fellow's mind and keeps him out of trouble he would get into if he were on the streets. It also benefits the government on the projects that have been completed. I hope it keeps going for others as well as myself.

Enrollee Bogach, Barracks 3B, Company 1280

I think that the CCC is a good undertaking. I've spent 19 months in camp and having no home it has served me well. I trust that it keeps going for three-fourths of the members are in the same circumstances.

Enrollee Hockenjos, Barracks 4B, Company 1280

Two years in the CCC taught me that any man capable of living with other men in an outfit of this kind without being disagreeable to his fellow workers belongs here. The CCC is a place where all men can learn to take care of themselves. Also, if a man has a little common sense, he can learn plenty, which will benefit him when he leaves here. Just saying <u>C</u>lean, <u>C</u>heerful <u>C</u>haracters.

Enrollee Korinek, Barracks 5B, Company 1280

I know the CCC is a wonderful organization because of innumerable reasons, mainly it clothes the fellows; it gives them a chance to keep their families as well as themselves; it provides outdoor life for building up rundown physical conditions and, last but not least, it assures us of THREE SQUARE MEALS A DAY."[6]

We Can Take It

Many former enrollees remember the difficulty of the physical labor, whether it was picking stone for a road bed, cutting brush, cutting trees, firefighting, building forms for the dam or quarrying stone. The CCC's unofficial motto was "We Can Take It," and the boys lived up to it. During one contest, sponsored in the "Happy Days" magazine to pick an official slogan for the CCC, a Company 216 enrollee, Albert Palumbo, suggested "Where Youth Marches On." Another enrollee from nearby Stokes suggested "Junior Forests of America." One of the nicknames the CCC acquired was the "Colossal College of Calluses."[7]

A project superintendent wrote proudly to NPS officials in Washington that new enrollees from the Forest Service were unable to keep up with the work being done by experienced enrollees at High Point: "Both camps received indirect compliments from enrollees who were sent here during January as replacements. They came from an abandoned Forest Service Camp. After being here for a week or so, they began to quit in groups of from two to nine claiming that they had to work too hard at these camps."[8]

Much of the work was done by hand, and it required stamina and muscle, and many men were not accustomed to hard labor. William DeGhetto, a member of one of the road gangs that built Sawmill Road, remembered clearing the bed for Sawmill Lake and manual construction methods used: "Before we could dig [out the tree stumps], you know we didn't have [any] machines in them days, we had to build a fire to thaw the ground out so you could pick it and pick at the soft ground ... chop the trees down. Then you'd have trucks, dump trucks - Chevy dump trucks. And a couple of rack body trucks, but most of them where all dump trucks. You'd tie a rope on it, dug around the stumps you know, because in them days you didn't have the equipment like you got now. Oh, it was a lot of work!"[9]

Another enrollee, John Malina, remembered the building of Sawmill Lake. He wrote: "We did build some roads and the part I was most connected with was the groundwork for the building of Sawmill Lake. The actual work to complete the lake was done after I had left. However, I worked with the man Mr. Paige, the engineer, on arriving ... I carried the transit, the tri-pod and took notes on the contour of the lake, drove in stakes at various spots, etc. It was all forest land with the exception of a small stream of water running through. I was in charge of a group of boys eighteen to twenty years of age, whereby we started a rock foundation for the dam. The present dam is where we started - without completion."[10]

Carl LoGrand remembered the construction of the dam at Sawmill and also what was probably a regular chore for many enrollees when the dam was being built, night duty: "I used to have this duty, night guard duty at Sawmill. Out in the woods, nothing around, all by myself, just a little tent. And I'd be sleeping there. In the morning, I'd wake up and there's rabbits, I'd see deer ... and that bothered me, all alone you know. I was miles away from High Point ... And no homes or nothing ... [I] was just put there just to watch the machinery ... like bulldozers and shovels and stuff like that."[11]

Enrollees were involved in other jobs that helped the camp to function like snow removal. Edwin Jakobowski remembered some of these details along with the duty of guarding equipment: "You wouldn't work Sunday, but if you missed a day during the week you had to work, make it up [on] Saturday. Like they had a rain day or something, in other words, you had to put in your time. We'd get snowed out, you know, if it snowed a lot. Well, we do a lot of plowing and shoveling and stuff too but, then we had guards, like at, the crusher we'd have a guard out there, so you ... had to take their food out to them. I used to like that because then the snow would be about three feet deep, you go out there with the truck and bring out his food. And where we [would] have any equipment, we [would] have a guard out there, you know to stay over night."[12]

Stone was quarried on park lands in several locations, to the east of Cedar Swamp Drive on the mountain side; at the Burrow's farm quarry located south of the ATT microwave facility; the shale pit which was near the proposed Shale Lake and another near the old maintenance yard on Route 23.[13] Stone for the campsites was quarried on Pochuck Mountain in Glenwood, New Jersey, not far from Warwick, New York.

Other jobs in the CCC required more mental acuity than physical prowess. One such job was on the surveying team. Under the leadership of the foremen, they staked out roads, building projects, parking areas and even skiing facilities. Enrollee Charles Wilbert was on a survey gang and remembered his experience: "We were doing the ditch ... some kind of a drainage ... I wasn't on that too long before ... a guy give me a break ... one of the leaders. I guess he liked me, I liked him so I asked him could I get on his crew. And then I got on his crew and he sent me with the surveyor. That's where I stayed ... And that was the best job.

"We would go out and he would tell us to cut stakes so long, pile them up, and then he would, lots of times he'd be doing other things. But he'd have to go somewhere else, but he would tell us now, make sure you don't get caught by the other leaders, the foremen. He says, you get your stakes and you can goof off if you want ... Yeah, we go out and cut the stakes ... pile them up and we just wait there till he come back."[14]

The CCC was a totally self-sufficient organization purchasing its own supplies and equipment. As such, it had a blacksmith on duty along with other mechanics. Edwin Jakobowski remembered: "We had our [own] garage, repair shop where we fixed the trucks and grease[d] them. Then we had a blacksmith there and he sharpened all the tools. We sharpened our own tools, axes, you know, drills and all that.

Whatever we used, we sharpened our own stuff ... We had our own sawmill there [at the maintenance yard on Route 23]. We made our own ... logs and stuff. Kids used to run that under supervision ... with the foreman."[15]

Sometimes projects required long hours of work like the pouring of concrete at the Sawmill Lake dam. Cook Michael Sagursky remembers having to make arrangements for food during the construction: "When we were building the dam, at the time when they started pouring the cement, that had to go on continuously like twenty-four, thirty-six hours and we'd have the youngsters there working. I remember hampering down and I would have to go out as a cook and feed them out there. We used to make bag lunches. Two sandwiches of various cold cuts, a fruit and then I'd bring the drinks out. It would all depend what time of the year it was – either a cold drink or a hot drink. And they were all well taken care of that way."[16]

The use of heavy machinery was new to many enrollees. Probably the most dangerous piece of equipment was the stone crusher. Because of the moving parts and also the amount of force it exerted, it could easily injure a man or crush him to death although the loss of a limb was more likely. Peter Lutz, remembered the stone crusher: "This stone crusher was very, very, dangerous to work. We would throw in stones, let's say some sizes were as big as a basketball, but not as round ... and these jaws would crunch them up and then there would be big piles of this crushed rock. And then the fellas would shovel it up, shovel it on the truck, the truck went along this particular road that I'm talking about to fill in certain areas, you see. Like swamp areas."17

Friends Of A Lifetime

For some, the friendships made at High Point lasted a lifetime. Consider the relationship between NPS foreman Albert Mastriani and Melvin Gemmill who later became superintendent of Camp Kuser. Sixty-seven years later Albert Mastriani said:

"I think my favorite memory is my lifelong friendship with Melvin Gemmill who was superintendent for about four years and who brought me into the office to do design work which enabled me to sharpen my drafting skills. I know almost everything there is to know about him, for we still keep in touch after these many years. When I was assigned to the CCC Camp in December of 1933 we shared a room together. He was three years older than me [twenty-four] and was like a big brother, teaching me the routine since I was very insecure being thrown in with experienced men up to fifty years old and one at least over sixty five, a Mr. Lewis. Except for the superintendent, we were all rated foremen.

"For a number of years Mel had a field crew as I remember before being assigned to the design office. He was a graduate of Penn State University. One of his brothers was an architect. His father was a railroad engineer on the Pennsylvania Railroad, the kind that operated trains ... Mel was responsible for the vast portion of the design work that came out of our office. When the original superintendent left ... Mel was assigned to that job, and that is when he put me in the design office.

After the camp closed down, he became a freelance illustrator and, at one time, told me that he had drawn 4,500 illustrations. I shall ever be indebted to him for allowing me to work in the design office, for that set me off on a career where I eventually became a registered professional engineer and still am to this day."[18]

Most enrollees, never saw their CCC friends again. Some had surprise meetings during the war or in the years following. Some tried to follow up on friends, but efforts led to dead ends. There was also a regular changeover of personnel due to end of enrollments, discharges or transfers. Occasionally, men were sent to other camps around the country, and enrollees from other companies were transferred to High Point. A substantial number of men who served at High Point also served in other nearby CCC camps.

Curiously, the men of both companies at High Point did not intermingle. No reason for that has ever been found. There is a lack of knowledge of the activities of Company 216 by members of Company 1280 and vice versa. Unfortunately, only one member of Company 216 was interviewed for this book. To many members of Company 1280, there is a general feeling that enrollees from Company 216 "were always out in the woods" when in fact they were creating some of the roads 1280 needed to get to their projects and even assisted in clearing trees from both lake sites.

Carl LoGrand describes the relationship between the two companies: "We never mixed with each other ... we only had our own gang. Each division would go work in one place and one [would] work at the dam where I was, and another would work up in the woods someplace you know, clearing paths and all. They all had their own section."[19]

The Weather At High Point

Most CCC enrollees who were interviewed by Friends of High Point member William Wurst in the late 1980s remembered the fierce cold during winter and major snowstorms that isolated the camp from the outside world for long periods of time. In January 1936, 2 ½ feet of snow fell during a two-week cold spell when the temperature hovered around the 0° degree mark. Michael Sagursky remembered the winter of 1935-6: "We must have had thirty-five to forty inches of snow! And we were snowbound for two days or three [days] and we all decided to take a walk up to the monument. Usually it would take us three quarters of an hour. It took us maybe five hours back and forth ... we were stumbling."[20]

Peter Lutz remembered the extreme cold at the camp along with some of the hardships it created: "Ooh, man it's cold up here! [In] February it was, 1937. It snowed for over a week ... everyday it would snow about a foot or so. And finally we had snow, it was almost, I would say about six foot deep. So we run out of ... food up at the camp. We had two hundred men on one side and two hundred men on the other side ... so we had to shovel out the snow by hand ... Into the camp, and we were shoveling downhill [on Route 23], that's quite a hill ... just so wide enough for a supply truck to get to us."[21]

Lutz also described the practical problems of working in the extreme cold: "Well normally, it was like 20° below zero and we just had to stick around because you couldn't possibly go out ... you'd have to have your ears covered and your face covered and just your eyes showing because High Point here in the winter time, the wind is very severe. And you would be eligible for a real good frostbite. It would go 20° below zero for weeks up in this area here. And you would go down to Branchville, and it would be maybe eight above, 10 above."[22]

Thomas Segar, another 1280 enrollee, remembered sledding down the long hill towards

Port Jervis and having the army trucks drag the bobsleds back to the top of the hill.[23]

In 1935, a three-day rainstorm hit the camp and flooded both lakes under construction and destroyed supplies in sheds at Steenykill lake. Torrential rainstorms occasionally damaged work on roads finished by C boys necessitating repairs on them.

Prized Jobs

One of the most coveted jobs for enrollees was to drive a truck. A clean driving record at a CCC camp meant jobs on the outside. Edwin Jakobowski was a driver at High Point and remembered: "After the road gang, I found out it's easier to drive a truck. I got a pass to go to the movies, take the kids down to the movies, down to Port Jervis and I'd get a free pass. You know, five bucks a month doesn't go far.

"Load[ed] up the trucks or worked on a quarry. KP, they teach you that, you learn that right away .... Then we'd come back, they'd have retreat ... Every weekend you'd have fire guard they'd call it, or guard duty you know, barracks duty ... So many people had to be in camp every weekend. So that's why I took the truck driver's job ... That would eliminate some of that other extra KP. I never got that no more, and I never got any guard duty, but I had to be on call for the truck in case I had to go someplace."[24]

We Can Take It!

Wildlife In The Park

Many enrollees were exposed to wildlife for the first time in their lives and their remembrances are particularly vivid after all these years. Edwin Jakobowski said: "Bobcat, there were a lot of wild[life]. We used to get good snares of rabbits and fox ... We'd put snares up and catch them. [The enrollees then gave the carcasses to men in Port Jervis.] Well, some of the old timers that lived down in Port Jervis, they kept the fur I guess.

"[There were] a lot of deer ... A lot of trout in Sawmill Lake. In the stream, we used to catch them by our hands. Rainbows, oh beautiful. I used to go down there early in the morning and see them coming down. You get down fast enough, you could grab one in your hand. Big ones. And, we would have trout for dinner."[25]

Company 1280 member Thomas Segar remembered helping to bury 200 deer in the winter of 1934 because so many died during the heavy snowfalls. Another feature of the park remembered by most enrollees were the elk the High Point Park Commission kept in a twelve-hundred acre fenced area near Route 23 at the main entrance of the park. This continued a tradition established by the Kusers when they owned the property.[26]

Peter Lutz remembered the bobcats: "Suppose you went to Port Jervis and you miss[ed] the truck going back ... at that time there was only an eight or ten foot wide shale road from Port Jervis. Now you have a three and a half lane road ... And as you would walk up this very lonely road ... in the middle of the night you would hear bobcats, or wildcats, screech like a train ... Just like that, you'd hear them 'meow!' And we used to put that big collar up because we were afraid [those] devils would jump out of the trees at us you know!"27

Many enrollees remembered the penned bears in the park. Peter Lutz had remarkably clear and poignant memories about the bears: "In the summertime ... there was a couple of bears. One was Jeff. I used to have his picture. And he had another boyfriend there I think, or two boyfriends. And every spring, Jeff, he wanted to, course he was looking for a girl and he would stretch those bars apart. I don't know if he was looking for a girl or just wanted to get loose. And he would get out and he'd roam all over, but he wouldn't get too far ... These bears were awfully strong. He would bend these bars apart so he could wiggle himself out ...

"They had local men from Space Farms who were very adept [with] wild animals, how they think and so forth and they used to, I don't know how they got Jeff back ... I know they didn't lead him back by the nose. Old Jeff, he was a tough old bird. How they used to feed old Jeff was, they used to get old loaves of bread from either the camp or slop from the camp and then there used to be a Port Jervis bakery who did a lot of delivery in the area. If he had extra bread, loaves of bread, then they would feed them to those bears. Bread, turkey heads, whatever, they would feed them to the bears! They were well fed and they were clowns and they would entertain the visitors."[28]

Time Off

Recreation and time off were anxiously awaited by the C boys. Many men went home on weekends, some by train, some hitch hiking and some even walked. Edwin Jakobowski remembered: "I had a motorcycle and a car. I couldn't bring it up to camp, [I] had to leave it three miles down. So I'd leave it in Colesville ... That's a little bit later on, but most of the time I walked up from Paterson ... I used to leave five o'clock Sunday night to come back to camp, and many of these roads weren't here yet ... So I had to go from Paterson up to Belmont Avenue, I think it is. Up to [Route] 23, press out on 23. Hitch hike or walk or sometime you get a ride. Most of the time I'd get in just in time for reveille, in the morning.

"[Things] got better. Like I said, I bought an old model A Ford and bike and I could ride up then ... but still, it was hard to do on five bucks a month."[29]

Albert Mastriani remembered: "For their evenings they had a recreation barracks in which pool tables, table tennis, card tables and a canteen were provided. There were movies at least once a week at which the educational director worked the projector and also once in a while, a live show by a road troop of actors sent by the government."[30]

One of the favorite pastimes was to frequent local bars known as "foam emporiums." While it was against rules to have alcoholic beverages in camp, it was not against the rules to drink alcohol off premises. Ads appeared in the newsletters along with comments about the drinking habits of some enrollees. One appeared in the February 1936 issue of Company 216's newsletter under the section "Jibs & Wisecracks": "Martin: What do you mean by coming back to camp in this condition? You're half drunk. Annette: I'm sorry, but I didn't have any more money."[31]

Most enrollees were under age so bars that allowed them to have an occasional beer were remembered fondly. Peter Lutz remembered one local bar:

"We used to buy that applejack down there ... I think, God bless his soul, Denton Quick used to make a lot of that stuff! ... He was a great guy, believe me! Dent had one fault you know? I would say it's a fault. He enjoyed his liquor, too, you know! But he didn't get boozed up like the rest of them. He was too damn smart. But he'd sell us applejack, and it was terrific ... It was very, very pure ... It was right in the general area of Colesville. It was on the right hand side. A little rambling shack and all of the hillbillies used to go down there, mountain people ... We'd be square dancing and they had a violin ... It was entertainment to the country people on Saturday night."[32]

There were other kinds of recreational activities in camp including swimming. John Malina, a company clerk in 1280, remembered: "We CC members did enjoy the swimming at Marcia Lake ... and we did become good swimmers and lifesaving members of the Red Cross."[33]

Carl LoGrand remembered using his time off in a number of ways after working a long day. He said:

"Well, then we go, we shower and all and relaxed a little bit. And about five thirty, they blow the bugle to eat. [We] used to line up before you eat and they'd look at us to see how we were, dressed and all ... Then after we ate, it was our time. Some played ping pong or different things ... they had movies, they'd show us movies and all. And most of us, we had our own games ... played cards. I used to go up to the monument a lot or walk around the lake ... I'm Italian. I love spaghetti ... I'd walk from up in our barracks down to Matamoras to a spaghetti place called Napoli ... I walked eight miles down and eight miles up ... takes me a good hour, hour and a half to do it ... I wouldn't do it now though.

"Port Jervis was then ... a hub of railroads. All these trains come in... Smokey Town I call it ...

And then we used to have trucks. Used to take us to town once a week to see the movie ... But I was looking for a good place for spaghetti, and I took that eight mile, sixteen mile round trip! ... Oh, when I got in the mood for spaghetti!

"Weekends ... I'll get a pass to go home ... Not every week, but weekends I enjoyed the crowds up here and I would go up to High Point park there and pick huckleberries you know. And I love huckleberries ... I ate them just like that. They're wild huckleberries, but they were good. Then other people, they're picking too you know? I don't know if it's still there, but right in back of the monument, plenty."[34]

The Fun Guys

Many enrollees, particularly rookies, fell for pranks. Some enrollees were, as Carl LoGrand called himself, the "fun guys." When interviewed by Debbie Fritter, a naturalist for High Point State Park, he had the following recollections: "I was one of these fun guys, and ... I kept the morale up here, I guess ... We used to play all these practical jokes ... I was one of the guys who would do it ... we used to short sheet the fellows and all ... Crazy stuff ... there's a fellow who always had a habit, when he comes finishing dinner, he'll come, he jumps on the bed you know, and I'll be sleeping ... So, I figured I'd cure him. So what I did, I took all the springs out and I tied it with string. So he come in after supper and boy he jumped on that bed and bang - he laid down! And now, after that happened, when he comes he checks the bed now and he doesn't jump no more, so I cured him!

"It was really fun. I was mean ... I was one of the trouble makers ... What I remember is the bugler ... he was a good sleeper. We took him and the bed outside ... while he was sleeping. So, I figured we won't have to hear that bugle, but he got up and blew the bugle anyway!"[35]

Other enrollees, who were considered "smart alecks," were exposed to initiations like one Peter Lutz described: "Once in a while, we would get some smart aleck and he would be mouthing off. We would bring him down to the north end of Lake Marcia, which was [a] swamp-like area. And we would tell him he was on a quail hunt ... sometimes if the wind wasn't blowing too hard, we would use a candle, like a plumber's candle. And the guy would stand there with a burlap bag and the candle would be down on a rock and he'd be holding the burlap bag [open] so, see the thing was the light would attract the quail.

"This is at night ... then he would swoop the burlap bag you see. Well it took maybe an hour or so before they get wise ... 'What am I doing here, this is stupid!' And they would come back, and they would be mad! Everybody would say, 'Gee, I don't know!' We would lie!"[36]

Most enrollees had never been exposed to dynamite and so most did not know dynamite by itself is a harmless gel in packaging. It was the blasting cap that made it dangerous. Only experienced enrollees, under the supervision of a foreman, could work with dynamite. Peter Lutz remembered another prank played on an unsuspecting enrollee who helped unload dynamite. "We used to have more fun with the dynamite. The truck would get in from Port Jervis off the train and be loaded with a big sign - Dynamite - So ... two guys are on the truck and they are throwing these little boxes ... of dynamite down. Some of the old timers who were with me, they knew that this guy is new, so he'd grab on and say 'look out, look out' here it comes! Bang and the dynamite would hit the ground and the kid thought that was the end of his life you know. Then of course, the driver would bring in the dynamite caps in a small box. That's the one you gotta watch. If you ever fall down, make sure it fits on your lap ... because hey man, you would be in pieces."[37]

On another occasion Lutz played a joke on the kitchen crew: "We wanted to get everybody in the kitchen, so we stuck sticks of dynamite in the stove and the guys were mad ... the dynamite wouldn't go off unless the caps were there. We laughed, you know."[37]

Lutz soon had the tables turned on him when he walked back from Port Jervis on a night off after having missed an army truck: "We have to walk [back to camp] so when we got back home as we call it, so [you] look for your bed and the bed is not there! So you say to your buddies, everybody is asleep, of course, they left in the truck, 'Hey, where the heck is my bed?' They say, 'I dunno.' (sic) So you head for the latrine and where is it? The bed would be fully made up sitting on top of the latrine roof.

"Now how did that bed ever get up there? There'd be two, three beds up there. So how would the bed ever get up there!? So that was one of the, the mysteries of the CC camps. So we'd get, a couple guys ... to get up there and we would put a rope around the bed and pull the darn thing off. We'd maybe sleep on the springs because the comforter would be all wet ... if it was snowing."[39]

Sometimes the fun came at the expense of other enrollees. While surveying the park's boundary, Neil Thiede recalled the private properties either in or along the park's boundary. At that time, as there are now, there were farms and hunting camps neighboring the park. Thiede remembered: "There would be a plot of ground, not in the middle of the park or near the border, down toward Deckertown Pike ... It belonged to some individual who never wanted to sell or couldn't be persuaded to sell it. Maybe he had a hunting camp there. So we're in the vicinity one time and there's this little shack in the woods. I won't mention any names, but one of our members peeked in the windows. First thing you know, he's got a bottle of whiskey in his hand. He got very, very drunk and sick."[40]

Nicholas Hanisak, an enrollee during the last two years of the camp's operation, remembered a humorous story about Sharkey Unangst, who operated the NPS power shovel. He was showing them how complicated the machine was. He recalled: "I understand that Sharkey Unangst took the steam shovel apart one time ... and he looks at the guys ... young fellows naturally, and he says, 'all right you guys, I'm getting out of here. You guys put it all together again.' Well he came back a couple of hours later and nothing was done. He said 'what's a matter with you guys - you stupid?' He says give me that part over there, they bring that over to him, puts it where it is supposed to go you know, give me that little part down there."[41]

The Wise Guys

All enrollees remembered the army's presence, and how it seemed like a military operation. Because of the discipline officers could bring to bear, there was also a collective distaste for enrollees whose actions reflected badly on the barracks population. The "wise guys," as Edwin Jakobowski called them, were segregated in their own unit. He said: "They were very strict. In fact, like in my barracks ... there were wise guys – we'd throw them out you know. They'd ask me to, who do you want, take this guy in the barracks, if I didn't like him, I'd say no, we don't want him. Because if he didn't have a clean barracks he'd get [unintelligible] like, because you're under army supervision. So you'd get extra KP or you wouldn't be able to go home over the weekend. And I said I don't want no goof offs. So we segregate the people like, sort of. Keep out the wise guys, we have a wise guy barrack down there. Go down there and they never go home. They don't want to do nothing."[42]

Sometimes enrollees simply could not handle the physical labor or could not adapt to the lifestyle. For them their term in the CCC was relatively short. Frank Seddio remembered another way "wise guys" were handled: "We had a few that ... came up here; they thought that they were big operators, you know, from the city and all that stuff. They['d] always find somebody to try and bulldoze ... Well we just let them shoot their mouths off and then eventually we get wise to them and if they got too, too active, we got rid of them. Dishonorable discharges."[43]

Other enrollees, while not "wise guys," ran afoul of army officers and were disciplined. Enrollee Robert Wilber remembered how an incident changed his plans for going to CCC camp in the West: "After you were in six months, you could go out West. So me and my buddy from Barnegat, we were in the mess hall one night on duty cutting potatoes and ... doing the dishes. Another guy was in there and ... he got us all teed off, so we give him a hard time and he went crying up to the commander. So we couldn't go out West. The commander hauled us up to the office ... and says, well you know for your punishments you can't go West. So that's why we come out in six months."⁴⁴

In other cases enrollees felt they were being picked on by army officers. In March 1935, John Spinarelli wrote to his Congresswoman Mary Norton, a personal friend of President Roosevelt's, to complain about treatment he was receiving: "I am not the kind to complain or ask favors but I'm in very serious trouble up here [High Point]. It seems that I don't get along very well with the Captain. He seems to treat me in the worst way. Most of the fellows have the same feeling against him as I have. I do my work and other tasks, and still I can't get along.

"Ever since we Jersey City boys arrived here, we've been treated in the worst way. I would like to reenlist, but the Captain won't let me. As my mother and the rest of the family need the money very badly, I would like to know if you can help me in this terrible predicament."⁴⁵

Because this letter went to a Congressional representative, who in turn brought it to Robert Fechner's (the CCC's Director) attention, it was given the highest priority. CCC Assistant Director James McEntee followed the chain of correspondence. In late March, Oswald Brown, project superintendent for Company 216, who had to deal with requests for information from higher officials, wrote: "Mr. George O'Neill, foreman of ECW SP Camp #1, states that Spinarelli, who was a member of Mr. O'Neill's work crew for a period of three weeks, was lazy, indifferent and insolent. Mr. O'Neill states that he constantly soldiered on the job and did the tasks assigned to him in a careless and indifferent manner.

"Spinarelli was finally turned in to the company commander by Mr. O'Neill for being insolent and for not working. He was then transferred to Foreman Saltsman's work crew and, according to reports of Mr. Saltsman, has been doing all right."[46] Mrs. Norton, upon receipt of the report, wrote back to McEntee and apologized for having caused so much effort to be wasted on someone who was having trouble in the CCC.

Another enrollee, Wladyslaw Kmiolek, from Company 1280, wrote to CCC headquarters trying to find answers to a number of questions concerning fines enrollees were being given for infractions while in camp. He also questioned other CCC policies including whether it was proper for special details to be undertaken after regular duty hours were completed and whether the LEM's would have to go on special details. After an investigation officials concluded there was no wrong doing.[47]

Red Sacco, an enrollee who served in both companies 216 and 1280, was from Brooklyn, New York. He remembered being transported in an army truck for a work crew when another C boy put his head into a milk can to get a drink. Just as he did that the truck hit a bump and his head got stuck in the can. They had to take the young man to the doctor where he proceeded to hacksaw the can off his head. Sacco said the boy was never the same after that.[48]

Local place names that have lost their meaning include "Platt's Boulevard" for the street that divided the two companies, named by a CCC boy for the camp's first project superintendent, Howard Platt. It was also known as "Platt's Street." A name that has been mispronounced for years is Lake Marcia. Every enrollee interviewed clearly remembers it as rhyming with "Garcia" which is how Dr. William Kitchell meant it to be said when he wrote his lovely poem and named the lake for his proposed bride, Marcia, in the mid-nineteenth century.[49]

One family that has long been associated with the park is the Fuller family and they too had their memories of the CCC. Men of the family worked for the park for decades. Florence Fuller's family lived on the park grounds and as a thirteen-year old, she remembered a hot shot army officer, Lieutenant George Keenan, the man who oversaw the construction of the camp. She recalled he occasionally flew a plane so low over the park that she could see him as he went overhead. She also remembered not being allowed anywhere near the CCC camp.[50] Her sister married a CCC enrollee, George Anderson.

Farewell To The CCC

For many who left the CCC at the end of their enrollment, it was a sad time. Farewell parties were given and, at the end of the first enrollment period at High Point, a program was given that included music provided by the Port Jervis Band, led by Charles Turner, secretary of the Port Jervis YMCA.[51]

On leaving Company 1280 in October 1938 an enrollee wrote: "I think it would do for every boy to spend at least six months in the C's. It instills a feeling of confidence. It builds you up mentally and physically, gives you a new perspective on life and teaches the value of a dollar."[52]

As enrollees left High Point, they occasionally wrote a piece for the company newsletter. These young men realized they were leaving a special organization. While many were going on to a new job or the military, they had grown to love the CCC. Phillip Auchard wrote this in the spring of 1939:

Farewell To The Boys
The days come and the days go;
The time for parting draws near.
The old-timers dislike it so
To embark from High Point so dear.

There are times when we may curse a place,
When we allow our spirits to fall.
But after the rain, the snow peers through space,
And spreads a new spirit over all.

Peter Osborne

> It sort of gets you, this outdoor life
> To be out in the fresh air so clear
> It's retreat from this world torn with strife
> And it ushers us into life without fear.
>
> In these few words, we say farewell
> To those that leave us soon.
> We know that when they leave the camp
> They'll be humming the tune of the C.C.C.[53]

The memories of enrollee Rudy Polise seemed to sum up best what so many felt when they left High Point. In 1939, upon leaving 1280, he wrote:

> Reflections Upon Leaving the CCC
>
> I thought I would never see
> A place where I would love to be
> A place where I would love to roam
> A place I'd love to call my home.
>
> Out I went to seek this place
> I thought I ran a losing race.
> All though I ran from sea to sea
> I found a place for you and me.
>
> Up in High Point you will see
> A camp they call the CCC
> With barrack light that shine 'till nine
> Then to a bed that's warm and fine.

We Can Take It!

On the D.I. Truck you will see
A seat that was built for me.
A special shovel and pick
Lots of hard work that's the trick.

The C's will build you up and make you fine,
And give you muscles just like mine.
After 6 months of night and day,
I pack my grip and am on my way.

I stand by the entrance of the gate
For my pals I've got to wait.
Salted tears run down my cheeks
Just like a water pipe that leaks.

Back on the decks from where I'd come
Considered as another bum
And watching a ship sail out to the sea.
I think of the chance that sailed from me.

The reason you all do know
For since I left the C.C.C.'s
I realize the value of
Wearing O.D.'s given to me.

I've been accepted: now I'm back
Back with Fat, Joe, Slim, and Mack.
Yes, having fun with all the boys,
No chance of missing all the joys.

Peter Osborne

> A chance to learn more and more
> I'm in and not such a bore,
> Yep! That's the very life for me
> That the Life - the C.C.C.[54]

One of the most poignant themes that runs through the memories of old men who were once C boys is their enthusiasm for the CCC decades after they served. Many recalled the days spent in the C camps as the most fruitful of their lives. Some fifty-two years after being at High Point, William DeGhetto, a member of Company 1280, said about his experience: "At that time, when they first opened, anybody could join it, and I was in there 'til '35 when somebody got me a job home in Passaic in a packing house. I quit. I came out of the CCs and I missed it so much that two years later, in 1937, I went to sign up again, and the first thing they asked me, is your family on relief? Because that was the height of the depression, '36, '37, '38, and I couldn't get in again so I still had my job.

"In them days you couldn't get a job. The only reason I got the heck outta [the CCC's] ... was because somebody got me a job back home. Otherwise, I would have, probably been in there till the war started. Because ... I enjoyed it. It was better than hanging around the house, you know, and out in the streets. That's why Roosevelt done it. To me, I think he done a good thing, doing that. They should have something like it today ... I think it'll cut down the crime.

Just think if we didn't have that. Maybe we would have been in the same, would have been hooligans too you know?"[55]

Edwin Jackobowski said: "The food was good and the clothes were warm. I never had it so good! ... Oh, they did a lot, they should have never stopped it ... It was the best thing they ever did. Like I said, some of the kids got good jobs out of this."[56] Michael Sagursky said: "Best three years of my life, and if they started today, I'd be right back again!"[57]

Frank Seddio, who was from Lyndhurst, New Jersey when he joined the C's, met his wife in Port Jervis and continued to live in Port Jervis until he died said: "I enjoyed myself up here [at High Point]. I mean, I really enjoyed CC camp. And like I say, I met my wife and we've been married forty-eight years. And Port Jervis has been good to me."[58]

Carl LoGrand, who was from Passaic, New Jersey, in the heart of the metropolitan New York area said: "The whole experience, it's a healthy life. And nothing like the outdoors. I enjoyed it. And once it gets in your blood, you always want to come back! I love the country. I don't like the city at all, but this is a good life. I felt like, like Hercules up here! ... You know, the air, the food and the work you know. And I felt great ... After I left the CC's ... got home, and then I always worked outdoors. I never wanted an inside job. And I wind up driving a bus so I could be outdoors and I went different places you know. I had a tour bus, I went cross country ... I went to Yellowstone National Park.

"I learned how to do everything — how to wash clothes. I was never that sure. It's a good thing. I wish they had it today for some of these kids, you get them off the streets. Really something good for them."59

Back In The Barracks Again

For many C boys it was only a matter of time before they were back in a barracks - a military barracks, fighting a world war. In the years leading up to World War II, there was a concern C boys would be taken from camps and drafted into the military, but President Roosevelt denied that would happen. The anti-war feeling was widespread, and enrollee Robert Wilbert had interesting recollections about this: "I was told that Roosevelt wanted us to have training, but the mothers got up in arms over it. They were opposed to it, the mothers. And then later on they said a lot of them was probably sorry that they didn't let the boys have training because when the war come they had to go right, right in. A little training and then right on over, so. But they put up a big squawk and so he didn't give us training."60

Edwin Jakobowski was drafted into the war effort after 1941 and reflected upon the value of his CCC experience: "It was the best time of my life, I think. And it helped me survive the war. I was in Patton's army, 80th Division, and out of 185 guys, there was only eight of us left out of my outfit when we reached Bastone. So all this training, between this and the other camp I was in, I was in forestry, that was like scouting you know, climbing all them mountains ... put me in shape."[61]

Frank Seddio remembered the value of his experience in the C's when he was in the army: "... One thing I do remember is that I belonged to the 1280th CC camp, and I went away in the service and I was in the 1280th Combat Engineers ... I went out on [a] cadre as a cook, and I become a mess sergeant in the service, through my experience in the CC camps. And still do it like as a hobby. Not as a professional, as a hobby, cooking."[62]

CHAPTER 13

Good Will Towards All And Malice Toward None

It will be the policy of this paper to print all the news of the camp in the spirit of "Good will towards all and malice toward none." In gathering and editing the news, the feature columns, we will endeavor to keep our eyes and ears attuned to the popular demands. All contributions will be welcome.

-The High Pointer, Company 216

Camp papers have been born in this company many, many times, but some unknown malady has generally caused them to sicken and finally die, usually at the second issue. This time, a very hearty youngster has given life and it is up to you men to make it grow, and be the strapping fellow to which we may point with pride ... it will indeed become issue on issue, an accurate record of events during our stay in the triple C's.

-Current Camp Capers, Company 1280

Every Saturday, a national newsletter called "Happy Days" was published for CCC camps across the country. The "Happy Days Are Here Again" song was the musical theme of President Franklin D. Roosevelt's first presidential election campaign. It was a newsy publication, telling of the exploits of CCC companies and stories about enrollees. There were occasional messages from the president and advertisements selling items to enrollees.

Company 1280 made it into the national publication at least twice. In the April 14, 1934 edition, Ludivico Ayala was said to have found a solution for moving rocks from the roadside to the road bed under construction. He used saplings as a slingshot to hurl rocks to the road bed. In the November 1934 edition, George Smith, the camp's education advisor, made a suggestion that a competition be created for excellent photography. Each camp that had a darkroom would send its photographs from camp to camp and have them judged.[1]

Company 216 also made the national newsletter on several occasions. In March 1934, enrollee Corcoran rescued an ice cream truck that got stuck in ice. He was given a free quart of ice cream and made the newsletter. Company 216 had a radio club that went on the air in 1934, and a 216 Army officer, J. King Wallace, created a new steam dish washer for use at High Point, and the plans were made available.[2]

Each company was encouraged to have its own newsletter and they provide an interesting window on company life. Newsletters at High Point were supposed to be published monthly although they were irregular because someone did not aggressively push for it like an Army officer. Also, the work of putting it out by volunteers proved to be too much. One editorial in a High Point newsletter also complained of a lack of cooperation from the members of the camp.

The newsletters were written by enrollees, and the editorial team consisted of eight or ten reporters or as few as two or three. Artists in the ranks were encouraged to contribute, and some were quite talented. The material was compiled and edited and then typed and proof-read. Stencils were cut and the publication was mimeographed in the company office and distributed for free. Additional copies could be obtained for two cents each.

When the camp's mimeograph machine broke down, John Gibbons, the executive secretary for the park commission, let the camp use his. On several occasions the newsletter was professionally typeset, probably by a local print shop. These were anniversary issues done in April of each year to coincide with the open houses taking place at the camp in honor of the creation of the CCC.

Company 216 had the distinction of being the first company in the Second Corps Area to have a newsletter.³ In December 1933, a publication called the "Columns" appeared for the first time and was the official journal of the camp's activities. The original editor was Lt. William Kuhn, along with Lt. W. H. Baetz, both officers at the camp. No copies of this initial newsletter survive. In February 1936, a new publication appeared named "The High Pointer." The next newsletter for the company did not appear until February 1937, and by June, the company was disbanded.

Company 1280 was better at keeping its newsletter going although there are gaps. There was a semi-regular publication for the company from 1935 until the summer of 1941. Its name was "Current Camp Capers." The name was not arrived at easily and took several months of solicitation before it was chosen.

The publications reveal much about each company and while it may appear they had continuity, actually, the life of each company was a fluid situation with men coming and going with each enrollment period. A popular enrollee in a given year was gone the next and the focus of the newsletter humor was turned toward someone else.

The newsletters often reveal the character of each company. For example, the motto for Company 216 was:

"216th Company - A Winner in Any Class"

Peter Osborne

The Company theme song, hummed or sung to the tune of "Mother," for Company 1280 was:

S is for the spuds we get for breakfast
H is for ham we never see
O is for the onions that they feed us
V is for a verse composed by me
E is for the end of our enlistment
L is when I leave dear old twelve-eighty

Put them altogether
They Spell SHOVEL
The emblem of the CCC

The newsletters are a combination of articles, jokes, crossword puzzles, updates about members, poems, short stories, advice for the lovelorn, artwork, moral advice, health advice, construction reports, safety exhortations, editorials, sports events, pep talks and an occasional list of enrollees. They reflect the atmosphere of any kind of a long-term camping situation like a Boy Scout or Girl Scout camp or the military.

Aside from taped audio interviews of enrollees in the park's archives, the newsletters provide the best account of what the CCC was like at High Point. Each newsletter reflects the personality of the enrollees or officers who wrote it. The meaning and humor of many of the "in" jokes or articles have long since disappeared. They were written under the auspices of the education advisor. Some of the individual barracks had their own feature pages in which their exploits could be recounted.

Each camp had enrollees who stood out or were favorites. One man was Red Sacco who served in Company 216. The following article appeared in a winter newsletter and described a "stunt night": "Red Sacco, one and only, pride of 216, scored a hit Stunt Night by singing an Italian love song before a packed house to win the award of one canteen book donated by the Educational Advisor. It was Red's spontaneous humor that brought down the house with roars of laughter, and applause that put the final clinch on the prize. There were many other contestants with diversified talent to add to the gala event. Pakestein and Wronka proved the quality of their voices by singing "Nocturne." Yanish and Monica gave a novel performance by rendering several cowboy songs with a harmonica played to the accompaniment of spoon tapping."[4]

The newsletters reveal the richness of camp life often mentioning enrollees by their nicknames. There was "Stump" DeVaul, "Pop" Johnson, "Ducky" Dittman" and a favorite among enrollees, "Deacon" Burke, who was editor-in-chief of the newsletter.

Poems were included in newsletters and often reflect camp life and the great affection the C boys had for the camps. Also, the kinds of dreams young men have. They demonstrate the

Peter Osborne

literary promise of some of the enrollees including Owen "Black" Murray who wrote the following in February 1937:

> What if we sweat in the summer
> And what if in the winter we freeze
> Though we grumble and kick
> Somehow we stick
> To life in the CCC's
> When enlistment times comes around
> And we all get the urge to breeze
> A couple may go but the rest of us know
> We're home in the CCC's [5]

Murray wrote two other poems for the newsletter, the first entitled *"Darkness up in High Point"* and the *"Contentment."*

"Darkness up in High Point"

> The flowers stop their nodding
> Each bows its pretty head
> For there's darkness up in High Point
> They know it's time for bed.
>
> The birds all stop their singing
> And nestle close instead
> For there'd be darkness up in High Point
> They know it's time for bed
>
> The day is through and play is through
> All's been done and said

We Can Take It!

When shadows creep it's time to sleep
Time to go to bed

The wind itself is crooning
There are pleasant dreams ahead
For there is darkness up in High Point
And it's time to go bed.[6]

"Contentment"

These things I ask of life
I know I'm asking much
Are a simple life, a home and a wife
The thrill of a baby's touch.

To know the joy of working
How sweet this life can be
When someone is waiting - Anticipating
The safe arrival of me.[7]

Other poems appear in the 1280 newsletter written by "Pat" under the heading of "This and That" in 1938.

Prayer of the Unemployed

Oh my God, I pray that Thee
Will send a job, not Charity
Give me a chance to earn my bread
And a place to rest my head
If I could just find work again
I'd bow my head and say, Amen.[8]

Peter Osborne

This poem also comes from "Pat" and reflects a concern of the time.

Give Me Work

With weary heart and heavy feet
I tramp along the dusty street;
My throat checked by a sob
For tho' I look I find no job.

"No help wanted," employers say
Then I plod my weary way
I'm groping blindly in my grief
I want a job, not relief.

Of course I could live on a Dole
But work itself is a better goal;
With work I could keep my pride;
There'd be no grief for me to hide.

In work I could be content,
A job would be Heaven sent;
Then my heart would fill with glee;
For in work I'd find Security.[9]

    Newsletters contained ads for local bars, diners and sports' shops and of the coming attractions in Port Jervis theaters. If any fee was paid for advertisements, it seems likely the money was turned over to the general fund and used for camp purposes. The results of various tournaments including pool, ping pong and boxing matches, baseball and basketball games were reported in the newsletters.

Peter Osborne

Courtesy The Center for Research Libraries

Newsletters often reflect a wonderful sense of humor and artistic talent. The sense of camp humor is revealed in this drawing from a March 1938 Company 1280 newsletter. Nicknames were given to match some feature of an enrollee's personality or job.

We Can Take It!

Courtesy The Center for Research Libraries

Homesickness was part of a rookie's initial time at the camp. Young men's thoughts were often turned homeward.

CHAPTER 14

Grateful Communities

Park Camp Enrollee Rewarded for Good Citizenship by DAR: Robert Drimmer Given Medal at Anniversary Dinner at High Point
>   -*Sussex Independent*, Sussex, New Jersey, April 11, 1940

I met my wife in Port Jervis and my first daughter was born there.
>   -Albert Mastriani, National Park Service Foreman

My father forbid me to date any of the CCC boys.
>   -Zita Innella, A Port Jervis girl

CCC Lad on Rampage: Stickup of Port Jervis Cigar Store is Night's Climax
>   -*Sussex Independent*, Sussex, New Jersey, April 7, 1938

Most of this book is about the history, experiences and the work projects of the C boys at High Point. But what of local communities surrounding the park? How was the CCC received in the small towns near the park? Good, wholesome or perhaps the future of our struggling nation? Perhaps FDR's radio speech to the CCC boys is what people thought: "Through you, the nation will graduate a fine group of strong young men, clean-living, trained to self-discipline and, above all, willing and proud to work for the joy of working."[1] Indeed, that was the case most of the time. Albert Mastriani probably said it best when he wrote, "The CCC enrollees were no better or no worse than any other of the boys in town."[2] By far, most of the men that served at High Point did so admirably, received honorable discharges and did the corps and themselves proud.

Economic Impact Of The C Camps

The C camps impacted upon local communities in a number of ways - the arrival of hundreds of young men into small rural towns had many social and financial implications. Generally the C boys were welcome, but occasionally the locals had concerns about hundreds of strangers in their midst.

The first and most obvious impact was the increase in population the camps created in 1933. The camp at High Point was located within

Montague Township, a short distance west of the Montague-Wantage boundary line. The following tables show what the population was in Sussex County and Montague and Wantage townships, Port Jervis and the Town of Deerpark during the CCC era.

Year	Sussex County	Montague New Jersey	Wantage New Jersey
1920	24,906	534	1,899
1930	27,821	581	2,075
1940	29,712	602	2,376 [3]

Year	Port Jervis, New York	Deerpark, New York
1920	10,171	1,615
1930	10,243	1,779
1940	9,749	2,228 [4]

In Sussex County, there was population growth both in the county and the two townships that include all of High Point State Park, from 1920-1940. During the federal census, C boys were not counted as residents of Sussex County, but counted in their hometowns. Across the board, the population increase in Montague Township was forty-seven from 1920 to 1930, an 8 percent increase, and twenty-one from 1930-

1940, a 3 percent increase. At the time, Montague was a vacation spot for large numbers of summer boarders. A significant part of the town was included within the park boundaries. Prior to the park's creation only a small portion of the land had been tillable preventing more population growth.

Wantage Township to the east of the camp is much bigger and contains more flatland. It was and remains more tillable. Because of that feature, its population growth was more significant. In Orange and Sussex counties, as late as the 1940s, there were about five thousand dairy farms, making the area predominantly agricultural.

At High Point, there were about four hundred enrollees plus additional support staff from 1933 to mid-1937. From mid-1937 until late 1941, there were about two hundred enrollees at the camp although that number sharply declined after 1940. At Stokes State Forest there were an additional four hundred enrollees with support staff, bringing to the northwestern corner of Sussex County a population increase of almost one thousand young men in the mid-1930s. In the case of High Point, if enrollees had been included in the census count, they would have made up 40 percent of Montague Township's population.

As for Port Jervis and the Town of Deerpark, the statistics are somewhat different. Between 1920 and 1940, the city was losing population due to the economic depression and the decline of the railroads during that time. Port Jervis was the region's economic center and transportation hub. Through the 1920s and 1930s, it was known as the "Queen of the Shawangunks." Its rail yards were important for the Erie Railroad and New York & Ontario Railroad and most of the supplies used by the CCC were purchased in the city or shipped by rail and picked up in the city. However, the Town of Deerpark was in a different position as it was gaining population because many people moved back to family farms as the depression worsened.

Hence, the economic impact of the C camp on local economies was an important one, and local businesses benefitted financially from the C camps in a variety of ways. It has been estimated that each camp spent $5,000 locally, monthly.[5] Based on the average cost of running a camp, it is estimated the camp at High Point directly contributed about $720,000 to the local economy. If enrollee's salaries are factored into the equation, the economic value of the CCC to the area was probably close to $850,000 in 1930's dollars. It also demonstrates why local congressmen often lobbied Robert Fechner and President Roosevelt to keep camps open after a closure had been announced.

To feed three hundred thousand men in the CCC cost about $3 million dollars monthly.[6] Bars and eateries reaped the rewards of having C boys in town as did movie theaters, pharmacies, sporting goods and clothing stores. Some foremen rented apartments in surrounding towns. A bakery in Port Jervis supplied the camp with bread. Local farmers benefitted from the CCC because they were able to sell fresh goods like milk, eggs and chickens to the camps. A 1934 report said that the average number of eggs in storage had declined markedly, a result of purchases made by the camps.[7]

From this vantage point it is hard to realize how much the CCC camps helped local economies and the best way to illustrate this is to consider the cost of staples in those days. During the 1930s $.25 per hour was going wage, gasoline was between $.10 and $.12 per gallon. A pond of pork chops was sold for $.13 and a house could be rented for $20 per month.[8]

The CCC Through The Local Media

What most people heard about the C camp at High Point was probably through newspapers or seeing the men in Port Jervis, Franklin or Sussex on their time off. In the first year of operation, there was frequent mention of the CCC boys and programs in local newspapers, but as time went on fewer items were written. Locals got used to the idea of them being there, and they did not attract attention.

The *Sussex Independent* was particularly attentive to the camp at High Point printing regular articles about activities. John Stanton,

Peter Osborne

the executive secretary of the park from 1924-1934 was also the owner of the *Sussex Independent*. The *New Jersey Herald* and the *Port Jervis Union-Gazette* also reported on projects at the park. Newspapers carried news of national enrollment periods, lists of enrollees going elsewhere and excerpts from an occasional letter home from an enrollee who was stationed far away.

Officers of the camp were speakers at meetings of local civic organizations and were constantly promoting the local and national organization as well as the benefits of the program for young men.

When the C boys first arrived at Camp Kuser, one newspaper article suggested area residents with old furniture and rugs give them to the camp at High Point. It said trucks at the camp would make a pickup. "The boys will be happy to receive them" the article said.[9] A piano, books, magazines and games were also solicited and received. Enrollees were encouraged to bring back seeds, bulbs and plants from their homes in an effort to spruce up the camp.[10]

Another article in the *New Jersey Herald* reported that Major Cooksey, the camp commander, thanked the people of Sussex County for their cooperation in preventing any friction between the C boys and area residents and asked for further cooperation. Another article appears in a December 1933 edition and said: "A bus owned by F.F. Drew of Sussex, broke down on the way to Newark while taking a load of boys from the 216th Co. to the city for weekend leave. There was a delay of about an hour, during which time the boys built a fire by the side of the road to keep warm. Passing autoists saw this fire and reported to Butler officials that a car was on fire, causing for a while some consternation. The mistake was corrected, and the bus continued on its way."[11]

From the same article comes a more personal story: "Due to the fact that a four-day leave, which had been expected, was not granted to the members of the camp, the mess officer prepared a Thanksgiving meal to take the place of the 'meals that mother made.' Twenty six varieties of food were served. This will be a memory of long duration in the minds of the boys who enjoyed it."[12]

Grateful Communities

There are numerous citations in local newspaper accounts about grateful communities acknowledging C boys and their help. The Chinkchewunska Chapter of the Daughters of the American Revolution, based in Sussex County, gave its Good Citizenship Award to C boys at Camp Kuser. A canvass was made of the company and the five best enrollees were picked, reduced to two by the leaders, with the final selection made by the administration.

Charles Russo, leader of a construction gang, and William Hartley, a stone crusher operator were given the awards at a dinner at High Point in December 1940.[13] Robert Drimmer, an enrollee who rose through the ranks, and served for almost all of the time the camp was in operation, was also awarded the DAR's Good Citizenship award in April of 1940.

Mrs. Clarkson Potter of the Chinkwhewunska Chapter of the DAR said about him: "You, Robert Drimmer, have been selected the outstanding young man of this group, the considerations being Honor, Service, Courage and Leadership. The value of the medal is not great, but that for which it stands means much. Your duty as a Good Citizen is a lifetime duty. I sincerely trust you will realize its significance and continue to be an outstanding citizen in whatever community you may reside. My sincere congratulations and good wishes go with it."[14]

The award was given to Drimmer at High Point on the seventh anniversary of the creation of the CCC and during a special open house. About two hundred visitors came to camp for the day's events and top CCC officials attended.

CCC boys assisted in the hunt for lost persons including Horace Dunn of Binghamton, New York who disappeared near Big Pond in Huguenot, New York in August 1941.[15] They resuscitated drowning people and assisted Camp Sussex during the summer of 1941 when a fire destroyed the mess hall. The C boys helped get dinner for five hundred and twenty people on the evening of the fire and raised tents to be used as dining quarters.[16]

In the fall of 1940, they searched for the Pye children at Lake Stockholm, New Jersey.[17] They were commended by Captain William O. Nicol from Troop B. Company commanders occasionally received letters noting the efforts of C boys.

The Image Of The CCC In Local Communities

The most enduring memory of the CCC for most long-time Port Jervis and Sussex residents was the army trucks bringing the boys to town and the interaction between locals and enrollees. On average, a truck could transport 18 men. The interaction is best described by enrollee Michael Sagursky:

"If you were on good behavior, we had trucks going down I believe it was Wednesday, Friday, and Saturday. Friday was mostly for the youngsters that would go home by train. They would get a ride to Port Jervis, and the fare was like a buck and a half or something like that all the way down to Hoboken ... then we would go into Port Jervis to ... various activities there. They had a roller skating rink ...We used to go to Sussex, but Sussex was not too friendly with our boys. Port Jervis took us real well. Of course we had a few problems with police ... boys would get a little under the weather. I was delegated to go to police headquarters and ask them to [release them].

"I think the difference is ... Port Jervis is like a city, Sussex is farm people ... I had no problem wherever I went. I would go take a truck load. First of all, you had to be a leader to take a load of boys, it was twelve or fourteen on a truck and they all had to be on good behavior otherwise they would never go ... I went to Port Jervis, I had no problems. Occasionally, like I said, the kids would get a little rough, but in Sussex I acted the same as I did in Port Jervis, and they just didn't take to us. Well, first of all the kids had no money and they would walk the street and the public didn't like it. Down ... in Port Jervis there's more people. They didn't notice. Of course we wore our uniforms, but still, they didn't notice us much as in a farm territory."[18]

Men found another way to get to Port Jervis. William DeGhetto said: "We used to walk down to Port Jervis. Yeah, all the way down. Well that's only about ten miles, and it was still daylight in the summer, but coming up at night - Holy Cats! No lights there or nothing. And its not like it is now. It was only a country road back in them days. Like the two lane macadam road. Very dark."[19]

Another story concerns the former mining community of Franklin, New Jersey, which had one of only three movie theaters in Sussex

County. It was a rough town because of extensive mining operations located nearby and the large number of ethnic groups working there. When the CCC boys went to Franklin to see a movie, local police Chief Herbert Irons would meet the truck, unload it and make the boys march in single file into the theater to a block of seats specifically reserved for them. They were kept in their seats, not allowed to buy candy or refreshments and after the movie, they were escorted back to the trucks.[20]

That negativity from local communities was brought to the attention of the camp commander and discussed in an editorial in a May 1938 Company 1280 newsletter: "No one expects the use of microscopic or candid camera proofs to realize the delegates from Company 1280 are received with much distaste in the Town of Port Jervis. At least no person of average intelligence could affect not to notice it. The sideways look, the walking upon the opposite side of the street when observing the CCC uniform, these and more sink deeply home into the average heart, causing no elevation or exhilaration of spirits. The moral hate which the great majority of the people regard in the aforesaid town should serve to act as a warning guide-post upon your route.

"Why not rescind the habit of operating in groups of nine or ten and constrict your number to twos and threes? Would it be an unbearable hardship to allow a person of the feminine sex to approach and pass by a cluster of you in a mannerly fashion?"[21]

The committing of serious crimes by CCC boys was rare, not only in the local community but across the country. But there were always troublemakers and, occasionally, local newspapers reported on misdemeanors by enrollees. The worst crime by a CCC boy at High Point took place April 1, 1938, when an enrollee from Garfield, New Jersey held up a tobacco store in Port Jervis after breaking the windshield of a local dentist's car and firing a shot at the doctor after he yelled at the young man.

He then went to the tobacco store, held up the patrons and threatened to "drive the third button of one man's vest through his body with a bullet." When the police arrived to arrest him, he pleaded guilty and offered no explanation for his actions.[22] It is not known what happened to the young man.

Another episode occurred in Port Jervis in 1934 which involved two men wearing CCC uniforms. They hijacked a man and his car after he asked for their assistance. They knocked him out, and he was found the next day, dazed, in his car in Trenton, New Jersey. The only detail the man remembered was what the men were wearing.[23] There is no way of knowing if the men were from High Point because there were other CCC camps in the area.

Another incident concerned an enrollee who passed a counterfeit $10 bill to a merchant in

Sussex in 1934. Upon discovering the bill, the merchant went to High Point, met with the captain, confronted the enrollee and was given a legitimate bill. Presumably, the enrollee was dishonorably discharged, or at least severely punished. Most of the other crimes were minor, fights and altercations with locals or rowdy behavior.

Probably the most notorious former member of the High Point CCC was also one of its most well-known and well-liked army officers, Wilfred H. Baetz. He was a leader in the army corps area, getting the Company 216 newsletter's written and published and creating an educational facility. He was also active in the community. He sang in the choir in the Sussex Presbyterian Church and, as one article described him, he was "popular with the younger set in the northern end of the county."[24]

After he left High Point: "He boasted of his love affairs, of his ability to act, dance, sing and play the piano, and he said his presence was always sought at all sorts of private parties and social events ... he described himself as a champion ski-jumper and an expert at dancing, boxing and debating ... He also worked for a ladies escort service in New York, served in the Merchant Marine and, for a brief period, was given a part with the Rockettes in Radio City. At the outbreak of World War II, according to his story, he enlisted and was assigned to training at Camp

Edwards. After several months of training he injured his leg and received a medical discharge.

"He said he then returned to radio work. Those who were acquainted with Baetz describe him as very cultured, quiet and very considerate of everyone."[25]

Baetz, however, had a darker side and in September 1944 was convicted of arson in Massachusetts and one month later was arrested for attempting arson and sent to prison for a year. On April 10, 1946, eight people were burned to death in a fire in the Back Bay section of Boston, and Baetz was arrested and held for $10,000 bail. Baetz denied the charges and then disappeared from the pages of history.[26]

Dear Miss I Wanta Man

Company newsletters often reflect there were four hundred relatively young men at High Point in a setting which was similar to a military base and who obviously were attracted to the pretty young women of the community. Some comments from "Things That We'd Like to Know and See Around Camp" from a company 216 newsletter relating to local young women:

"The name of the dusky Port Jervis lass Parker F. is courting.

The love letters that Schneberger receives. (It is rumored he writes them himself and mails them in Port Jervis.)"

The name of the fellow who doesn't think Port Jervis is such a swell place since Annie isn't home anymore."

The name of the girl who draws "Baldy" Williams to Sussex every third night.

What is the big attraction that has the Captain's son going to Port Jervis every night for the past two weeks."27

Another section of the same newsletter entitled "Advice for the lovelorn had the following inquiries to "Miss I Wanta Man." The advice follows:

"Dear Miss Man:

I love a girl in Port Jervis; she also loves me. I'm a first cook in Co. 216. Should I marry her or continue towards my career. 1st Cook.

Dear 1st Cook

By all means, stay at your career.

Dear Miss Man:

I love a very charming girl in Unionville. She is fifty-five while I am sixty. Is marriage proper. Hill Billie Smith

Dear Hill Billie Smith,

By all means, forget the situation, you are too young to consider marriage. Wait a while."28

John Scully, an enrollee poet with Company 1280, wrote the following:

A kiss is such a little thing,
A dash, a flash of joy.
A brush of lips, of finger tips,
Pray whom does it annoy?

If taking a kiss is a crime,
I'll be an outlaw all the time
A dainty miss, a moments bliss.
Pray, what's the harm in just a kiss.[29]

Many C boys married local girls and stayed in the area for decades after their service. Albert Mastriani got married to a local girl, June Baldwin, who was from Port Jervis and he was invited to join and participate in affairs of the local Elks Club.[30] So did Melvin Gemmill, Frank Seddio and Red Sacco. The following is a partial listing of CCC marriages that occurred:

CCC Marriages
Melvin Gemmill & Dorothy Mayfield (Port Jervis)
Albert Mastriani & June Baldwin (Port Jervis)
Everett "Red" Sisco & Dorothy Gochenour (Port Jervis)
Tony Martinez & Mary Laconi (Port Jervis)
Henry Winters & Lucy Miglionico (Port Jervis)
Frank Seddio & Fannie Tortorini (Port Jervis)
George Ryder & Dorothy McDermott (Port Jervis)
Red Sacco & Katherine Trotta (Port Jervis)
George Anderson & Helen Fuller (Sussex)
Jerry Kutzler & Catherine Ziffino (Port Jervis)
Gus Graffe & Carmel Ziffino
Andy Ross & Eugenia Kwiatkowski (Port Jervis)
John Cole & Hedwig Kwiatkowski (Port Jervis)
Dan Perricone & Olga Ogrodnick (Port Jervis)

For local Port Jervis boys, CCC men coming to town provided competition for their lady friends. Leslie Crine, a Port Jervis resident who remembers the C boys, also recalled the concern of local lads who lost their girlfriends to CCC boys. Just like everywhere else, local boys were looking for ways to earn some money to take their girls out to the movies or on a date.[31] CCC men sent home the required allotment for their families, but they still had money in times when it was hard to come by. For local boys, that could only mean trouble.

For the young ladies of the community there were several levels of apprehension. Zita Innella remembered that her father forbade her to date the C boys. Indeed, even if her father had let her date them, she would have been reluctant to do so because the men were not locals.[32] Another problem was that some CCC men frequented the red light district in Port Jervis and the "houses of ill repute" that were also frequented by Erie railroaders.[33]

In the end, the relationship between the local communities and the C boys was a good one. Perhaps it was best said in a 1938 camp inspection report: "Community relations [were] good, although police at Port Jervis inclined to be too harsh in judgement on boys."[34] Communities benefitted financially from the camp and its purchases of supplies, enrollee's purchases and from increased access to park lands. Enrollees benefitted by the work the CCC provided, were

Peter Osborne

able to support their families at home or found themselves coming back to the region after their service was complete or after the war was over.

CHAPTER 15

A Rendezvous With Destiny

There is a mysterious cycle in human events. To some generations much is given. Of other generations much is expected. This generation of Americans has a rendevous with destiny.
-President Franklin Delano Roosevelt, June 27, 1936

Day is done, gone the sun
From the lake, from the hills
From the sky,
All is well, safely rest, God is nigh.

Fading light, dims the night and a star
Gems the sky, gleaming bright
From afar drawing nigh, falls the night
-Forrest Gaz, Enrollee, Company 128, Hinsdale, Massachusetts

A study of FDR's most popular New Deal agency reveals two distinct histories. The first is about the life of a typical CCC camp. High Point very much represents the thousands of camps located in the states and territories of this country. Enrollees, NPS employees and army officers came from similar backgrounds and worked under the same kind of conditions.

The second involves the creation and running of the corps on a national level. This book has attempted to tell both stories while placing the greater emphasis on the CCC at High Point. However, it is not complete without the larger story that involves the massive and multi-agency effort fraught with bureaucratic infighting, congressional hearings, and the vagaries of FDR's political whims. Many enrollees did not give much thought to the larger challenges of managing this unique agency and probably thought the CCC would always be there. However, the CCC's existence was a fluid situation which depended on Congressional support and FDR's own priorities.

The Politics Of The CCC

While politics did not play a major role in the operation of the CCC it was significant. It is important to remember, from the beginning, the CCC enjoyed widespread bipartisan support. In the 1936 presidential election, both the Republican presidential and vice-presidential candidates endorsed the CCC.[1] Typical of the bipartisan support the CCC enjoyed were comments made by Congressman J. Parnell Thomas of the 7th New Jersey Congressional District. In the spring and summer of 1937, debate in Congress focused on FDR's proposal to make the CCC a permanent agency. Thomas said:

"I still believe that the CCC camps have been a distinct aid to the youth of America and I hesitate to think the desperate plight that thousands of young boys might have faced in the darkest days of the Depression had not the government provided them with work, food, shelter and clothing.

"The camps not only have been of great benefit to the boys, but the work accomplished by the Civilian Conservation Corps has been a vital factor in the conservation of thousands of acres of forest land.

"Had the New Deal spent the taxpayer's money on its million and one other projects with the same degree of intelligence and constructiveness as it did in the case of the CCC, the financial structure of the United States today would not be in its present weakened state. Money has been and still is being squandered on various useless projects and eaten up by political grafters despite the fact that unemployment has been reduced and private industry is daily absorbing workers.

"I shall vote to maintain the CCC for another year because I believe it has accomplished much at a reasonably low cost to the taxpayers, but I shall remain opposed to most other New Deal projects until a semblance of an attempt is made to halt the continued spending spree."[2]

The opening of a camp was a source of great celebration for local communities for many reasons. From 1933 until 1935 there was a constant expansion of the CCC. By 1935 there were 502,000 men in 2,500 camps across the country, the high point in the CCC's existence. Senators and Congressmen from both parties were constantly lobbying Roosevelt, Fechner and Ickes to have camps placed in their districts.

The closing of a C camp in a politician's district could be politically dangerous.[3] In 1936, FDR ordered the number of enrollments be reduced to 300,000 men. While director Fechner argued against it, FDR pushed on with announcement that 489 camps would be closed. When the camps began to close, Republican and Democratic congressmen signed a petition urging Roosevelt to stop the closings. Congressmen also threatened additional problems with other relief programs, and the president relented.

Curiously, there is no correspondence to the president from anyone lobbying to keep Company 216 operating at High Point after the decision as to which camps were to close was announced in 1937. When the nearby Wallkill River water diversion project was threatened with closure, FDR was lobbied extensively. Perhaps local congressmen or the governor took the issue up personally with the president or Robert Fechner. Typically, when faced with such an inquiry, Fechner wrote back to a Congressmen the following: "The camp in question could be closed with the least harm to the general work program of the state."[4]

Another facet of the political side of the CCC that is not surprising is that it was a pro-Roosevelt organization. In camps around the country, framed pictures of Roosevelt were hung on barracks walls although at High Point, it was Theodore Roosevelt's picture that can be clearly seen in a rec hall photo.[5] The CCC became known as the *"Roosevelt Tree Army"* although there were other nicknames: *Woodpecker Warriors, Tree Troopers, Soil Soldiers and Peaveys.*[6] There was a strong feeling of gratitude on behalf of the enrollees for FDR's efforts to alleviate the suffering of so many during the Depression. Roosevelt's personal stamp was on the conservation effort more than any other relief program.

In 1935, an inquiring reporter from the camp newsletter asked enrollees if they thought the CCC was a good organization. Everett Sisco of Company 1280 responded: "I think the CCC is one, if not the best organization in this country.

It not only helps the CCC personnel and families, but the outside dealers who sell food to the camps. It will keep going as long as President Roosevelt is in the Presidential chair [sic]."[7]

At various times, a small number of Republicans attempted to repeal New Deal legislation including the CCC, but the savvy administrators of the CCC had created an agency with bipartisan support that was near and dear to the hearts of millions of Americans. By 1937, with many traditions and operations of the CCC standardized, FDR moved to make it a permanent government agency. Hearings were held in both houses of Congress and proceeded without controversy even as a poll showed 87 percent of all Americans approved of it.[8]

But in a surprising twist, as the hearings concluded, several Congressmen proposed extending the CCC for another two years only. It was a backlash against FDR's effort to expand the Supreme Court after it ruled against some of his New Deal programs. It was also the effect of conservative Congressmen who had blocked some of FDR's legislative packages. The final legislation included a provision that extended the life of the CCC for three more years, but it also cut Fechner's salary by $2,000 per annum, probably in response to his support of the court-packing plan. The legislation also encouraged for the first time that vocational education be included in the program. In 1939, when the bill authorizing the CCC came up again, Fechner's salary was raised to its original rate.

The battle for a permanent CCC, one that would live on long after FDR, was never won, mainly because its reputation was that of a relief organization that did useful conservation work. That reputation never changed in the common perception of the people.[9] The CCC never became a permanent agency, rather, it remained a coordinator of agencies.

It never had the luxury of planning ahead. It operated from year to year and from short-term political deal to deal. John Salmond, in his important work on the CCC entitled *The Civilian Conservation Corps, 1933-1942: A New Deal Case Study,* makes the argument that one of the principal causes of the end of the CCC was that it did not take advantage of its educational and vocational training.[10]

While the CCC was one of the most popular of the New Deal programs and was not subject to as much criticism as other parts of FDR's programs, it was still a part of the large "alphabet soup" of federal agencies FDR created to fight the Depression. As such, the *New York Herald Tribune* printed a piece that was reprinted in the *New Jersey Herald* in late December 1933. The article said:

"Q.E.D.

What with the N.R.A. at odds with the A.A.A. and C.C.C. troubled with members being A.W.O.L. and the "brain trust" down on the

I.C.C. and A.E.S. giving the C.W.A. a KO, and the farmers complaining that their SOS to the F.H.O.L. marked R.S.V.P., P.D.Q. has been passed on to the F.C.A. and thence to the R.F.C. with the notation N.G. and F.D.R. using the R.F.D. to send his OK to the E.C. and sever M.C.'s troubled with B.O. applying to the S.A.B. for an M.D., is it to be wondered that things are not altogether duck soup in D.C.? P.S. - How about O.M.W.S."[11]

Another article appeared in the *New Jersey Herald* in April 1934, again using the alphabet soup of agencies:

> "A young CCC lost his BVD
> So the PTA sent an SOS
> To the CWA who was CTQ
> As the FRA had put the CAN
> To the PWA with a near KO
> And the NRA was all FOB
> So the AAA sent it COD
> But the USA wired PDQ
> To the RFC for its IOU
> Now its all OK at the MTC
> For the CCC got his BVD."[12]

Criticism did come occasionally from unusual places. Frank L. Hague, the powerful and well-known mayor of Jersey City, New Jersey, an area where large numbers of CCC boys at High Point had come from, agreed with a 1939 assessment from a commission in Massachusetts that

"Communists were creating dissatisfaction in the camps."[13] This opinion is not reflected in company newsletters or by the men who were interviewed for this book.

The CCC evolved, to some degree, from its initial "emergency conservation work" and work relief purpose to an organization that became as much a training center for young men. By the end of its life, there was a proposal in New York to have enrollees spend half their six-month term in conservation work and half their time in intensive training in an occupational school.

One of the criticisms leveled against the CCC nationally was its cost. The cost per enrollee was about $1,000 a year while the Works Progress Administration cost per enrollee was between $770 and $800 per year. The National Youth Association was between $400 and $700 per year. The idea of "future value" is not included in any of these estimates. Nor is the impact it had on the men who served, particularly in the CCC.[14]

Despite the popularity of the CCC, it did get embroiled in the national debate over budget deficits and whether it should even remain in existence. In June 1938, four junior technicians at High Point, all making $70 per month, were notified their positions would revert back to the pay scale of enrollees at $30 per month. They were allowed to become assistant leaders and leaders, raising their pay to $36 or $45 per month. While it would seem the decision to leave and get another job would be an easy one, jobs were still scarce and most of them stayed on.[15]

By 1940, there were efforts to cut the number of camps from fifteen hundred to twelve hundred and the number of enrollees from three hundred thousand nationwide to two hundred and twenty-five thousand. The cuts did not come to pass and there was a decided lack of interest nationally to debate this issue and very little mention of the CCC can be found in the newspapers of the time.

As the 1930s passed, there was an occasional mention of the growing problems in Europe in company newsletters at High Point. As war clouds hovered over Europe the C boys at High Point reflected the isolationist feelings held by the majority of the nation's citizens. When war began in Europe in late 1939 and 1940, it impacted on the C boys more and more as they heard of the German invasion of Poland.

A national committee called "America First" was formed, and one of its most outspoken representatives was Charles Lindbergh, the young hero who flew his plane solo over the Atlantic in 1927. The cover of a 1941 Company 1280 newsletter used the group's logo as its cover. Increasingly, articles in newsletters discussed patriotic issues and the cover of the January-February 1941 issue proclaimed "America First," a popular notion across America.

The End Of The CCC

From its beginning, CCC officials sought to assure people that it was not militaristic, not a future army in waiting. But, as the situation worsened in Europe, there were calls to support military training in the CCC. By late 1938, 75 percent of Americans supported training in the camps.[16] Congressmen even introduced legislation supporting the idea.

In 1940, FDR declared a limited national emergency as Hitler's troops advanced into France, and the draft was begun. Soon, CCC camps across the country became more engaged in national defense. Increasingly, America watched the war engulfing Europe and became worried about its own security.

As such, the focus of many C camps became national security although that did not happen at High Point. Non-combatant military training was being given and, by late 1940, was being done in all camps and incorporated into the education program. By 1941, many camps were doing defense work like constructing communication lines, building roads and undertaking tasks that soldiers had done previously.

Enrollment in the CCC declined significantly in 1941, from three hundred thousand enrollees to one hundred sixty thousand by year's end in nine hundred camps. A major factor in the decline was the economy being geared towards military spending to support the Allies. Enrollees were leaving the CCC at the rate of nine thousand per month to take jobs in industry.[17]

Another factor in the decline was that many potential enrollees believed they might be drafted right from the CCC. There was even discussion nationally of calling the CCC units into the military intact although the CCC regularly assured enrollees that it was not a military organization and that the military had higher standards for enrollment and consent was required for those under twenty-one. Occasional articles appear in the newsletter describing the branches of military service.[18] There was also growing pressure to abandon the concept of the CCC by politicians in Washington as the main need for the program, work relief for young men, was gone. Suddenly, the CCC lost some of its popularity.

CCC officials tried a number of ideas to breathe new life into the organization including increasing the number of African-American enrollees, merging the CCC with the NYA into an organization called the Civilian Youth Administration and a policy of continuous selection for enrollees. All efforts were to no avail.

The final blow came on the morning of December 7, 1941, when the Japanese bombed Pearl Harbor and America entered World War II. The question became - was the CCC necessary to win the war? On January 1, 1942, all conservation work ended as thousands of men left the CCC to join the military as the nation prepared for war. FDR wanted to continue with a reduced number of camps, but the House voted to end appropriations on June 30, 1942, in a vote of 158-151. After that date, the CCC went out of existence. Its assets were liquidated and the CCC became a part of American history. Liquidation would continue until 1948.

As 1941 wound down, the CCC operation at High Point began to dwindle. Enrollees were leaving to enlist or to answer the draft notices or to take jobs in the private sector. In the final year before the closing of the camp, 126 men were discharged before the end of their term, and seventy-four were given discharges that were labeled administrative desertion. There were no dishonorable desertions and only five honorable desertions.[19]

Company 1280 was rapidly going the way of so many. The company's morale declined to such a point it was rated only "fair" by the camp inspector, along with the technical service quarters, its garages and officers' quarters. Five of the ten technical service's trucks were rated unserviceable and four were about to be condemned as permanently unserviceable. One of two of the army's trucks was considered unserviceable. The camp no longer had an ambulance and had to rely on the ambulance at Stokes State Forest for emergencies.

The numbers of enrollees in the company dropped to a point where the camp could not be justified or sustained. According to the October 1941 camp inspection report, ninety-six men were left in the company, the lowest level since 1933. Sixteen men were on detached service, twenty-four men were required to maintain the camp's overhead, three were sick, four were away without leave and seven were on authorized leave.[20]

When the trucks left the DI garage in the morning, only forty-two men were available for work projects. Even David Traub, the long-time educational advisor, had left for Louisiana where he took charge of U.S.O. activities in four camps. It created a situation at High Point where the camp inspector described the education program as below average. Traub had been at High Point for five years and had lived in Port Jervis.

Camp Kuser was ordered closed November 15, 1941 by the United States Department of Interior.[21] It was just three weeks before the attack on Pearl Harbor by Japan. From various recollections it is believed that the orders came to simply close the camp. The construction of the Shale Lake Play Area was only 75 percent complete and work on Shale Lake had just begun when Company 1280 shut down operations. In the minutes of the commission, the ending of this productive effort was noted by the president. "The president spoke of the excellent work accomplished by the C.C.C. camp in this area."[22]

The camp's equipment was inventoried, loaded onto trucks and taken to a central warehouse and motor pool in Shelton Station, New Jersey.[23] At least one story is that a park employee was told to bury the remaining tools in an effort to dispose of them. He left them uncovered in a pit, and somehow neighbors of the park found out, took the tools, and the next day, park employees returned to find nothing left.[24] Albert Mastriani, who was involved in the final disposition of the tools, questions that account because of the wartime effort that was well underway by 1941.[25]

There are also differing accounts as to what happened to the power shovel, one of the major pieces of equipment the CCC used at High Point. Albert Mastriani stated that it was either borrowed or used on another CCC project in either 1940 or 1941 and never returned. Nicholas Hanisak believes it was sent to Camp Drummond in New York. John Keator, superintendent at High Point, heard it was sold, and the person who bought it used it in a construction business near Beemerville.[26] Rick Strain, a former park employee, believes it might have been left on site, between the Annandale unit and the Shale Lake area and just rusted away until it was cut up and sold as scrap.[27]

Copies of the records of the NPS and CCC necessary for future maintenance and planning, were apparently turned over to the executive secretary of High Point, John Gibbons, and probably included copies of maps, drawings and miscellaneous project files. Those drawings, which number about one hundred, are now in the park's archives. The project files have been purged from the archives.

The remaining records including inventory books and other important NPS files all stored in two metal file cabinets, were taken to the Morristown National Historic Site in Morristown, New Jersey. Morristown was the nearest NPS facility in New Jersey and it seems logical that the records were sent there as camps were being rapidly demobilized in 1941 and 1942. It is not known what happened to the two file cabinets as there are currently no records at Morristown that either indicate they were brought there or that they were disposed of.[28]

The only piece of evidence of what their final disposition may have been may also be the answer as to why there is little CCC material around the state, including the archives of the Division of Parks and Forestry. The remaining clue is an internal NPS memorandum dated July 14, 1983 that states: "Many of the CCC records for New Jersey were destroyed in a fire and additional detailed information may not be easily available."[29]

As for the other records, those of the enrollees, it is believed the army took personnel records and camp operational files back to their regional headquarters. Those files like so many of the World War II veteran's files were destroyed in a huge fire in St. Louis after the war.

As NPS trucks left High Point in November 1941, so ended the most constructive and productive period in the park's history. Within weeks, many enrollees, foremen and army officers were inducted into service. This activity at High Point coincidentally came as a series of hearings in Congress to abolish the CCC began several weeks later and concluded on Christmas Eve. By April 1942, 54 percent of the population thought the *Roosevelt Tree Army* should be disbanded.[30]

The War And The CCC

Veterans of the C camps were in the years leading up to the war sought out because of their useful and practical work experience. They were perfect candidates for military service because they had a head start on other young men and were accustomed to a military life style. In 1939, a recruiter came to High Point and seven enrollees enlisted.[31]

Many officers who gained experience at the CCC camps used it to lead America's military to victory. The majority of the C boys found themselves in military service after Pearl Harbor. About 70 percent fought in the European and Pacific theaters. When they came home in 1945,

Americans had largely forgotten their earlier conservation service, and the plans to create five thousand new camps were never discussed again.

The CCC Remembered

After the announcement of the closing of the camp, the High Point Park Commission voted to authorize the executive secretary to contact the Department of Interior so that the state could take possession of the remaining buildings and equipment.[32] On August 1, 1942, the army took control of the buildings from the National Park Service with a plan to recondition them for use by troops. The commission made this action subject to discussion with them.[33]

On December 29, 1942, the CCC acknowledged receipt of Gibbons' previous request and approved it after the army made its wishes known. The Federal Security Agency, the agency under which the CCC was then included, signed off on the transfer in January 1943. At the time of the transfer there were still twenty-five buildings standing and whatever equipment remained, mainly miscellaneous items like electrical fixtures, glass reflectors and fire fighting equipment. The property was valued at $15,000. Finally, in May 1943, the transfer was reported complete to the director of the CCC.[34]

What happened to the camp after 1943 is somewhat unclear and not well documented. In

1944, one of the remaining buildings at Camp Kuser was taken apart and rebuilt at the camp for the blind along Park Ridge Road. In June 1946, a public auction to sell the remaining buildings was announced in the local newspaper.[35] While it is not known if any of the buildings were sold at the auction, by 1951, all of the buildings were gone except for the Camp Meeting Hall and the Educational Building, both of which stood at the far northern end of the camp.[36] Ronald Slate, a neighbor of the park, concurs with those dates.[37]

In 1954, a plan was announced to establish a camp for groups from the state's correctional institute at Annandale. Up to fifty boys could be sent to High Point for the last ten weeks before their release, and during that time they would work in the park.[38] The boys were to use the two remaining buildings in the old camp as a reformatory. When the plan was revealed, there was a local public outcry against it.[39]

Despite the outcry, the CCC buildings were used as a work center by the North Jersey Reformatory until 1958. At that time, they were considered to be unsightly according to a report prepared by Dryden Kuser. He suggested that they be torn down. In 1958, a new facility was created by the Department of Institutions and Agencies, just off of Route 23. It operated until 1999, and the whole facility has since been demolished.

The remaining two buildings stood until 1961 and were taken down sometime before 1969.[40] It is believed that at least one of the CCC buildings was dismantled and the materials used to build a mess hall for the new correctional facility. A park neighbor, Rick Strain, believes that the old CCC blacksmith shop was moved to the park's maintenance yard and converted to a lunch room and is still in use.[41] When the remaining CCC structure was demolished or taken off site cannot be determined.

Curiously, no one has any recollections of the demolition of the buildings happening prior to 1951. It is believed that several of the camp's buildings are still standing in new locations scattered around Sussex County and being used as private residences or outbuildings. John Keator remembered being told that the person who bought the power shovel, purchased a CCC building which he used in a construction business near Beemerville.[42] A building on Route 519, near the 4H camp entrance, could be the one he described and might be one of the barracks buildings.

Recently, the last documented structure built for use by the CCC remaining in the park, the incinerator in the shale pit, was demolished by park employees. Foundations remain on each side of Cedar Swamp Drive for several buildings including the chlorinator and latrine. However, most of the buildings sat on concrete posts and there are no foundations remaining. Chunks of concrete are scattered throughout the area. Several concrete pads remain where the shops for Technical Services were, as well as a loading dock that abuts the road. Former paths lined with rocks around and through the camp can still be seen.

At some point after the CCC's departure from High Point, it is not known exactly when, the remaining records of National Park Service were placed in storage at Stokes State Forest in Branchville, New Jersey. In the mid-1960s, what remained of the records and memorabilia of the CCC camp at High Point, still in their original CCC footlockers, was taken from the loft of a barn at Stokes State Forest and burned. Other CCC items were taken to a burning pit near the pine plantation along Struble Road and destroyed.[43]

The destruction of the CCC camp's files, the removal of records to Stokes and the disbursement of the High Point Park Commission's files at the Kuser Mansion after it was closed are a great loss because those items probably included Olmsted materials, old project files, camp newsletters and memorabilia that is irreplaceable. The park's historical files that were located in the Trenton offices of the State Parks agency have been purged as well. The cumulative effect of these actions is a great loss for historians, CCC alumni and the citizens of New Jersey.

Peter Osborne

There have been a number of efforts in recent years to preserve what remains of CCC records and projects. The single most important action was the nomination of High Point State Park to be listed on the United States Department of Interior's National Register of Historic Places. The nomination, prepared by Ronald J. Dupont, Jr., is the most valuable piece of research ever done on the structures and features of the park and will serve as the foundation on which future histories are written. Current Park Superintendent John Keator has a long-standing interest in the CCC and has continued to collect materials about the CCC at High Point.

During the course of this project the remaining blueprints were sorted, filed and placed in archival folders and then into a new cabinet built for CCC archives. The Friends of High Point have undertaken a long-term effort to preserve the extensive photograph collection in the park's archives, many of which were taken in the CCC-era. Tapes of interviews with surviving C boys have been transcribed. There is a relatively complete collection of both company's newsletters at the Center for Research Libraries in Chicago and the surviving company newspapers were acquired and are available for research, due to the generosity of the Friends.

A review of the CCC collection in the National Archives at College Park, Maryland revealed that many administrative materials still survive, including inspection reports, work progress reports, superintendent's reports and a variety of other records. A number of local historical organizations have tidbits of history relating to the park and the CCC.

Most CCC-era projects at High Point have survived and continue to be used. Camping areas, lakes, hiking trails, roads and buildings stand as a testament to the effort and fine workmanship of the *Roosevelt Tree Army* of the 1930s. Unfortunately, other projects have been demolished or suffered from lack of maintenance including the grand boardwalk, boat dock, float and bathhouse located at Sawmill Lake. The beautiful stone fire places are gone as well as the handsomely bordered parking areas at Sawmill. The service road leading into Sawmill is now closed to traffic and overgrown. The Shale Lake complex remains uncompleted and until recently was home to a state correctional facility.

The greatest tragedy in recent memory was the demolition of the Kuser Mansion, the former home of Colonel Anthony and Susan Kuser who donated the park to the State of New Jersey. Their home served as park headquarters for many years, including the time the CCC was at High Point. The loss of the building was an insult to all residents of the state because of the generosity of the Kusers.

And, finally, there is the issue of time's passing. When this project was begun in 1999, anyone who served in the CCC was at least seventy-six years old. Typically, he would have been born in 1924. If he served in the first year of the CCC's existence, he would have been born in 1916 and would now be eighty-four years old. Albert Mastriani is now eighty-eight years old. Mastriani, Neil Thiede and Peter Lutz had remarkable memories, but they were in the minority. Melvin Gemmill, the project designer whose work we still admire, died while this book was being written.

In the 1980s, many of those men were in their mid-60s and still had clear memories of those days. Fortunately, Bill Wurst and Debbie Fritter interviewed a number of them on audio tape, and their remarks provided an important resource. However, one cannot help but wonder at how much more information might have been gathered if the efforts to remember the CCC had begun earlier.

Some CCC enrollees who served at High Point are disappointed that more than sixty years after their dedicated hard work, there are no signs in the park describing the important contributions the CCC made at High Point. Nor is there any sign saying that the park is a National Historic District. Hopefully this book and the effort by the many who made it possible will in some small way address those oversights. There are plans in 2002 to begin installing signage around the park calling attention to the CCC's efforts.

Neil Thiede is typical of enrollees who recalled his feelings about the park and his time there: "It has always been a favorite little excursion of mine to go back there and sometimes take a couple of sandwiches along and see what's better than it used to be. Well, you know what my big disappointment was? I rode in and rode past Lake Marcia to where the entrance to the camp used to be and there is nothing. A couple tables here and there. And I say 'now here was barracks 2B.' I guess they could have left it standing, but it seemed to me it would look nice if it was still there. I'd sit there and I'd say, 'now the barracks was here and the path ran down this way and another barracks here.' I was disappointed that it was all gone. But I figured, well, I guess they deteriorated and they needed to tear them down."[44]

In 1979, Rudy Polisi, who obviously took great pride in his work in Company 1280, wrote the following letter:

"I have always thought of the days I spent at High Point (New Jersey, Company 1280, SP-8). Every time I went north, I swore that I would go back to see the place where our camp was. Then something would happen and I would have to put it aside till the next time. Well, last year [1979] I made up my mind it was Co. 1280 or bust. Then after forty years I was finally nearing High Point Park past Newton, then Franklin, then I saw it in the distance. The High Point Monument standing two hundred twenty feet tall on the highest peak in New Jersey.

"Then I got scared. I was afraid to go on, afraid of what I would find or would not find. Perhaps after all these years, I traveled fourteen hundred miles chasing a dream. I started to turn around and go back to Florida. But the group I was with would not have any part of it. My wife said that after hearing me talk about the CCC for thirty-eight years and getting so close, there was no way for me to turn back. Well, we turned at the stone house on the hill and started down into the camp.

"The first thing I saw was a toll booth in the middle of the road. It cost one dollar to get in the state park. The bear cage was still there. I guess the bear had to be a different one. Then came Lake Marcia; the old ice storage house was gone. Then the camp site came in view. The place had grown up. There were picnic tables all over. All that was left of the camp was some blocks that the barracks floor sat on. We went to the monument. I rode over the roads that I helped build.

"We visited two artificial lakes that the CCC boys built. The roads that looked so wide while we were building them were now narrow but still in good shape. The waterfalls or spillways we built by hand out of large rock looked beautiful. Then, as we left, I felt sorry and glad at the same time. Sorry because there was not one sign or anything telling tourists that the roads they were riding on or the lakes they were fishing in were built by the Depression army. For this, I will always be sad.

"Then I felt glad and happy because after all these years a part of me will always be at Co. 1280, SP-8, High Point Park, New Jersey. Then I had no right to expect the camp and everything else to remain the same. Perhaps I went back there expecting to find my youth again, or something to rekindle a fire in a lamp that will for all outward purposes slowly dim then go out. But until that light goes out, I will always remember the time spent in the CCC."[45]

Epilogue

Across the country the CCC had a profound effect on the landscape and the numbers are staggering. The entire program cost $2.969 billion and $662 million of that was sent home to families in the form of allotments. Three million C boys, supervised by 263,000 supervisors, built eight hundred state parks, two hundred city and county parks, restored 3,980 historic structures, beautified many Civil War battlefields, built forty-two wildlife refuges and worked on an additional 257. The C boys built sixty-three thousand buildings, erected four hundred and five thousand signs, built 204 lodges and museums and 8,045 wells and pump house. Three of the most popular byways were either built or improved by the C boys including Skyline Drive in Virginia, the Pacific Crest Trail and the Appalachian Trail.

Some 2.5 billion trees were planted (having a value of $75 billion today), 248,000 acres of swamp were drained, 7,622 lakes were built, 814,000 acres of graze land replanted, 21 million acres of diseased trees cleared, 972 million fish were restocked, 126,000 miles of road, thirteen thousand miles of trail built and eighty-nine thousand miles of telegraph wire strung. More than fifty-two thousand acres of campgrounds were created.

Some 17 million people were directly employed by or economically benefited from the CCC. Two

We Can Take It!

billion 1942 dollars of infrastructure were created, much of which is still used, and 7.1 million days of labor were provided to fight forest fires.[46] Almost eight thousand men died in the C camps for a variety of reasons, although none perished at High Point.

The region's parks and forests also benefitted tremendously from the CCC. In New Jersey, state parks and forests were developed along with construction of countless public amenities like cabins, lakes, roads and campsites. The number of work projects completed is an impressive list.

Bridges	199
Dams	47
Fences & Guard Rails (Rods)	57,102
Number of Trees Planted	21,745,080
Forest Stand Improvement (Acres)	52,641
Tree & Plant Disease Control (Acres)	152,032 [47]

At the program's height, 91,500 men from the state were enrolled, and there were on average twenty-five camps in operation. Over the program's entire operation, thirty-six camps were operated in the state. The state committed almost $47 million towards the effort.[48] More than $18 million went home in the form of allotments to enrollees' families.[49]

In neighboring Pennsylvania, many state forests and state farm lands were improved, and a number of new parks were established. Gettysburg National Park was restored by C boys and almost one hundred and ninety-five thousand men worked at seventy-four camps with the state committing almost $127 million dollars. Several companies were stationed at Promised Land State Park and worked in the large state forests.[50]

New York state had 220,700 enrollees - the largest number of men enrolled. They operated sixty-eight camps and the state committed more than $134 million to the projects. The state's large parks and forests benefitted greatly from the CCC.[51] Four companies worked in the Wawayanda and Middletown, New York area. One of the companies was made up of World War I veterans and the other three companies were made up of African-Americans. The CCC very much reflected its time, and segregation was the norm. One of the largest CCC endeavors undertaken was the flood control project on the Wallkill River in Orange County, New York. The CCC dug a channel 4.5 miles long and twenty feet deep that drew off flood waters in the black dirt area, one of the finest farming areas in New York State.

In the end, the *Roosevelt Tree Army* advanced the cause of state and national conservation programs by fifteen to twenty-five years. In the decades that followed, every state and national park in the country has suffered from budget cutbacks as staffing levels have declined and historic and cultural resources are left to benign neglect.

The CCC Today

In the years after the war, it was obvious that the parks needed the kind of assistance the CCC had provided. However, there was never any federal effort on the level that had been achieved from 1933-1942. Many people like FDR saw the need for a permanent agency. Dryden Kuser wrote in 1960: "If the CCC were reestablished as a permanent agency, we would go far toward providing better facilities in our parks and it should serve as a most valuable antidote for the steadily mounting delinquency which is far too prevalent."[52]

The CCC remains alive today in various forms. There is the National Association of Civilian Conservation Corps Alumni (NACCCA) located in St. Louis, Missouri formed in 1977. The organization, which has more than seven thousand members, promotes the conservation and work ethic of the CCC and encourages CCC-like programs in federal, state, county and local government agencies. Several of the men from the C camp at High Point are members.

Another organization called the Brotherhood of ex-CCCers, is managed by Joseph Toltin. It is a separate organization from the NACCCA and maintains one of the largest private collections of CCC memorabilia in Toltin's home in Florida. They have records of men who served at High Point.

Another way the CCC is being remembered is on the Internet. A growing number of websites are dedicated to the efforts of the men of the three C's. Some are managed by private individuals who served, and others, like state government agencies, have web pages. For example, Oregon, Georgia and Idaho all have material on the CCC in their states. Some chapters of the NACCCA have their own web pages.

There have been a number of efforts since 1942 to build on the CCC legacy including the Job Corps, a major piece of President Lyndon B. Johnson's war on poverty. In 1978, the Young Adult Conservation Corps was established and worked on projects across the country including some remodeling of the Grey Rock Inn. A camp was established at High Point, but the agency was abolished in 1981 by President Ronald Reagan. Another federally funded group called the Youth Conservation Corps also operated during the 1970s and 1980s. The Americorps of President Bill Clinton is also rooted in the ideas generated from the CCC.

A number of states have tried programs that emulate the original ideals of the *Roosevelt Tree Army* including the Ohio Department of Natural Resources Division of the Civilian Conservation

Corp. Some fifteen thousand young men have been employed since 1977 in the program. California also has the California Conservation Corps which has benefitted thousands of young men over the years. The Michigan Civilian Conservation Corps was established in 1984, and it provides an employment experience for young people and conducts work on public lands.

There are at least three museums within driving distance of High Point dedicated to the memory of the CCC. The first is at Promised Land State Park Museum in Greentown, Pennsylvania. It has the most important collection of CCC materials in the region, related mainly to Camp Pocono (S-139) that was located there. The collection reflects the work projects and personal mementos and has administrative manuals and books used in running the camp. The park sponsors an annual reunion of former CCCers that draws more than one hundred people. The 2000 reunion saw more than fifty former C boys attend with families. The museum is located in the former officers quarters building.

The Pennsylvania Lumber Museum in Galeton is located in a CCC-era log building. Finally, the NACCA Chapter 170 maintains the Northeast Civilian Conservation Corps Museum in Stafford Springs, Connecticut. The museum is housed in a CCC building and has a large collection of materials.

Peter Osborne

One of the few monuments dedicated to the CCC in the eastern part of the United States is located at Stokes State Forest. The full sized replica of an enrollee about to go off to work was dedicated on November 4, 1996, at Montclair State University's New Jersey School of Conservation in Branchville and was rededicated on June 5, 1999. The statue is located on the parade ground of Camp S-71 that housed companies 218 & 1266.[53]

As the 70th anniversary of the creation of one of President Roosevelt's pet projects approaches, the legacy of the CCC continues to make our lives better. Almost all C boys have said the experience was one of the best of their lives and, to a man, they are proud of the work they accomplished. Almost all thought the program had an important effect upon their lives.

For those of us who use and love our nation's parks and forests, we can never express our gratitude enough to the *Roosevelt Tree Army* or to President Franklin D. Roosevelt who had a far-sighted vision about conservation and young men and acted upon it. Some CCC boys understood what they were doing went beyond the building of roads or lakes or even a paycheck. They saw a larger purpose. Peter Lutz reflected upon that mission: "We were from the city, and we realized what we were doing, see, we were building that park for our next generation, see we knew that. And we were only kids, we didn't have anything, we were from the city and we had no toys, Christmas didn't mean a thing to us. And so we thought, well, when we get married and have children we want them to be able to see what nature is all about."54

When we drive over the roads of High Point, camp at one of its beautiful sites or canoe on its lakes, we can tip our hats to men like Messrs. Gibbons, Gemmill, Mastriani, Thiede, Lutz, Polisi and the others who made it possible. We remember, as Ray Hoyt said in his history of the CCC, *"We Can Take It"* that life in CCC camp was a great adventure.

APPENDIX

Great Benefactors To The Park

I saw the results of the work done by the CCC. The achievements of this agency began to dot city and rural areas alike. Soil conservation and forestry work went forward, recreation areas were built ... It is true they cost the people of the country vast sums of money, but they did a collective good and left tangible results which are still evident today.

-Eleanor Roosevelt

This I Remember

The CCC was a truly brilliant idea. Here was the agency to care for the new generation of young men who discovered that the place they had hoped or expected to take in commercial or industrial life did not exist. The CCC besides aiming to relieve unemployment had a secondary purpose: to preserve the nation's natural resources and to develop areas filled with nature's beauty so that they might become more easily accessible to the general public.

-*Sussex Register,* Sussex, New Jersey, April 13, 1939

Because the complete set of CCC records for Camp Kuser no longer exist, there is no known listing of all the people who worked for the CCC at High Point. The author has attempted to compile a listing of the men who were stationed in the camp including the Army officers, NPS personnel and CCC enrollees. It is as comprehensive as is possible with the surviving records that are scattered across a number of archives. The names come from many sources including the camp's newsletters, NPS drawings, the archives and files at HPSP, taped interviews, the National Archives, newspaper clips and materials at the President Franklin D. Roosevelt Library.

The task of creating a complete list of those who worked at High Point is probably an impossibility without the official camp personnel records. As many as twenty five hundred men may have passed through Camp Kuser from 1933 until 1941 although the number is probably lower than that. The dates cited are for known service only. The men may have served for a longer period of time, but available resources, most of which are incomplete, indicate those dates.

Some names are suggested because of documentary evidence. If a line appears before a last name it indicates the first name was not known. Names in quotations are nicknames for the C boys. Anyone with further information may write to the author.

Peter Osborne

High Point Park Commission Executive Secretaries
(During CCC era)
John Stanton, 1933-1934
John Gibbons, 1934-1941

(Mr. Gibbons served this position long after the CCC left High Point State Park)

Camp Kuser

Camp 2A
Camp 216, SP-1
Lusscroft Farm Site
Permanent Site

Camp Superintendent
Major Richard W. Cooksey (Cookin) (1933)

U.S. Army Officers
First Lieutenant A. Merkie (1933)
Army Instructor, Fordham University
First Lieutenant John R. Culleton (1933)
Field Artillery, ROTC, Cornell University

Cooks
Mess Sergeant Clitus Swann (1933)
1st Cooks
Louis Farone (1933)
John Clancy (1933)
2nd Cooks
Dan Bellanti (1933)
Joseph Ritchie (1933)
Julius Roinell (1933)
Anthony Borelli (1933)
First Aid
StephenCrist (1933)

We Can Take It!

George Morrow (1933)

Camp SP-1/Company 216 - Camp Kuser

Camp Commanders
Major Richard Cooksey (1933)
1st Lieutenant R. H. Grinder (1933)
Coast Artillery Reserves
Captain Henry Woyton (1933-1934)
Engineer, Reserves
Captain Alonzo M Couvert (1934-1935)
36th Infantry Reserve
Captain William C. Halpert (1935)
Captain Benjamin Perricone (1935-1936)
Quartermaster Reserves
1st Lieutenant Clyde F. Marion (1936-1937)
Infantry Reserves

U.S. Army Officers
1st Lieutenant John R. Culleton

1st Lieutenant R. H. Grinder (1933)
Coast Artillery Reserves
(Lt. Grinder was in charge of Company 216 in 1933)
_____ Schwartz
1st Lieutenant J. King Wallace (1933-1934)
(Q.M.)
(Lt. Wallace was in charge of Company 216 in 1934)
2nd Lieutenant William F. Kuhn (1933-4)
(Mess Officer)
Coast Artillery Reserves
Winfred H. Baetz (1933)
(D.S.A.)
Lt. Kenneth Gaul (1934)
Lt. Stickney (1935)

Peter Osborne

Lt. Paul L Petty (1935)
Lt. Rolland G. Scott (1936)
1st Lieutenant Clyde F. Marion (1934-1937)
Infantry Reserves
(Mess Officer - 1935, Commanding Officer - 1936)
*(Lt. Marion was in charge
of the company in 1935-1937)*
Lieutenant Robert T. Craig (1934, 1935, 1936)
307th Infantry
(Property Officer - 1936)

Camp Surgeons & Doctors
Lt. Herbert F. Gross (1933)
Captain William Zuckerman (1933)
Dr. J. D. Haggerty (1933)
1st Lieutenant, Dr. Harry T. Kassell (1934)
1st Lieutenant, Dr. Lester R. Eddy (1934-1935)
Lieutenant Alan A. Freed (1935)
Captain Anthony G. Sabin (1936)
Medical Reserves
1st Lieutenant Theodore D. Spritzer (1937)
Medical Reserves

Camp Education Advisors
George D. Smith (1934-1936)
Edwin H. Wintermute (1936-1937)

Project Superintendents
Oswald W. Brown (1933-1937)

National Park Service Foremen
Ralph Bratberg, Landscape Foreman
(1934-1937)
Edwin L. Brawley, Landscape Foreman
(1934-1937)
George Davis, Cultural Foreman (1934-1935)
Charles Henkel, Landscape Foreman

We Can Take It!

(1933-1935)
Herman Hornecker, Foreman (1935)
Elmer Miller, Cultural Foreman (1934-1937)
George H. O'Neill, Cultural Foreman (1934-1937)
Arthur Parker, Landscape Foreman 1934-1935)
Leigh Saltsman, Cultural Foreman (1934-1937)
George H. Schmierer (1934-1937)
Oliver Wells (1933-1936)

(* - These men were listed in some documents as foremen but they were not actually foremen but performed the jobs as noted. + - This indicates the following status that they were junior technicians)
+*Benjamin Demerest
(1935-1937, Mechanic)
+*Abe Kooistra
(1935-1937, Blacksmith)

Civilian Conservation Corps
Enrollees
(Some of these names may be duplicates of the names listed below however there names are from resources where the date cannot be determined.)

James Hascup

1933

____ Bartlett	____ Kaminski
____ Belcher	____ Kannaley
____ Bierbaum	____ Krank
____ Bishcop	____ Martin
____ Cifelli	Walter Morris
____ Corcoran	____ Polyak
George "Stumpy" De Vaul	____ Scazzafava
____ Gaska	____ Trykoswki
____ Gaul	____ Werner

Peter Osborne

1934
Edward "Deacon" Burke

1935
Edward "Deacon" Burke
Robert Ellendorf
Joe Martin
Harold Williams

1936 & 1937
(Some of these names may be duplicates of the names listed below when members of Company 1217 were transferred into this unit in February 1936)

_____ Addeo
_____ Annett
Edward "Deacon" Burke
_____ Bicskey
_____ Blewett
_____ "Major" Bowes
Bob "Pep, Wim and Wigor" Brasher
_____ Budz
_____ Clark
J. P. Collette
_____ Conniry
_____ Cooper
_____ "Smile A wile" Doyle
_____ "Red Nose" Dwyer
_____ "Da Da" Elliot
_____ Fallen
_____ Haggerty

Jack Coykendall
_____ De Mario
George "Stumpy" De Vaul
G. Decker
W. Decker
_____ "Smokey" Dekmar
_____ "Sparks" Dedovitch
_____ Denges
_____ Deste
_____ "Ducky" Dittman
Joe Hass
O.J.
_____ Jones (Assistant Leader)
_____ "Bull" Johnson
_____ "Pop" Johnson
_____ Kaberter

We Can Take It!

_____ "Bill" Lemon
George Lesslie
_____ Lowenstein
John "Goldie" Macken
"Eddie" Manning
N. "Mickey" Markovich
"Mickey" Marks
(Asst. Company Clerk)
Joe Martin
_____ Miskovic
_____ McCarthy
_____ Missouri
_____ Monica
Owen "Black" Murray
_____ Nuttal
_____ "Fu Manchu"
O'Brien
Charles Pak
C. Pakestein
Dave Palumbo
F. Parker
_____ Paserchia
_____ Prussack
M. Petro
Anthony Rocco
_____ Rosenthal

"Red" Sacco
_____ Saltzman
_____ Schneberger
_____ Scott
_____ Shanahan
_____ Shaper
_____ Shaurger
Harry Silverman
_____ Smitty
_____ Straub
_____ Stroolman
_____ Tango
_____ Traubman
_____ Van Keuren
_____ G.I. Wallace
_____ Walker
(Mess Steward)
_____ Walsh
_____ "Baldy" Williams
_____ Wolverton
Alexis Wronka
_____ Yanish

February 1936

(The following enrollees were transferred from Company 1217, Camp S-71, Branchville, New Jersey)

James Dwyer
Anthony Martinez
John Morrow
Stanley Naber
Alfred Nilsson
George Nuttal
Vincent O'Brien

John Pappas
Gordon Pittman
Jacob Polinsky
Victor Porcaro
Max Prussach
Joseph Rabowski
Elmer Rage

Peter Osborne

Anthony Reichert
Peter Robando
Sidney Rosenthal
Robert Ryan
John Sawalla
Francis Scot
Walter Skupski
Harry Silverman
John Silvia
Thomas Sogar
Valentine Sok
Henry Sokulski
John Sommerfield
John Sottosanti
James Soutwick
William Tobay
Samuel Tedino
Carl Tutino
John Wesbecki

Camp 2B
Camp 1280, SP-8
Permanent Site

Camp Commander
Captain Milton Heilfron (1933)
62nd Coast Artillery
Captain Harold Hotten (1934)
Field Artillery Reserves
Captain Donald McGrayne (1934)
Field Artillery Reserves
Captain Francis J. Grueter (1935)
Coast Artillery Reserves
2nd Lieutenant Walter S. Schaefer (1935)
C.A.R.
1st Lieutenant Robert T. Craig (1935)

307th Infantry
Captain Benjamin Perricone (1935-1936)
Quartermaster Reserves
Captain Russell P. Westerhoff (1937)
C.A., Reserves
Captain Harry S. Ryskind (1937-1938)
Infantry, Reserves
1st Lieutenant Clyde F. Marion (1937)
Infantry Reserves
1st Lieutenant Robert Parry (1938, 1939)
Engineer, Reserves
1st Lieutenant John G. Crawford (1938)
1st Lieutenant Louis Ebert (1938-9)
Infantry, Reserves
Captain Samuel J. Loyd (1939-1940)
Engineer - Reserves,
Civilian Camp Commander
Captain Louis A. Smith (1941)
U.S. Cavalry Reserve
Civilian Camp Commander
Captain ____ O'Brian (1941)

U.S. Army Officers
First Lieutenant Donald McGrayne (1933)
(F.A.)
Second Lieutenant George F. Keenan
(1933-1935)
(A.C.)
Lt. ____ Strauss (1934)
1st Lieutenant Robert T. Craig (1934, 1935-1936)
307th Infantry
(Commanding Officer - 1935-1936)
Lieutenant Thomas F. Sullivan (1934-1936)
Warrant Officer, USCG
(Mess Officer, Transportation Officer and Post Exchange Officer)
2nd Lieutenant Walter S. Schaefer (1935)

C.A.R.
(Supply and Finance Officer)
Lt. _____ Scott (1936)
1st Lieutenant Leo H. Hecht
Infantry - Reserve
(Commanding Officer - 1937)
1st Lieutenant Clyde F. Marion (1935-1937)
Infantry Reserves
(Commanding Officer - 1937)
1st Lieutenant John G. Crawford (1938)
(Mess and Motor Transport Officer, Supply Officer)
1st Lieutenant Robert G. Parry (1938, 1939)
Engineer, Reserves
(Commanding Officer - 1938)
1st Lieutenant Louis Ebert (1938-1939)
Infantry Reserves
(Commanding Officer - 1938-1939)
1st Lieutenant John G. Crawford (1938)
(Supply Officer)
(Commanding Officer - 1938)
First Lieutenant Louis Ebert (1938-1939)
(Post Exchange Officer)
*(Lt. Ebert was in charge of
Company 1280 in 1939)*
1st Lieutenant Frederick M Udall (1938-1939)
Infantry, Reserves
(Junior Officer)
Captain Louis Smith (1940-1941)
*(Captain Smith was in charge of
Company 1280 in 1940)*
Captain Samuel J. Loyd (1939-1940)
Engineer - Reserves
*(Captain Loyd was in charge of
Company 1280 in 1940)*
Lieutenant Nat Bender (1939-1940)
Sub-Altern
Captain Louis A. Smith (1940)

We Can Take It!

U.S. Cavalry Reserve
Subaltern
*(Captain Smith was in charge
of Company 1280 in 1941)*
Luke Gray (1941)
Subaltern
Alexander Gregory (1941)
Subaltern

Project Superintendents
Howard Platt (1933-1939)
Melvin Gemmill (1939-1941)

Assistant Project Superintendents
Melvin Gemmill (1938-1939)
Oliver W. Wells (1940-1941)

National Park Service
Technical Services
Designers
Eric Flemming - 1933-1936(?)
Emmett L. Paige - 1934
Edward Taubert - 1935-1936
George Schmierer - 1936-1937
George Hill - 1936
Melvin Gemmill - 1936-1939
Albert Mastriani - 1939-1941

National Park Service Foremen
Morrie Atkins, Landscape Foreman,
(1933-1937)
Frank X. Clark (1939-1940)
Raymond Evans, Senior Foreman (1940)
Melvin Gemmill, Landscape Foreman
(1933-1936)
C. Hefelfinger, Cultural Foreman
Charles Henkel, Landscape Foreman

Peter Osborne

(1935-1937)
Lawrence S. Jones, Cultural Foreman, Senior Foreman
(1933-1941)
C. Laube, Cultural Foreman (1933)
H. W. Lewis, Cultural Foreman (1933-1934)
Albert Mastriani, Cultural Foreman (1933-1941)
Emmett Paige, Landscape Foreman (1933-1936)
Richard Potter, Cultural Foreman (1935)
Joe Sweeney, Landscape Foreman (1933-1935)
Edward Taubert, Landscape Foreman (1935-1936)
John Thorpe, Cultural Foreman (1935)
Theodore Turner, Landscape Foreman
(1938-1939)
Oliver Wells, Cultural Foreman (1935-1941)

(- These men were listed in some documents as foremen but they were not actually foremen but performed the jobs as noted. + - This indicates that they were junior technicians)*

+*John Bowblis (1938) Foremen's Helper)
*Allen Grinder (1935-1940) Blacksmith, tool foreman)
*Cline "Chubby" Harris (1933-1939, 1940-1941) Mechanic, truck foreman)
*Gordon Grinder (1938-1939)
*John Kruppa (1938) Heavy Equipment Operator)
+*Richard Molle (1938-1940) Blacksmith Helper, Officers Orderly

+*Everett "Red" Sisco (1938) Tractor Operator, Heavy Equipment Operator
*Arthur "Sharkey" Unangast (1936-1940) Heavy Equipment Operator 1935-1936, Power Shovel Operator & Independent Contractor
+Henry Winkler (1938) Mechanic's Helper, Junior Technician

We Can Take It!

Civilian Conservation Corps Enrollees

(Dates of Service Unknown)

George Anderson
Christopher Ayers
Carmen Antinello
Edward Bundro
Carmen Degaetano
Nick Degaetano
Stanley Fork
Amoveno Fracaro
Joseph Gallo
Michael Giamongo
____ Haiden
William Hartley
Maurice Healy
Nicholas Hanisak
(Office Clerk)
Edwin Jakobowski
Alec Kovach
Jerry Kutzer
William Lenahan
Firpo Lemma
Carl LoGrand
Peter Lutz
Tony Martinez
Cimerino Minvide
Edward Moran
Robert Mudd
Edward Nolan
Michael Novak
Charles Pakestin
Stanley Pierce

Alfred Rullo
Charles Russo
John Saski
Joseph Schaffhouser
William Scully
Frank Seddio
Fred Tavener
Joseph Titus
Shine Vega
Rolland Walker
Robert Wilbert
____ Winters
Joseph Zavatsky
Stanley Zink

1933
Edward "Deacon" Burke
____ Flannagan

1934
Ludivico Ayala
Hilton Babcock
Edward "Deacon" Burke
William DeGhetto
Andy Helancy
G. Meyers
John Pinko
Blackie Railio
Thomas Segar

Peter Osborne

1935

- ____ Bohetz (2nd Clerk)
- Vito D'Angelo
- William DeGhetto
- John Dewan
- Jim Diamond (1st Sergeant)
- ____ Dougherty (2nd Cook)
- Ben Johnson (Supply Sergeant)
- Adolph Korinek (2nd Cook)
- ____ Langridge
- Anthony Lategola (Mess Steward)
- Robert Lieber
- John Malina (Company Clerk)
- Tom Murphy (1st Cook)
- Alexander Nester (1st Cook & Mess Steward)
- ____ Olin (Baker)
- Alfred Patino (2nd Cook)
- ____ Randsteid (Assistant Education Advisor)
- Nathan Schnaars (1st Cook)
- ____ Simpson
- Samuel Smitheran (Storeroom Clerk)
- ____ Sobeck - (Infirmary Attendant)
- John Spinarelli
- Thomas Stewart
- Steve Swetz (Mess Steward)
- August Torck
- Nicholas Villano
- ____ Wallace
- Art Walsh (Canteen Stewart)
- Michael Zagursky (1st Cook)

We Can Take It!

Fall 1935 Roster

Senior Leader
John Hayden

Leaders
Roy Decker
Robert Hockenjos
Abraham Koman
John Kruppa
Robert Simpson
Everett "Red" Sisco

Assistant Leaders
Michael Bachure
John Bogash
Vito D'Angelo
John Dewan
Edward Doyle
Robert Drimmer
Ernest Eisman
Earl Harriss
Jacob Langereis
Salvatore Salute
John Strauch
Nicolas Villano
James Wallace

Enrollees

Carl Alessandra
Carl Anderson
Joseph Anzalone
Larry Anzalone
William Apmick
Carmen Baccarella
George Baldauf

Emil Balleriai
Clarence Berry
Walter Bittner
Benard Blace
Charles Bopura
Norman Bowen
Robert Brooks
Edward Burke
Raymond Burke
Joseph Calvacca
Edmund Cambra
Orlando Capicotto
Joseph Carreteunto
Edward Christ
Kenneth Clouse
Everett Conklin
Edward Costello
Paul De Feo
Harold De George
Samuel Dimeo
Philip Dunn
Frank Di Stefano
Thomas Dobbin
Joseph Famular
Philip Ferraro
Ralph Ferraro
William Ford
Amos FreemanJoseph
Frontauria
Steve Fulgo
Harry Furman
Paul Gebbia
John Gemon
Norman Germaine
Abe Goodman

Peter Osborne

Paul Grange
Louis Grasso
Edgar Greco
Harold Grodjesk
George Grube
George Hallestien
Harry Hazen
Frank Heater
Fred Hoffman
William "Shanty" Hogan
Chester Hrabovsky
Chester Hovaney
Wallace Hurd
Harry Irwin
Edward Kapulka
Joseph Kapusta
J. Karlick
F. Kazaren
J. Kempka
K. Kenneth Kern
Herman Kimble
Louis Kleso
Michael Kimick
Peter Kinney
Walter Kmiolek
Walter Kochis
Felix Kowalski
Wilbur Krause
Phillip Lagattuta
William Lamb
Wilbur Lapp
Leroy LaRue
Edmund Lauder
John Lauro
Robert Lieber

Rudolph Lo Guidice
George Losey
Walter Losey
Donald McDonald
D. Macejka
M. Machuga
William Mackerly
Louis Majka
George Malek
Andrew Mangini
Paul Manto
Adolph Mantzke
Charles Marchese
John Martin
Stanley Matuesich
John Matushak
George Mayer
John Meyers
Robert Myers
Richard Molle
John Mucha
George Newell
John Nicholas
Cammelo Nicosia
Andrew Novak
Micheal Novak
Vincent O'Brien
John Ochab
Ernest Oddy
John O'Donnell
James Passantino
Grant Payne
Matthew Pelka
Joseph Piekarski
Joseph Piowlski
Albert Plevier

We Can Take It!

Francis Pohlman
Rudolph Polise
Mike Prester
Joseph Presti
Andrew Prunchak
Francesco Re
Richard Reichert
Joseph Rera
Charles Rieder
James Ripel
Bruno Rogalek
Lester Romaine
George Rothman
Bruno Ruchalski
John Rudio
Ettare Rusconi
Sylvester Sawyer
Paul Scheffel
Walter Schneider
John Shedosky
Everett Salzman
George Shupak
Arthur Simon
George Smith
Sonny Staudt
Thomas Stewart
Harold Struble
John Strauss
John Sudol
John Szkole
Glenn Taggert
Alex Teich
Morton Terwilliger
Bruno Thomas
Grove Thompson
Alfred Todisco
Agust Tork

James Totaro
Frank Troise
Walter Tuers
Alfred Turchetto
Mario Tuzzo
Henry Van Gelder
Andrew Vasile
Joseph Vernuccio
Albert Voros
Theodore Wadowski
Herman Werlitz
Alex Westlake
Allan Wilson
Harry Wilson
Henry Winkler
William Zoller

1936

_____ Blok
_____ Clouse
_____ Dougherty
_____ Drimmond
_____ Fotaro
_____ Gormine
_____ "Shanty" Hogan
Wladyslaw Kmiolek
Peter Lutz
_____ Patino
_____ Rubber
Michael Sagursky
_____ Schmarra
Frank Seddio
Neil Thiede
Walter Tueres
Alan Wilson

1937
Harold "Football Head" Bailliee
____ Bogash
Edward "Deacon" Burke
(Assistant to Education Advisor)
Dominick Coppolla
Edwin Jakobowski
John Kruppa
Carl LoGrande
Peter Lutz
James Malizia
Thomas Morgan
Michael Sagursky
Frank Seddio
Neil Theide
Joseph Terry
Transferred from Company 216
1938
George Anderson
John Anderson
John Antonik, Jr.
Phillip Auchard
____ Ayers
____ Baginski
Harold "Football Head" Bailliee
Benny Ballone
____ Banks
George "Baldy" Bauldauf
(First Sergeant & Senior Leader)
Michael Belanski

Alfred Bell
John Ben
____ Black
Mike Bobrunko
____ Bonner
Eddie Borkowski
____ Borngesser
____ Bosco
Frank Brain
____ Brown
____ "Fat" Bizukewicz
Edwin "Deacon" Burke
(Assistant to Education Advisor)
Jack Cambell
Michael Capua
Frank Carpita
M. Cataliotta
____ Chester
____ Ciasco
John Cinsco
John Clause
Richard Criss
(Mess Steward, First Cook)
Louis Czick
____ "Man Mountain" Dean
B. Delarsky
____ DePasquale
____ Dorinek
Edward "Slim" Doyle
(Canteen Steward)
Robert Drimmer
Metro Duda
Wallace Dudeck

Joe Dudik
James Duffy
James Dwyer
____ Eckel
Ernie Eisman
Vincent Esposito
Nick Falise
George "Bats" Fallahee
____ Fallagee
____ Fazio
John Fiorillo
____ "Baggy" Foran
____ Fortes
____ Fredericks
____ Gagliano
Charles Gallagher
John Gemon
____ Geodon
Frank Gerado
____ Gerardo
Michael Giamongo
Warren "Tex" Glynn
Thomas Godino
Chalres Godley
William Gonzalez
____ Gosslin
August Grafje
____ "Turk" Grasso
____ Gulardo
Arnold Guerriero
James Hackett
Joseph Hackett
____ "Farmer" Haeffely
Robert Halsey

Norman "Butch" Hanns
____ Harris
____ Haverick
Maurice Healy
____ Herell
Sylvester Herold
(Assistant Leader)
____ Hingsten
William "Shanty" Hogan
George Hohle
Wallace Hurd
____ Iosco
____ Iurato
Edwin Jakobowski
Joseph Janski
____ Jaromin
George Johnson
Herbert Johnson
(Assistant Leader)
Ikay Johnson
Red Kenny
Henry Knoemeller
William Knoble
Abraham Koman
(Supply Sergeant)
Edward Kornacki
Adolph Korinek
____ Kornek
Nick Koske
____ Lagara
____ Langaris
____ Latour
Edmund Lauder
____ Laverty
Joseph Lazarczyk

Peter Osborne

____ "Stratosphere"	____ Muller
Leach	Frank Nardone
William Leahy	____ Nementh
____ Lebiedz	____ "Red" Neubert
"Tiny" Lalek	____ Newell
____ "Punchy"	____ O'Donnell
LaTour	____ Oswald
Steve Lisowski	"Shorty" Noferio
Carl LoGrande	____ Pankewicz
Joe Lombardo	____ Papp
____ "Punchy" Lomka	Joe Pappaterra
Bruno Maciejewski	____ Perlman
____ Maggi	Salvatore Perrone
John Manella	____ Petecki
Alfred MacKinnon	(Assistant Leader)
David McDonald	Pete Pleva
____ McNaney	____ Pessi
Al MacKay	____ Poley
John MacNeney	____ Pohlman
Vic Macek	Clifford Polo
Frank Mack	Andrew Popovich
James Malizia	Joe Poteck
(Office Clerk)	Rudolph Polise
John Manella	____ Prendergast
Francis McAleer	____ Prussia
____ McCluskey	____ Regan
____ McElroy	____ "Red" Richtermoc
____ McKenna	____ Rieder
John F. McNenny	____ Royek
____ Mendyk	____ Rullo
____ Mericle	____ Russell
____ Michael	E. Ryan
Joe Miller	John Sabo
Edmund Monahan	Paul Scheffel
Robert Mooney	John Sculley
Joseph Moran	Frank Seddio
____ Morgano	____ Semkow

We Can Take It!

_____ Sexton
Frank Sharry
Harry "Hockshop" Silverman
_____ Slowlik
_____ Sondaj
Barney Sparnon
George "Woosey" Strauch
John "Barney Oldfield" Strauch
_____ Stumpf
Henry Swensen
Frank Tabano
Clement "Chow Hound" Tassi
Jimmy Tataro
_____ Taylor
Mike Taylor
Charles Tedeschi
Neil Thiede
_____ Tomalo
_____ Torino
Raymond Trygar
Walter Tuers
Joe Uhnak
(Mess Steward)
Albert Urciuloi
Frank Vergo
Francis "Percy" Waldman
Bill Walker
Michael Walsh
Ralph Weber
Glen Wedmere
Alvin Whitlow
Jack Whittaker

Alto Williams
_____ "Slim" Willis
Alan Wilson
Charles Winnik
Stanley Winnik
Samuel L. Woessner
Kenneth "Solitaire Kid" Wood
_____ Yurko
William "Red" Zoeller

1939

Hank Adams
Carmen Attinello
Phillip Auchard
_____ Auche
_____ Baker
George "Baldy" Bauldauf
(First Sergeant & Senior Leader)
Jim Baker
Benny Ballone
Samuel Buonauro
_____ Barney
_____ Batholomew
_____ Bendek
_____ Bernardine
_____ Berger
Walter Blum
Mike Bobrunko
_____ Branisisk
_____ Browers
_____ Brown
_____ Bugler
_____ Callahan

Peter Osborne

_____ Carroll
_____ Carmella
_____ Castner
_____ Chitko
Nick Ciasco
_____ Cella
Eugene Clayton
John Coyle
_____ Coyne
_____ Culbert
_____ D'Kerkado
William Degethoff
_____ DeLuce
John DeVries
Henry DelVavero
_____ Derda
_____ Dimmick
Edward "Slim" Doyle
Robert Drimmer
Metro Duda
James Duffy
John B. Dunne
_____ Duris
_____ Dzuibeck
_____ Eckle
_____ Fabian
Neil Farley
_____ Ferris
_____ Forys
Charles Gallagher
Edward Gallagher
James Garnet
John Gemon
_____ Gertz
_____ "Shorty" Gelemb
T. Gibbert
(Leader)

_____ Gjertsen
August Grafje
_____ Haeffely
Joe Handze
_____ Hanisak
_____ Harrison
W. Hartley
(Assistant Leader)
_____ Havel
_____ Hehlo
Sylvester "Blubber" Herold
(Assistant Leader)
Robert Hill
_____ Hughes
_____ Iosco
Edwin Jakobowski
Joseph Janski
_____ Jiorle
_____ Joyner
_____ Kanter
_____ Kimble
_____ Kinsella
_____ Kirgan
Harry Kisselback
_____ Klem
Joseph "Joe Blow" Klusowixz
Henry Knemoller
William Knoble
Abraham Koman
Nick Koske
(Leader)
_____ Kosko
_____ Kosminsky
_____ Koszare
Albert "Red" Kubas

We Can Take It!

Johnny James Kukles
_____ "Whitey" Kutas
_____ Kutzler
James Lanaris
Jake Langeries
(Assistant Leader)
_____ Lasco
Richard LaTour
James Laverty
_____ Lazuray
Lew Lehr
_____ "Whitey"
Lizowski
Carl LoGrande
_____ "Punchy" Lomka
_____ Lusk
_____ "Porky" Maerz
John Manella
_____ Manual
_____ Maransak
John MacNeney
(Leader)
_____ McAleer
Charles McCarthy
Alex "Junior" McCluskey
Joseph McNicholas
_____ Meazaros
_____ Melnyk
Bruno "Bull Head" Michota
Casper "Dr." Milquetoast
_____ Miller
_____ Minardi
Robert Mooney
_____ Muller

_____ Murphy
_____ Nicholson
Robert O'Connor
John O'Donnell
_____ Olozowey
Frank Orden
_____ Oswald
_____ Patire
_____ Patla
_____ Piatti
Zazu Pitts
Pete Pleva
_____ Pokraska
Rudolph Polise
Frank Ponack
(Assistant Leader)
Andrew Popovich
_____ Potignano
Alfred Poyer
_____ Price
_____ Prussia
_____ Pupura
_____ Ragucci
Frank Reich
_____ Reider
_____ "Red" Richtermoc
_____ "Skippy" Roberts
Phillip Roth
_____ Royek
_____ Ruggucci
C. Russo
(Assistant Leader)
Clarence Rutan
Edward "Becky" Ryan
_____ Rygg
John Sabo

Peter Osborne

____Scarfo
Edward Scheell
Paul Scheffel
John Sculley
____ Seeweed
N. Semkow
(Leader)
____ Sepuch
____Sexton
Roy Spencer
William Spencer
____ Stacey
____ Stacey
____ Stalzer
____ Stelte
George Strauch
____ Stroupe
____ Sweeney
J. Sullivan
____ Syfor
Clem Tassi
Chester Taylor
Mike Taylor
(Assistant Leader &
Leader)
____ Todd
____ Van Atta
____ Vargo
Bill Walker
____ Wargo
____ Whip
____ Willis
Kenneth Wilson
Kenny Woods
(Assistant Leader)
____ Yanci
____ Yoda

____ Yokum
Mickey Yurko
Emil Zoeller
William "Red" Zoeller

1940

____ "Jughead"
Adams
Hank Adams
____ Alonzo
Carmen Attinello
George "Baldy"
Bauldauf
(First Sergeant &
Senior Leader)
Raymond Bannon
____ Baronsky
Bill Batholomew
Douglas Bennett
____ Bitterle
Walter Blum
Joe "Poo Poo"
Branisisk
John "Hank" Brower
Samuel Buonauro
Charles Butler
____ Callahan
____ Carey
George Carson
Albert Casella
William Christ
Eugene Clayton
Frank Clymer
____ Cooke
____ "Greek" Czura
____ Dedeo

We Can Take It!

John DeVries
____ Despot
____ Dimmick
____ Dinks
Edward "Slim" Doyle
Robert Drimmer
Metro Duda
James Duffy
John B. Dunne
William "Blackie" Duris
James Emery
____ Ferreri
____ Francone
Harold Gjertsen
Luke Gray
____ Grover
____ Hanisak
Harry Harper
____ Harrison
William Hartley
(Assistant Leader)
____ Hillmuth
____ Hotminsky
Dominic Jiorle
Rasmus Jonson
____ Kavenagh
____ Kennedy
William Kinsella
William Kirgan
____ Kinsel
Harry Kisselback
Joseph "Joe Blow" Klusowixz
William Knoble
____ Kohler
Nick Koske

(Leader)
____ Kosminsky
____ Koszare
____ "Smokey" Kupferschmidt
Johnny James Kukles
____ "Whitey" Kutas
James "Greek" Lanaris
____ "Whitey" Lizowski
Joseph Lombardo
____ Lueck
____ "Porky" Maerz
____ Marruna
John MacNeney
(Leader)
____ McDonald
____ McGinty
Joseph "Curly" McNicholas
Chris Miller
____ Minardi
____ Nemeth
Roy Nesom
____ Passonato
____ Pawluchik
____ Penyak
John Perrotta
____ Peyer
Frank Pietshman
Andrew Popovich
____ Porosky
____ "Fat" Potignano
Alfred "Shorty" Poyer
George Puzzo
____ Rapp

Peter Osborne

____ Reardon
Frank Reich
____ Reynolds
Charles Russo
(Assistant Leader)
____ Scarfo
Nick Semkow
(Leader)
____ Shine
Eddie Siegler
James Snow
____ "Ben Blue" Stout
Frank Stalzer
(Leader)
Lawrence Thomas
____ "Pop" Todd
____ Urbaniak
Richard Wagner
Bill Walker
Robert Wilbert
____ Wickward
____ Williams
Kenneth Wilson
____ Wylandt
____ Yoda

Summer 1940 Roster
<u>Leaders</u>
Carmen Attinello
George Baldauf
John Campbell
Edward Doyle
Robert Drimmer
James Dwyer
John MacNeney
Charles Russo
Frank Stalzer

William Walker

<u>Assistant Leaders</u>
Raymond Bannon
Douglas Bennett
Harry Harper
Gethin Harrison
William Hartley
William Kinsella
Ernest Kohler
Joseph Lombardo
James Murphy
John Pappagallo
George Raynor
Howard Reed
Stephen Sopko

Members
Henry Adams
Manual Alonzo
Steve Barnowsky
Harold Barrett
Henry Binghi
John Blizak
Steve Bobick
John Bonus
Emil Bowinski
Joseph Bransiak
Joseph Brienza
Joseph Cammarata
Carmin Carbone
Charles Carey
Albert Cassella
Joseph Cheaney
William Christ
Frank Clemer
Nicholas Colella

Stevens Cooke
George Critchfield
David Cronin
Theodore Czura
Joseph Darabant
Nunzie Dedko
Federick Dimmick
William Dolan
William Duris
Patrick Flood
Antonio Ferrante
Peter Francavilla
William Francone
Henry Furman
Joseph Gecik
Harold Gjerstsen
Edward Goldyn
Charles Grant
John Groenhoff
John Grover
Walter Gumulak
Sygment Gwiazdzinski
Stanlislaw Gwiazdzinski
Nicholas Hanisak
Arthur Harabin
Warren Hillmuch
Lawrence Hisko
William Hober
Joseph Homyak
Albert Hopkins
Casper Impellizer
Jack Inscho
Edward Irwin
Dominick Jiorle
Joseph Johnson
Rasmus Johnson

Steven Joseph
Charles Kacska
Alphonse Kandrat
Joseph Kaspereen
Steve Kazmer
David Kennedy
Joseph Kerekes
William Kirgan
Harry Kiscelback
Stanley Klusewicz
Kalman Kodila
Joseph Krisanits
Sigmund Kupfershimd
Jere Kutzler
Irving Lansky
Edwin Lauer
Martin Laxer
Roman Lopatecki
Peter Lozar
George Lueck
Frederick Luttgens
Francis Lynch
William Mahoney
John Marune
Angelo Marranca
Robert Meyer
Christopher Miller
Richard Molle
Carmine Montalbano
Joseph Morris
Joseph Munkacsy
Joseph Murphy
Robert McDonald
Christopher McGinity
Roy Nesom
George Newell
Robert Newhard

Peter Osborne

Graciano Nieves
Carl Parker
James Paulino
George Pawluchik
Edward Peake
Frank Pietschman
Andrew Pokrivabak
Peter Porosky
Harold Powell
Alfred Poyer
Joseph Premock
Thomas Rapp
Thomas Reardon
John Regiec
Thomas Regiec
Julius Reina
Hexter Reyes
Harold Reynolds
Juliano Rigatti
Gregory Rivera
Luis Rodriguez
Mario Rubino
Enrique Salgado
John Salzman
Arthur Schnittman
Fred Seigler
Albert Shapiro
Tony Skakal
John Sheedy
Micheal Sillet
Harold Smite
James Snow
Frank Soltys
John Sosinski
John Stacy
George States
Joseph Steekovich

John Stout
Leo Supera
Ralph Tedesco
Willard Todd
Moses Tondi
Vernon Travis
Joseph Travaglio
Anthony Vaccaro
William Vigus
Angelo Vitanza
Benny Wiacek
Robert Wilbert
Franklin Williams
Edward Winston
Harold Witt
John Wylandt

1941
William Adler
Charles Ames
Carmen Attinello
George "Baldy" Baldauf
(First Sergeant & Senior Leader)
____ Barber
____ Bobich
Emil Bowinski
Harold Brown
Ray Chasm
William Christ
Steven Cooke
David Cronin
Joe Cronin
____ DeGroat
Edward "Slim" Doyle
Jim Dwyer

We Can Take It!

____ Everhorn
William Finkenstadt
"Flash" Gorden
____ Grimaldi
Stanley Gwiazdizinki
Daniel Gyorf
Hugh Hara
Harry Harper
William Hartley
(Leader)
Bernard Hershey
Bernard "Shorty"
Husky
David Jacobs
____ Kasmer
Aaron Leo Karten
William Kirgan
(Canteen Stewart)
Michael Korsak
Raymond Krine
____ Kutz
____ Kutzler
John Lada
Manual "Blackie"
Laura
Raymond Lopatesky
Sal Macaluso
William Mahoney
Nicholas Mare
James McDermott
____ McDonald
Arthur Milo
____ Miniello
James Mulvaney
____ Muruskj
____ Newell
____ Nieves

George Nilson
____ O'Donnell
Adam Paluszec
Thomas Patti
Joseph Perone
John Perretta
J.C. Polock
____ Prestler
George Puzzo
Charles Rickley
Thomas Rinaldy
____ Rivera
Charles
____ Ryder
Paul Schinstin
____ Sheedy
Harold Smith
Floyd Solt
Harold Stollman
____ Thomas
____ Truilo
Richard Wagner
Harry Weinberg

Camp Education Advisor
M.E. Young
(1934)
George D. Smith (1934-1935)
Edwin H. Wintermute (1936-1937)
David E. Traub (1937-1941)

Camp Surgeons & Doctors
Dr. J. D. Haggerty (1933)

419

(Dentist)
Lt. Meyer N. Goldstien
(1938-1939)
(Dental Officer)
1st Lieutenant Jacob B. Alter
(1938-1939)
(Camp Surgeon)
Dr. Thomas D. Monte
(1939-1941)
Dr. T. V. Hammond
Dr. Lester R. Eddy
New York Headquarters
Department of Interior
Procurement Office
L. B. Sexton

Head Supervisor CCC
Selection Agency
Gertrude Van Ryper

NOTES

Abbreviations

FDRL   Franklin D. Roosevelt Library, Hyde Park, New York.
HPSP   High Point State Park, Sussex, New Jersey.
MVHS   Minisink Valley Historical Society, Port Jervis, New York.
NARA   National Archives and Records Administration, College Park, Maryland.

In citing works in the notes, short titles have generally been used. Works frequently cited have been identified by the following abbreviations:

ECW/CCC - General Records of the Emergency Conservation Work and Civilian Conservation Corps,1933-1942, Records Group 35, NARA.
NPS/CCC - Records of the National Park Service, Records Group 79, NARA.
Mastriani - Albert Mastriani, Letters to author, January 1, 2000 - July 31, 2001.
Minutes Minutes, Commissioners of High Point Park, 1923-1945, HPSP.
NJH - *New Jersey Herald*, Newton, New Jersey.

Newsletters 216 - The Civilian Conservation Corps Camp Papers. Civilian Conservation Corps Company 216, The Center for Research Libraries, Chicago, Illinois.

Newsletters 1280 - The Civilian Conservation Corps Camp Papers. Civilian Conservation Corps Company 1280, The Center for Research Libraries, Chicago, Illinois.

Nomination-Dupont, Jr., Ronald J., "Nomination for Inclusion of High Point State Park on the Register," Registration Form, National Register of Historic Places, Sussex County Historical Society, Newton, New Jersey.

OF268 Official File on the Civilian Conservation Corps, OF 268, 1933-1942, FDRL.

Osborne/CCC Osborne, Peter. ed. "We Can Take It: The Roosevelt Tree Army at High Point State Park 1933-1941: Interviews With Former Civilian Conservation Corps Enrollees, Camp Kuser, Companies 216 & 1280." Interviews by Peter Osborne. vol. 2. rev. ed. 2000. MVHS & HPSP.

PJUG *Port Jervis Union Gazette,* Port Jervis, New York,
SI   *Sussex Independent,* Sussex, New Jersey
SR   *Sussex Register,* Newton, New Jersey
WR   *Wantage Recorder,* Wantage, New Jersey,

Wurst/CCC - Osborne, Peter. ed. "We Can Take It: The Roosevelt Tree Army at High Point State Park 1933-1941: Interviews With Former Civilian Conservation Corps Enrollees, Camp Kuser, Companies 216 & 1280." Interviews by Debbie Fritter and William Wurtst. vol. 1. rev. ed. 2000. MVHS and HPSP.

Chapter 1: The Dirty Thirties

David M. Kennedy, *Freedom from Fear: The American People in Depression and War 1929-1945* (New York: Oxford University, 1999),104.

Stan Cohen, *The Tree Army: A Pictorial History of the Civilian Conservation Corps, 1933-1942*, rev. ed. (Missoula, Montana: Pictorial Histories Publishing Company, 1996), 6.

1. John Blum et al., *The National Experience: A History of the United States since 1865,* 3rd ed.(New York: Harcourt Brace Jovanovich, 1973), 615.
2. Ibid., 615.
3. William E. Leuchtenburg, *Franklin D. Roosevelt and the New Deal* (New York: Harper and Row,1963), 52.
4. Blum, The National Experience, 615.
5. John A. Salmond, *The Civilian Conservation Corps, 1933-1942: A New Deal Case Study* (Durham, North

Carolina: Duke University Press, 1967), 3.
6. Ibid., 3.
7. Blum, The National Experience, 615.
8. Ibid., 623.
9. Ibid., 624.
10. Studs Terkel, *Hard Times: An Oral History of the Great Depression* (New York: Pantheon Books, 1986), 222.
11. Kennedy, *Freedom from Fear*, 194.
12. Mead Stapler, letter to author, August 21, 2001.
13. Kennedy, *Freedom from Fear*, 134.
14. Ray Hoyt, *We Can Take It: A Short Story of the CCC* (New York: American Book Company, 1935), 16.
15. Edgar B Nixon, ed., *Franklin D. Roosevelt & Conservation 1911-1945*, vol.1 (Washington: US Government Printing Office, 1957), 4.
16. Adam Hubbard, *"Gifford Pinchot's Influence on FDR and the Formation of the Civilian Conservation Corps* (capping paper, Marist College,1996), 11-12.
17. Salmond, *The Civilian Conservation Corps*, 7.
18. Nixon, *Franklin D. Roosevelt & Conservation 1911-1945*, vol.1,109-110.
19. Ibid., 99-100.

20. Hubbard, *Gifford Pinchot's Influence on FDR*, 6.
21. Salmond, *The Civilian Conservation Corps*, 5.
22. Stapler, letter to author, August 21, 2001.
23. Salmond, *The Civilian Conservation Corps*, 5-6.
24. Hubbard, *Gifford Pinchot's Influence on FDR*, 13.
25. Nixon, *Franklin D. Roosevelt & Conservation 1911-1945*, vol. 1, 299.
26. Perry H. Merrill, *Roosevelt's Forest Army: A History of the Conservation Corps 1933-1942* (Barre, Vermont: Northright Studio Press, 1981), 4.
27. Promised Land State Park, "*Interesting CCC Facts,*" (Greentown, Pennsylvania, undated, photocopy).
28. The word "act" does not appear in the title of the original legislation hence the title of ECW throughout this book.
29. Salmond, *The Civilian Conservation Corps*, 14.
30. Hoyt, *We Can Take It*, 11.
31. Nixon, *Franklin D. Roosevelt & Conservation 1911-1945*, vol. 1, 431.
32. Salmond, *The Civilian Conservation Corps*, 14-25.
33. Ibid., 31.

34. Hoyt, *We Can Take It*, 19. Salmond, *The Civilian Conservation Corps*, 27-28.
35. Salmond, *The Civilian Conservation Corps*, 28.
36. Ibid., 74-75.
37. Ibid., 82.
38. Ibid., 29.
39. Ibid., 31-32.
40. Ibid., 38.
41. Ibid., 39.
42. Ibid., 41.
43. Ibid., 38.
44. Nixon, *Franklin D. Roosevelt & Conservation 1911-1945*, vol. 1, 345-347.
45. Frances Perkins, *The Roosevelt I Knew* (New York: Harper and Row Publishers, 1946),179.
46. Cohen, *The Tree Army*, 176.
47. Salmond, *The Civilian Conservation Corps*, 45.
48. Hoyt, *We Can Take It*, 32.
49. Shary Page Berg, *The Civilian Conservation Corps: Shaping the Forests and Parks of Massachusetts - A Statewide Survey of Civilian Conservation Corps Resources* (Boston: Department of Environmental Management, 1999), 6.
50. "Civilian Conservation Workers in New Jersey," NJH, January 25,1934.

Chapter 2: For The Boys Are Coming

"Life in Civilian Conservation Corps Camp," SI, July 21, 1933.

Whenever a quote from an interview or letter has an omission or if the editor needed to insert a phrase for clarification the change is indicated by a bracket.

1. *Your CCC: A Handbook for Enrollees* (Washington, D.C. Happy Days Publishing Co., Inc., 1940), 11.
2. Ibid., 13.
3. Nomination, sec. 7, 2.
4. Ibid.
5. Mastriani, February 28, 2000.
6. "New Requirements for C.C.C. Camps," NJH, July 1, 1937, Leslie Crine, interview by author, January 7, 2000.
7. Cohen, *The Tree Army,* 176.
8. Promised Land State Park, "*Interesting CCC Facts,*"(Greentown, Pennsylvania, undated, photocopy).
9. *Your CCC,* 6-7.
10. Salmond, *The Civilian Conservation Corps,* 91-92.
11. "CCC Enrollment for Specialized Training Increases in July," PJUG August 6, 1941.
12. Box 1, 1/33-7/33, OF 268.
13. Ibid.

14. *The CCC in Idaho.* Boise, Idaho: Idaho Public Television, 2001.videocassette.
15. "Freeholders Association at High Point Park," NJH, October 12,1933.
16. "Franklin," NJH, January 18, 1934.
17. Salmond, *The Civilian Conservation Corps,* 34.
18. Ibid., 35.
19. Ibid.
20. Frank Dale, "Good Guys, Bad Guys, Memories of the Civilian Conservation Corps," Book No. 8, Warren County Chronicles, (Washington, NJ:Eckert Printing, April 1999), 13.
21. Report dated, March 13, 1933, OF 268, Box 1, 1/33-7/33.
22. *Your CCC,* 68.
23. "Reforestation Workers Called For Examination," SI, June 2, 1933.
24. Salmond, *The Civilian Conservation Corps,* 181.
25. Camp Inspection Report, April 14,1934, SP-8, HPSP, ECW/CCC, NARA.
26. Ibid.
27. "C.C.C. Men Learn Fast," SI, August 25, 1933.
28. Ibid., "C.C.C. Officer Tells of Conservation Plans," SI, September 1,1933.
29. "Changes Made In Forestry Camps," NJH, October 9,1933.

30. *Your CCC*, 10-11.
31. "Sixth Anniversary of C.C.C. Will Be Observed at High Point Camp," SR, April 18, 1939.
32. *Your CCC*, 9.
33. Newsletters 216, February 2, 1936.
34. Superintendent's Report, SP-1, HPSP, December 1935, NPS/CCC, NARA.
35. Ibid., February 1936.
36. Salmond, *The Civilian Conservation Corps*, 86.
37. Florence Fuller, letter to author, undated.
38. "Visit High Point: German Notables Make Inspection Tour of C.C. Camp," SI, November 24, 1933.
39. Mastriani, April 29, 2000, *Your CCC*, 13.
40. Nicholas Hanisak, interview by author, tape recording, December 17, 2000.
41. Mastriani, June 23, 2000.
42. Ibid., February 18, 2000, February 28, 2000.
43. Hanisak, December 17, 2000.
44. Mastriani, June 23, 2000.
45. Ibid., April 22, 2000.
46. Ibid., June 23, 2000.
47. Hanisak, December 17, 2000.
48. Mastriani, February 14, 2000.
49. Ibid., February 28, 2000.
50. Ibid., April 29, 2000.

Peter Osborne

51. Ibid., March 28, 2000.
52. *Your CCC,* 36.
53. Ibid.
54. Monthly Work Progress Report, SP-1, HPSP, July 1937, ECW/CCC, NARA.
55. Ibid.
56. Monthly Work Progress Report, SP-8, HPSP, May 1937, ECW/CCC, NARA.
57. Camp Inspection Report, SP-1, HPSP, May 1934, ECW/CCC, NARA.
58. "German Officer Visits CCC Camps, SI, September 27, 1935.
59. Clyde Marion to Charles Kenlan, October 9, 1938, Camp Inspection Report, SP-8, HPSP, ECW/CCC, NARA.
60. Ibid.
61. Ibid.
62. Camp Inspection Report, SP-8, HPSP, June 1938, ECW/CCC, NARA.
63. Ibid.
64. Mastriani, July 14, 2000.

Chapter 3: Life At Camp Kuser

Eleanor Roosevelt, *This I Remember* (New York, Harper Brothers), 1949, 135.
Cohen, *The Tree Army,* 10.
1. "High Point Notes," SI, June 2, 1933.
2. Lawrence King, ed., *Our Wantage Heritage: By People of Wantage*

(Baltimore, Maryland: Gateway Press, 1976), 14.
3. "Forest Workers Here: Unit of 200 in Camp at State Farm at Lusscroft," SI, June 16, 1933.
4. Monthly Work Progress Report, SP-1, HPSP, November 1933, ECW/CCC, NARA.
5. *The CCC in Idaho,* Boise, Idaho: Idaho Public Television 2001, videocassette.
6. Report dated, March 13, 1933, OF268, Box 1, 1/33-7/33.
7. Rodney Brink to Louis Howe, June 15, 1933, OF268, Box 1, 1/33-7/33.
8. Superintendent's Report, SP-1, HPSP, undated, NPS/CCC, NARA.
9. "Forest Workers Here: Unit of 200 In Camp at State Farm at Lusscroft," SI, June 16, 1933.
10. "Forestry Camps Change Made In," NJH, October 5, 1933.
11. Ibid., Mastriani, February 4, 2000.
12. Monthly Work Progress Report, SP-1, HPSP, December 8, 1933, ECW/CCC, NARA.
13. "C.C.C. Camp News," SI, December 8, 1933.
14. Monthly Work Progress Report, SP-1, HPSP, December 8, 1933, ECW/CCC, NARA.
15. "Branchville," NJH, December 14, 1933.

16. "Four New Projects Started in Sussex County," NJH, December 28, 1933.
17. Mastriani, February 4, 2000.
18. Nomination, sec. 7, 2-3.
19. "Camp About Ready: Lusscroft Outfit Will Move to High Point Park Soon." SI, November 17, 1933.
20. Mastriani, January 24, 2000.
21. Osborne/CCC, 8.
22. Wurst/CCC, 13-14.
23. Ibid., 80.
24. *Your CCC*, 26-7.
25. Newsletters 1280, September 1939, 1-2.
26. Mastriani, February 14, 2000.
27. "Vast Amount of Good Being Done," NJH, March 1, 1934.
28. Newsletters 1280, February 1938, 4.
29. Newsletter 216, Febraury 1937, 2.
30. Newsletters 1280, June 1938, 6.
31. Perkins, *The Roosevelt I Knew,* 180.
32. "Life in Civilian Conservation Corps Camp," SI, July 21, 1933.
33. Ibid.
34. Mastriani, February 18, 2000.
35. Mastriani, March 9, 2000.
36. Hanisak, December 17, 2000.
37. Mastriani, February 14, 2000.
38. Osborne/CCC, 12-13.
39. Ibid., 19-20.
40. Mastriani, February 14, 2000.
41. Wurst/CCC, 86.

42. Ibid., 181.
43. Ibid., 181-182.
44. Superintendent's Report, SP-1, HPSP, November 1935, NPS/CCC, NARA.
45. Supplementary Camp Inspection Report, SP-8, HPSP, April 9, 1934, ECW/CCC, NARA.
46. "Civilian Camps in New Jersey," NJH, August 17, 1933.
47. Supplementary Camp Inspection Report, SP-8, HPSP, October 2, 1940, ECW/CCC, NARA.
48. *Your CCC*, 25.
49. Wurst/CCC, 106.
50. Ibid., 36-37.
51. Ibid., 72.
52. Ibid., 177-178.
53. Ibid., 104-105.
54. Osborne/CCC, 12.
55. Wurst/CCC, 146.

Chapter 4: Education And Recreation

John Gabriel Hunt, ed., *The Essential Franklin Delano Roosevelt: FDR's Greatest Speeches, Fireside Chats, Messages and Proclamations* (New York: Gramercy Books, 1995), 112.

1. "Sixth Anniversary of C.C.C. Will Be Observed At High Point Camp," SR, April 13, 1939.
2. Merrill, *Roosevelt's Forest Army*, 11.

3. Newsletters 1280, December 1939, 6, "*CCC Establishes School For Uneducated Campers,*" NJH, March 20, 1941.
4. Salmond, *The Civilian Conservation Corps.* 51.
5. Ibid., 48-49.
6. "C.C.C. Camp News." SI, December 8,1933.
7. Wurst/CCC, 49-50.
8. "CCC Enrollment Next Monday," NJH, April 15,1937.
9. Wurst/CCC, 59.
10. Newsletters 1280, April 1939,1.
11. Ibid., February 1938, 4.
12. Merrill, *Roosevelt's Forest,*19.
13. Wurst/CCC, 35-36.
14. Ibid., 49-50.
15. Hanisak, December 17, 2000. During the author's interview with Mr. Hanisak he allowed the author to make a copy of an early resume. A photocopy can be found the in the MVHS CCC project files.
16. *Your CCC,* 24.
17. Osborne/CCC, 46. Camp Inspection Report, SP-8, HPSP, June 23, 1938, ECW/CCC, NARA.
18. Salmond, *The Civilian Conservation Corps.* 144n.
19. Hanisak, December 17, 2000.
20. Wurst/CCC, 178.

21. Salmond, *The Civilian Conservation Corps.* 141-2.
22. Mastriani, February 14, 2000.
23. Wurst/CCC, 151.
24. Osborne/CCC, 19.
25. Ibid., 181.
26. "Sussex," NJH, October 25, 1934.
27. "Smoker Date Changed: Entertainment Planned for CCC Workers in High School." SI, December 12, 1933.
28. "C.C.C. Camp News: Competition in Sports Adds Spice to Life of Foresters," SI, August 25, 1933.
29. "The Week in Sussex," SI, December 22, 1933.
30. "CCC Camps To Observe Sixth Anniversary," NJH, March 23, 1939.
31. Newsletters 1280, October 1938, 1.
32. "CCC Camps Urge Inspection By Public," NJH, November 1, 1934.
33. "Open House Program At High Point Camp," SI April 13, 1939.
34. Newsletters 216, February 1937, 1.
35. Wurst/CCC, 149-151.
36. Ibid., 147.
37. Osborne/CCC, 13.
38. Newsletters 1280, October 1938, 9.
39. E. B. White, "One Man's Meat," *Harpers: An American Retrospective, Writing from Harper's Magazine 1850-1984,* ed. Ann Marie Cunningham,

(New York: Harper's Magazine Foundation, 1985), 55.
40. "C.C.C. Camp News: Competition in Sports Adds Spice to Life of Foresters," SI, August 25, 1933.
41. Newsletters 216, February 1937, 1.
42. Ibid., February 1936
43. Newsletters 1280, January 1938, 8.
44. "Company 1280 Baseball Champs," SI October 1, 1936.
45. Newsletters 1280, May 1938, 1.
46. Newsletters 1280, June 1938.
47. Camp Inspection Report, SP-8, HPSP, April 9, 1934 ECW/CCC, NARA.
48. Mastriani, February 14, 2000.
49. Newsletters 1280, September 1938, 4.
50. Newsletters 1280, June 1938.
51. "No Fingerprints For CCC Enrollee," NJH, February 29, 1940.

Chapter 5: The Golden Age of Parks and Forests

Paul Russell Cutright, *Theodore Roosevelt: The Naturalist* (New York: Harper Brothers, 1956), 72.
Ibid., 175.
1. Nixon, *Franklin D. Roosevelt & Conservation 1911-1945*, vol. 1, 323.
2. Ronald J. Dupont, Jr., letter to author, August 22, 2001
3. "Warren Lauds Use of CCC To Develop Streams," NJH, December 7, 1933.

4. "High Point to Have Music on Sunday, Jun. (sic) 11," PJUG, June 8, 1933
5. Nomination, sec. 8, 3.
6. Minutes, *11th Annual Report of the Commissioners of High Point Park, 1933*, Commissioners of High Point Park, 1923-1945, HPSP.
7. Newsletters 1280, April 1938.
8. "High Point Park Disrepair Mild, Survey Shows," *Newark Sunday Call*, August 29, 1937, various letters to the editor, *Newark Sunday Call, Newark, New Jersey,* September 26 & 30, 1937.
9. "High Point Park Disrepair Mild, Survey Shows," *Newark Sunday Call*, August 29, 1937.
10. Olmsted Brothers, Landscape Architects, *High Point Park, New Jersey: A Report Concerning Its Development* (Brookline, Massachusetts, 1923), 5.
11. Witold Rybczynski, *A Clearing in the Distance: Frederick Law Olmsted and America in the Nineteenth Century* (New York: Scribner, 1999), 409.
12. Minutes, *12th Annual Report of the Commissioners of High Point Park, 1934*, Commissioners of High Point Park, 1923-1945, HPSP.
13. Rybczynski, *A Clearing in the Distance*, 423-426.

14. Ibid.
15. Phoebe Cutler, *The Public Landscape of the New Deal,* (New Haven, Connecticut: Yale University Press, 1985), 65.
16. Minutes, December 12, 1923.
17. John Stanton to J. W. Kempson, February 8,1924, High Point Park Commission Correspondence, 1923-1924, The Private Collection of Wayne McCabe, 83 Main Street, Newton, New Jersey.
18. Minutes, A. R. Kuser to Felix Fuld, November 30, 1923.
19. Olmsted Brothers, *High Point Park, New Jersey.*
20. "Development of High Point Park: Report of Olmstead (sic) Bros., Noted Engineers Makes Many Suggestions," SI, February 8, 1924.
21. Ibid., March 14,1924.
22. Nomination, sec. 8, 3.
23. Box 1, 1/33-7/33, OF268.
24. Robert Fechner to Louis Howe, May 27, 1933, Box 1, 1/33-7/33. OF268.
25. Dupont, August 30, 2000, "John L. Kuser," SI, August 19,1937.
26. *A. Van Doren Honeyman, ed., Northwestern New Jersey: A History of Somerset, Morris, Hunterdon, Warren and Sussex Counties, vol. iv* (New York: Lewis Historical Publishing

Company,1927), 446, Dupont, letter to author, August 22, 2001.
27. Nomination, sec. 8, 7-8, Honeyman, *Northwestern New Jersey*, 446.
28. Charles Pack to FDR, May 3,1933, Box 1, 1/33-7/33, OF268.
29. Owen Winston to FDR, January 19, 1934, President's Personal Files, File No. 316, FDRL, Elliot Roosevelt, ed. *FDR His Personal Letters: Early Years* (New York: Duell, Sloan and Pearce,1947), 484.
30. Hoyt, *We Can Take It*, 24.
31. Olmsted Brothers, *High Point Park, New Jersey*, 18.
32. "New Civilian Conservation Camps," NJH, November 23, 1933.
33. Herbert Evison to C.P. Wilbur, December 28, 1933, President's Personal Files, File No. 316, FDRL.
34. High Point Park Commission, *High Point Park: On the Roof of New Jersey* (Newark, New Jersey: The Essex Press, 1928), 9.
35. Superintendent's Report, SP-1, HPSP, November 1934, NPS/CCC, NARA.
36. Ibid.
37. High Point Park Commission, *High Point Park*, 9.
38. Ronald J. Dupont, Jr. and Kevin Wright, *High Point of the Blue Mountains* (Newton, New Jersey:

Sussex County Historical Society, 1990), 35.
39. Plot Plan, Insurance Schedule Layout, October 1933, General Park History Files, HPSP.
40. Ibid. There are four picnic shelters shown on this map. See Chapter 11 for further discussion about when and who may have constructed them.
41. Camp Inspection Report, SP-8, HPSP, December 1,1934, ECW/CCC, NARA.
42. "Camp About Ready: Lusscroft Outfit Will Move To High Point Park Soon," SI, November 17,1933.
43. Dupont, August 22, 2001.
44. Minutes, February 6, 1934.
45. Dryden Kuser, *History of High Point State Park, Sussex County, New Jersey* 1960, 22. The original copy of this unpublished manuscript is in the possession of the Jane Gibbons Proctor, the daughter of John Gibbons and step-daughter of Dryden Kuser. A photocopy is in the collection of the author's files that were created for this book.
46. "Park Official Takes Charge High Point (sic)," SI April 6,1934.
47. "Deaths and Funerals: John J. Gibbons," PJUG, January 12,1956.
48. Nomination, sec. 8, 2-3.
49. Minutes, March 6, 1934.

50. Mastriani, February 9 and 14, 2000.
51. Minutes, October 3, 1933
52. Salmond, *The Civilian Conservation Corps*, 40.
53. Minutes, March 6, 1934.
54. Ibid.
55. Mastriani, July 30, 2000.
56. Superintendent's Report, SP-8, HPSP, December 1, 1934, NPS/CCC, NARA.
57. Minutes, October 14, 1934.
58. Nomination, sec. 8,5.
59. "High Point Lodge Becomes Hotel," *Hotel World-Review*, April 24, 1937.
60. "*Maps to Aid High Point Visitors To Identify Surrounding Sections*," Unidentified newspaper article, March 13, 1937, The newspaper clip can be found with the author's collection of materials donated to MVHS.
61. Robert Fechner to FDR, January 18, 1937, Box 1, 3/36-97/37, OF268.
62. Memorandum From FDR to All Governors, December 8, 1936, Box 1, 3/36-97/37, OF 268.
63. Minutes, December 14, 1940.
64. Newsletters 1280, April 1938, 3.
65. Minutes, *12th Annual Report of the Commissioners of High Point Park, 1934*.
66. "Deaths and Funerals: John J. Gibbons," PJUG, January 12, 1956,

RoseMary Conklin, interview by author, telephone, October 26, 2000.

Chapter 6: The Roosevelt Tree Army

Wurst/CCC, 52.
Ibid., 115.
1. Ibid., 52.
2. "Lakes Set Like Jewels Amidst High Point Greenery," *Newark Evening News,* September 23,1936.
3. Wurst/CCC, 175.
4. Ibid.,172-173.
5. Ibid.
6. "High Point Notes," SI, August 25,1933.
7. "Four Million Forest Tree Seedlings Ready," NJH, December 28,1933.
8. Ibid.
9. Superintendent's Report, SP-1, HPSP, November 1934, NPS/CCC, NARA.
10. Superintendent's Report, SP-1, HPSP, July 1933, NPS/CCC, NARA.
11. Mastriani, February 28, 2000.
12. Wurst/CCC,115.
13. Ibid.
14. Ibid.,175-176.
15. "Forest Fires in Park And Near Ogdensburg," SI, May 3,1935.
16. "State Park Fire," SI, July 16,1936.
17. "Thirteen Trucks, Car Burned in Garage Fire," SI, November 26,1936.

18. Osborne/CCC, 18.
19. "Fire Destroys CCC Camp Building at High Point," NJH, March 10, 1938.
20. Wurst/CCC, 85.

Chapter 7: We Can Take It!

Wurst/CCC, 101.
Ibid.,135.
1. Newsletters 1280, 1938.
2. Ibid.
3. Wurst/CCC, 125-127.
4. Superintendent's Report, SP-8, HPSP, December 1,1934, NPS/CCC, NARA.
5. Camp Inspection Report, SP-8, HPSP, June 23, 1938, ECW/CCC, NARA.
6. Superintendent's Report, SP-1, HPSP, 1934, NPS/CCC, NARA.
7. Wurst/CCC,168.
8. Ibid.,17.
9. Ibid., 169-170.
10. Ibid., 55.
11. Ibid., 101-102.
12. Ibid., 101.
13. Ibid., 64.
14. Ibid., 135.
15. Minutes, June 19, 1938, December 10,1936.
16. Nomination, sec. 7, 1.
17. Superintendent's Report, SP-1, HPSP, November 1934, NPS/CCC, NARA.
18. Dupont, August 22, 2001.

19. "C.C.C. Camp News," SI, December 8, 1933.
20. Dupont, *High Point of the Blue Mountains*, 6.

Chapter 8: The Splendor Of Our Lakes

Wurst/CCC, 16.
High Point Park brochure, circa 1940, HPSP
1. Cutler, *The Public Landscape of the New Deal*, 65-66.
2. Ronald J. Dupont, Jr., "A History of Mashipacong Pond,", 1994, 9-10. This unpublished manuscript provides a detailed account of why the pond never became part of the state park.
3. Nomination, sec. 7, 23.
4. Mastriani, April 8, 2000, May 29, 2001.
5. Newsletters 1280, May 1938, 5.
6. Nomination, sec. 7, 23. Roberta Bramhall, a long-time visitor to the park believes that the Sawmill facilities were gone before the 1970s and that the shelter was burned down in the 1960s. She believes that the YACC also worked on the Sawmill dam.
7. Olmsted Brothers, *High Point Park, New Jersey*, 10.
8. Dupont, *High Point of the Blue Mountains*, 37.

9. Minutes, October 22, 1935, "Underway at High Point," SR, March 17, 1932.
10. Camp Inspection Report, SP-8, HPSP, June 23, 1938, ECW/CCC, NARA.
11. "Lakes Set Like Jewels Amidst High Point Greenery," *Newark Evening News*, September 23, 1936.
12. Ibid.
13. Nomination, sec. 7, 14.
14. "Want Park Waters Opened For Fishing," NJH, March 21, 1940.
15. Untitled newspaper clip, *Newark Sunday Call*, Newark, New Jersey, April 4, 1937.

Chapter 9: Conveniences To Make A Return To Nature Easier

High Point Park brochure, circa 1940, HPSP Ibid.

1. Sawmill Lake, as it is presently known, was called "Sawmill Pond" in all NPS documents related to High Point during the CCC era, but for the sake of consistency in this manuscript it has been called Sawmill Lake instead of Sawmill Pond.
2. Minutes, February 4, 1936.
3. Dupont, August 22, 2001.
4. John C. Keator, letter to author, August 29, 2001.
5. Dupont, August 22, 2001.

6. Keator, August 29, 2001.
7. The shelter can found on the Sawmill Lake drawings at HPSP archives.
8. "Lakes Set Like Jewels Amidst High Point Greenery," *Newark Evening News*, September 23, 1936.
9. "The Long Brown Path," *New York Evening Post*, August 24, 1936.
10. Minutes, February 4, 1936.

Chapter 10: The High Water Mark

John G. Allee, ed., *Webster's Dictionary* (Ottenheimer Press, 1975), 282.
Wurst/CCC, 55.
1. Cutler, *The Public Landscape of the New Deal*, 84-85.
2. Ibid.
3. Ethan Carr, *Wilderness by Design: Landscape Architecture & The National Park Service* (Lincoln, Nebraska: University of Nebraska Press, 1998), 268.
4. Ibid., 251.
5. Ibid., 290.
6. Ibid., 269.
7. Olmsted Brothers, *High Point Park, New Jersey*, 9.
8. Ibid.
9. Ibid., 8.

10. "Concert at Park," SI, June 9,1933, "High Point to Have Music, Jun. (sic) 11," PJUG, undated news clip, probably June 1933.
11. Osborne/CCC, 39-40.
12. Box 1, 3/1933 - 6/1933,OF 268.
13. Osborne/CCC, 17.
14. Ibid., 8-10, Dupont, August 22, 2001.
15. Ibid.,12.
16. Ibid., 15 and 41.
17. Salmond, *The Civilian Conservation Corps,* 55.
18. Newsletters 1280, January 1939, 4.
19. Newsletters 1280, January 1938, 7.
20. Osborne/CCC, 22.
21. Newsletters 1280, January 1939, 4.
22. "CCC Worker Injures Leg," SI, April 5,1935.
23. Newsletters 1280, February 1938, 8.
24. Newsletters 1280, March 1938, 8.
25. Wurst/CCC, 51.
26. John Keator, Superintendent, HPSP, interview by author, January12, 2000.
27. Minutes, July 22,1939, "Lakes Set Like Jewels Amidst High Point Greenery," *Newark Evening News,* September 23,1936.

Chapter 11: What Might Have Been

Roosevelt, *This I Remember,* 135.

Carr, *Wilderness by Design: Landscape Architecture & The National Park Service*, 123.
1. Olmsted Brothers, *High Point Park, New Jersey*, 11.
2. Ibid., 16.
3. "Explanatory Statement," NPS Master Plan - High Point State Park, 1938, HPSP. In a letter to author dated August 29, 2001 John Keator, the superintendent of HPSP, wrote that he had heard that the large ball field with the bleachers was to have been home to a minor league baseball stadium.
4. "Lakes Set Like Jewels Amidst High Point Greenery," *Newark Evening News*, September 23, 1936.
5. Minutes, October 22, 1935.
6. "Explanatory Statement," NPS Master Plan - High Point State Park, 1938, HPSP.
7. Ronald J. Dupont, Jr., "*High Point: New Jersey's First State Park*," HPSP, 9.
8. Dupont, August 22, 2001 and corrections to original manuscript.
9. "High Point - Conservation Practiced In The Blue Mountains", PJUG, February 27, 1992. This article was included in the Directions special section of the newspaper.
10. Dryden Kuser, Consultant, *Report on High Point State Park*, 1958. The

original copy of this unpublished manuscript is in the possession of the Wayne McCabe. A photocopy of the important sections on the CCC is in the author's files.
11. Ronald J. Dupont, Jr., "Vandalism at High Point Not A New Thing," *Advertiser-News,* North Edition, Vernon, New Jersey, December 11, 1997.
12. Keator, August 29, 2001. In the same letter John Keator noted that efforts had been made in the 1990s to reintroduce the irises at the site but were completely eaten by the Canada Geese.
13. Ronald J. Dupont, Jr., "Off-limits Lake Rutherford Rich In Beauty, History," *Advertiser-News,* North Edition, Vernon, New Jersey, April 16,1998.
14. Nomination, sec. 7, 15.
15. "The Long Brown Path," *New York Post,* New York, New York, January 1937.
16. Nomination, sec. 7,12, Dupont, August 22, 2001,Keator, August 29, 2001, Plot Plan, Insurance Schedule Layout, October 1933, HPSP. It is believed that at the time the CCC arrived at High Point that there were four existing stone picnic shelters. The stone picnic shelters at the main

entrance to the park are two of them. The third shelter is believed to have been on the location where the present log Deer Run shelter is now. What happened to it is not known. A fourth shelter was near the playground area where the comfort station was located at the southern end of the Lake Marcia. That shelter was demolished in 1983. Ronald J. Dupont, Jr. remembered in his manuscript corrections that the late Jim Flynn, the chief ranger at HPSP, believed that the Deer Run shelter was built in the late 1940s.

17. Newsletters 1280, May1938, 2.
18. Nomination, sec. 7, 3.
19. 19., Port Jervis Quadrangle, Topographic Map United States Geological Survey, Washington, D.C., 1906, Olmsted Plan Map, 1923, HPSP, Dryden Kuser Map of High Point State Park, 1947, HPSP. In a letter to author dated August 29, 2001 John Keator, the superintendent of HPSP, wrote that he had heard from predecessors that there had been a red barn on the site when the property was acquired by the park and hence the name Red Barn Pond. It was also believed that pond was built at the same time as the barn. A friend of the author's,

We Can Take It!

Harry Leek, from Port Jervis, New York always called it *Catfish Pond*.

Chapter 12: Memories

Newsletters 1280, December 1935, 7.
Wurst/CCC, 54.
Mastriani, February 4, 2000.
1. Wurst/CCC, 74.
2. Ibid., 84-85.
3. Salmond, *The Civilian Conservation Corps,* 76.
4. Wurst/CCC,166.
5. Ibid., 107 and 109.
6. Newsletters 1280, December 1935, 7.
7. James F. Justin Civilian Conservation Corps Museum, Justin Oral History Center, http://members.aol.com/famjustin/cccroster.html.
8. Superintendent's Report, SP-1, HPSP, January 1936, NPS/CCC, NARA.
9. Wurst/CCC, 16.
10. John P. Malina to William Cerynik, Superintendent, High Point State Park, June 2,1982, CCC Files, HPSP.
11. Wurst/CCC, 99.
12. Ibid., 57.
13. Nomination, sec. 7, 1, 3, 13 and 19.
14. Wurst/CCC, 136.
15. Ibid., 58.

16. Ibid., 42.
17. Ibid., 174.
18. Mastriani, February 4, 2000 and February 18, 2000.
19. Wurst/CCC, 106.
20. Ibid., 51.
21. Ibid., 170.
22. Ibid., 171.
23. Thomas Segar, interview by author, August 19, 2000.
24. Wurst/CCC, 56-57.
25. Ibid., 66-67.
26. Thomas Segar, interview by author, August 19, 2000, Dupont, *High Point of the Blue Mountains*, 27.
27. Wurst/CCC, 187.
28. Ibid., 183.
29. Ibid., 67-68.
30. Mastriani, February 18, 2000.
31. Newsletters 216, February 1936.
32. Wurst/CCC, 188-189.
33. John P. Malina to William Cerynik, Superintendent, High Point State Park, June 2, 1982, CCC Files, HPSP.
34. Wurst/CCC, 112-113.
35. Ibid., 94-98.
36. Ibid., 187.
37. Osborne/CCC, 46.
38. Ibid.
39. Wurst/CCC, 187-188.
40. Osborne/CCC, 26.

41. Nicholas Hanisak, interview by author, tape recording, December 17, 2000, MVHS.
42. Wurst/CCC, 70.
43. Ibid., 87.
44. Ibid., 130.
45. John Spinarelli to Mary Norton, March 19, 1935, Camp Inspection Report, SP-1, HPSP, ECW/CCC, NARA.
46. O.W. Brown to C. H. Kenlan, March 25, 1935, Camp Inspection Report, SP-1, HPSP, ECW/CCC, NARA.
47. Wladyslaw Kmiolek to CCC Bureau, August 2, 1938, Camp Inspection Report, SP-8, HPSP, ECW/CCC, NARA.
48. Red Sacco, interview by author, March 12, 2000.
49. Dupont, *High Point of the Blue Mountains*, 15.
50. Florence Fuller, letter to author, undated.
51. "Forestry Camps Change Made In," NJH, October 9, 1933.
52. Newsletters 1280, October 1938, 3.
53. Newsletters 1280, February 1939.
54. Newsletters 1280, January 1939. "DI" represents Department of Interior and "OD" specifies olive drab, the color of the CCC uniforms.
55. Wurst/CCC, 10 and 32.
56. Ibid., 54 and 75.

57. Ibid., 53.
58. Ibid., 92.
59. Ibid., 118.
60. Ibid., 139-140.
61. Ibid., 73.
62. Ibid., 90-91.

Chapter 13: Good Will Towards All And Malice Toward None

Newsletters 216, February 1937, 2.
Newsletters 1280, December 1940.
1. Camp Inspection Report File, SP-8, HPSP, ECW/CCC.
2. Camp Inspection Report File, SP-1, HPSP, ECW/CCC.
3. The only complete collection of newsletters from both companies are located at the Center of Research Libraries in Chicago, Illinois. A microfiche copy has been purchased and is now in the High Point State Park's CCC archives.
4. Newsletters 216, February 1937, 1.
5. Ibid., 5.
6. Ibid.
7. Ibid.
8. Newsletters 1280, January 1938, 14.
9. Newsletters 1280, February 1938, 14.

Chapter 14: Grateful Communities And Malice Toward None

"Park Camp Enrollee Rewarded for Good Citizenship by DAR:Robert Drimmer Given Medal at Anniversary Dinner at High Point," SI, April 11, 1940.
Mastriani, February 18, 2000.
Zita Innella, interview by author, January 13, 2000.
"CCC Lad on Rampage: Stickup of Port Jervis Cigar Store is Night's Climax," SI, April 7, 1938.

1. Cohen, *The Tree Army*, 10.
2. Mastriani, February 4, 2000.
3. *Population Data 1920-1940, Sussex County*, Sussex County Department of Planning, Development and Human Services, Newton, New Jersey.
4. D. N. Raynor & R. B. Coler, *Where the Rivers Meet: Golden Jubilee 1907-1957* (Port Jervis, New York: Golden Jubilee Committee, 1957) 13.
5. Salmond, *The Civilian Conservation Corps*, 111.
6. Ibid.
7. "Montague," NJH, April 5, 1934.
8. Mead Stapler, letter to author, August 21, 2001 and corrections to original manuscript.
9. "C.C.C. Camp News," SI, December 8, 1933.
10. Newsletters 1280, May 1938, 3.

11. "C.C.C. Camp News," SI, December 8,1933.
12. Ibid.
13. "Citizenship Medals to High Point Enrollees," SI, December 26,1940.
14. Park Camp Enrollee Rewarded for Good Citizenship by DAR," SI, April 11, 1940.
15. "CCC Joins Trooper Today In Search For Horace Dunn,"1941. PJUG, August 5,1941.
16. "Fire Destroys Camp Sussex Mess Hall Monday Afternoon," PJUG, August 5, 1941.
17. Newsletters 1280, September 1940.
18. Wurst/CCC, 47-48.
19. Ibid., 18.
20. Louis Cherepy, Interview by author. Telephone, January 26, 2000. Mead Stapler, letter to author, August 21,2001 and corrections to original manuscript. Mead Stapler has suggested that the police protection was as much for the CCC boys as from the CCC boys because Franklin was then considered to be a very rough mining town.
21. Newsletters 1280, May 1938.
22. CCC Lad on Rampage: Stickup Port Jervis Cigar Store is Night's Climax," SI, April 7,1938, "Holdup Man From

CCC Camp Nabbed In Hornbeck Store," PJUG, April 1, 1938.
23. "Montague Man Found In Auto in Trenton," SI, August 24, 1934.
24. "7 Burned to Death in Boston Back Bay," NJH, April 11, 1946, "Boston Arsonist Was CCC Camper At High Point," NJH, April 18, 1946. The author wishes to acknowledge Ronald J. Dupont Jr. who found this strange and sad story during his research on the park and shared it with the author.
25. "Boston Arsonist Was CCC Camper At High Point," NJH, April 18, 1946.
26. Ibid.
27. Newsletters 216, February 1936.
28. Ibid.
29. Newsletters 1280, June 1938.
30. Mastriani, February 4, 2000.
31. Leslie Crine, interview by author, January 7, 2000.
32. Zita Innella, interview by author, January 13, 2000.
33. Louis Cherepy, interview by author. Telephone, January 26, 2000.
34. Camp Inspection Report, SP-8, HPSP, June 23, 1938, ECW/CCC, NARA.

Chapter 15: A Rendezvous With Destiny

Hunt, *The Essential Franklin Delano Roosevelt*, 113.

Forrest Gaz, Enrollee, Company 128, Hinsdale, Massachusetts, Found at Civilian Conservation Corps Resources on the Internet at http://pages.prodigy.com/reunion links.htm. (Cited September 1, 2001) The original bugle melody that this was sung to was written during the Civil War.

1. Salmond, *The Civilian Conservation Corps*, 68-69.
2. "Favors C.C.C. Camps," SI, April 29, 1937.
3. Salmond, *The Civilian Conservation Corps*, 104.
4. Box 4, 3/36-9/37, OF268.
5. Many letters can be found in the OF268 files from individual camps asking for a visit by the president or giving him some gift.
6. "*Interesting CCC Facts*," Handout, Promised Land State Park, Greentown, Pennsylvania.
7. Newsletters 1280, December 1935, 7.
8. Salmond, *The Civilian Conservation Corps*, 151.
9. Ibid., 63, 207.
10. Ibid., 219.
11. "Q.E.D." NJH, December 21, 1933.

12. "Major Freelance: As He Sees Things," NJH, April 5, 1934.
13. Salmond, *The Civilian Conservation Corps,* 192.
14. Ibid., 128-129.
15. Newsletters 1280, May 1938, 1.
16. Salmond, *The Civilian Conservation Corps,* 193.
17. Ibid., 210.
18. Newsletters 1280, 1940-1941.
19. Camp Inspection Report, SP-8, HPSP, October 16 & 18,1941, ECW/CCC, NARA.
20. Ibid.
21. Minutes, November 15, 1941.
22. Ibid.
23. Nicholas Hanisak, interview by author, tape recording, December 17, 2000.
24. John Keator, Superintendent, HPSP, interview by author, January 12, 2000.
25. Mastriani, January 5, 2001.
26. John Keator, Superintendent, HPSP, interview by author, December 27, 2000.
27. Rick Strain, letter to author, March 5, 2001.
28. Superintendents Monthly Narratives 1939-1947, Superintendents Annual Reports 1939-1967, CRM Archives, Central Files, Boxes 2 & 3, Administrative Records, Morristown

National Historic Park, Morristown, New Jersey.
29. "Civilian Conservation Corps activities in Morris County," July 14, 1983, CRM Archives, Central Files Box 5, CCC, 1933-1940, Morristown National Historic Park, Morristown, New Jersey.
30. Salmond, *The Civilian Conservation Corps,* 213.
31. Newsletters 1280, December 1939, 4.
32. Minutes, November 15,1941.
33. Minutes, August 8,1942.
34. Records of Liquidation Unit, 1933-1942, HPSP file, ECW/CCC, NARA.
35. "To Sell Buildings At CCC Camp SP8," NJH, June 6,1946.
36. 1951 Aerial Survey of New Jersey, Department of Environmental Protection, Tidelands Management Bureau, Trenton, New Jersey.
37. Ronald Slate, interview by author, January 8, 2001.
38. Kuser, *History of High Point State Park,* 27.
39. "Reformatory Center in High Point Park Opposed in Sussex," NJH, December 9,1954, "Reformatory Plan Gets Opposition of Wantage, NJH, December 16,1954.
40. 1954, 1961 and 1971 Aerial Surveys of New Jersey, Department of

Environmental Protection, Tidelands Management Bureau, Trenton, New Jersey, Rick Strain, letter to author, March 5, 2001. In this case the aerial photography does not match the recollections of so many because in 1961 only two buildings were still standing. They remained until 1969. If one of them was indeed used for the correctional facility it would have had to been taken down after 1969 but before 1971 when the buildings are gone from the photographs.

41. Rick Strain, letter to author, March 5, 2001. The author does not agree with Mr. Strain on this issue. He believes that the existing lunch building was not built by the CCC but rather during the CCC era. It is similar in design to the oil and paint building which is known to have been built by the park.
42. John Keator, Superintendent, HPSP, interview by author, December 27, 2000.
43. Louis Cherepy, interview by author. Telephone, January 26, 2000.
44. Osborne/CCC, 36, 37 and 41.
45. Cohen, *The Tree Army,* 177.
46. Merrill, *Roosevelt's Forest,* 196.
47. Ibid.,151.
48. Cohen, *The Tree Army,* 152.
49. Merrill, *Roosevelt's Forest,* 151.

50. Cohen, *The Tree Army*, 152.
51. Ibid.
52. Kuser, *History of High Point State Park*, 22.
53. Program, 50th Anniversary Event, Rededication Ceremony: CCC Statue, June 5, 1999, Stokes State Forest, Branchville, New Jersey.
54. Osborne/CCC, 45.

Appendix

Roosevelt, *This I Remember*, 136.
"Sixth Anniversary of C.C.C. Will Be Observed At High Point Camp," SR, April 13, 1939.

BIBLIOGRAPHIC ESSAY

The author's entire collection of notes, letters, photocopies and various records generated by this project were placed in four binders and given to the Minisink Valley Historical Society at the end of the project. Copies of most of the footnoted materials can be found in this collection at its library archives.

There were a number of sources that were of great value to this project with regard to researching an individual CCC camp. In particular were *The General Records of the Emergency Conservation Work and Civilian Conservation Corps, 1933-1942,* which can be found in Records Group 35, at the National Archives and Records Administration in College Park, Maryland. Monthly work progress reports, inspection reports and various division reports are also available there. *The Records of the National Park Service*, Records Group 79 can also be found at College Park and of particular interest are the superintendent's regular reports. Before using the records researchers should consult the two indexes of those collections including the *Preliminary Inventory of the Records of the Civilian Conservation Corps* compiled by Harold T. Pinkett, and the *Preliminary Inventory of the Records of the*

Peter Osborne

Civilian Conservation Corps edited by Douglas Helms.

The *Official File on the Civilian Conservation Corps* at the Franklin Delano Roosevelt Library provided a great deal of material on the national developments concerning the CCC and also contain correspondence that occasionally relates to individual camps or some problem related specifically to a camp. The personal correspondence of the president can also provide insights into particular camps or members of Congress who were lobbying for camps or against the closure of camps.

A collection of CCC company newsletters for most of the camps across America are housed in the Center for Research Libraries which is located in Chicago. Anyone interested in researching a particular camp's operation should obtain a microfiche copy of the records from the organization. They provide the single best contemporary source of the workings of a typical camp and give a flavor of what living in a camp was like. A complete copy of High Point's newsletters are available in the park's archives.

Another excellent contemporary resource on the CCC is the booklet entitled *Your CCC: A Handbook for Enrollees* and Ray Hoyt's book *We Can Take It: A Short Story of the CCC*. Both of them would have been available to enrollees when they were in the CCC. The National Association Civilian Conservation Corps Alumni has an excellent collection and web page.

Compiled on their web page is listing of all of the camps and the companies that worked in them. It publishes an excellent newsletter and has a good gift shop.

One of the most fascinating resources is the CCC boys themselves who for the most part had remarkably clear memories of the Roosevelt Tree Army. For this project the author interviewed several of them and duplicate copies of the transcriptions and tapes are in the MVHS and HPSP collections. Individual CCC service records can be obtained by writing the National Personnel Records Center in St. Louis, Missouri.

Local newspapers provided important perspectives on the CCC, particularly in the early years when the organization was new to the American people. As the years went by the work projects and the men who were doing them became part of the nation's fabric and so did not attract as much attention. In later years they often provided valuable data when major projects were completed.

For a general history of the CCC, Stan Cohen's *The Tree Army: A Pictorial History of the Civilian Conservation Corps, 1933-1942;* Perry Merrill's *Roosevelt's Forest Army: A History of the Conservation Corps 1933-1942* and John Salmond's *The Civilian Conservation Corps, 1933-1942: A New Deal Case Study* are all good sources. For a contemporary look at the CCC Ray Hoyt's *We Can Take It: A Short Story of the CCC* is an excellent source. An excellent book that relates the story of the National Park Service and the CCC is Ethan Carr's *Wilderness by Design: Landscape Architecture & The National Park Service*.

Another important source of CCC material was the Internet. Any search engine will turn up the web pages of many state government agencies across the country which have materials on the CCC and the camps that were located there. Another place to look for CCC materials is on http://www.ebay.com. This web site regularly contains CCC items that are being auctioned of by private individuals. It would be impossible to keep a list of all of the videotaped materials that are available but several do stand out, including *The CCC in Idaho* produced by Idaho Public Television, in 2000 and *The CCC: Roosevelt's Tree Army - The Story of the Civilian Conservation Corps during the Great Depression* by the State of Georgia's Department of Natural Resources in 1997.

There are several agencies that have displays of the CCC in the region. By far the most important collection is located at Promised Land State Park in Greentown, Pennsylvania. This museum has an excellent collection of materials relating not only to the CCC camp that was located there but memorabilia that was used in other CCC camps as well. An annual reunion of former CCC enrollees is held in the park every August. There is also the New York State CCC Museum; Gilbert Lake State Park, Laurens, New

York; the Pennsylvania Lumber Museum in Galeton, Pennsylvania and the Northeast Civilian Conservation Corps Museum. It is located at the Shenipsit State Forest which is operated by Connecticut Department of Enviornmental Protection at 166 Chesnut Hill Road in Stafford Springs, Connecticut. An original CCC camp building serves as headquarters for the NACCCA's northeastern region's museum collection.

On High Point State Park's history, Ronald J. Dupont Jr.'s collective body of work remains the standard. His nomination of the park for listing on the National Register of Historic Places and his *High Point of the Blue Mountains* are the most important resources on the history of the park ever compiled. He has written a number of other articles about the park over the years and many of them are listed in the bibliography. The park does not have a great deal of material concerning its history, perhaps one file drawer. Hopefully in the future the park will make a comprehensive effort to reach out to outlying communities to gather as much material about it as is possible because there is a much available in many of the region's historical societies.

Another important history of the park that was found and previously unknown to historians was one written by Dryden Kuser in 1960. It is entitled *History of High Point State Park, Sussex County, New Jersey*. He also drafted a detailed inventory of the park for the state in 1958 entitled *Report on High Point State Park*. In it he made recommendations for the park's future. Both reports provide a valuable look at the park in the late 1950s and 1960 and are the only surviving historical materials from that period. Because he was the son of Anthony Kuser, they also provide the family's view of the property and its history. William Wurst wrote a history of the park entitled *At The Top of New Jersey*. Both his book and Ronald J. Dupont, Jr.'s book are available for sale from the Friends of High Point State Park.

High Point State Park's archives have a fairly complete collection of CCC maps that number more than 100. Few of the original sketches remain but there are numerous blueprints. Almost all of the projects are represented. Curiously, the most important park-constructed projects are not well represented in the collection. There is a complete collection of blueprints of the Grey Rock Inn but there is not a single drawing of the Iris Inn. There are no drawings of the bathrooms at Lake Marcia or the picnic shelters. A complete set of drawings for the High Point Monument are in the collection. Witold Rybczynski's *A Clearing in the Distance: Frederick Law Olmsted and America in the Nineteenth Century* provides information on the Olmsted connection to High Point.

On FDR there is a tremendous wealth of material but his interest in the CCC is well documented in *Franklin D. Roosevelt &*

Conservation 1911-1945, edited by Edgar Nixon. For a general treatment of FDR during the Depression and war years David Kennedy's *Freedom from Fear: The American People in Depression and War 1929-1945* is an excellent source. On the Depression one of the most poignant books is Studs Terkel's *Hard Times: An Oral History of the Great Depression* which gives one a sense of how bad the Depression was on a personal level for many people. The best narrative history of the Depression is T.H. Watkins' *The Hungry Years* which does an admirable job of describing the nation's woes during the 1930s.

BIBLIOGRAPHY

Books

A Guide to Stokes State Forest. Branchville, New Jersey: Stokes State Forest, 1975.

Allee, John G. ed. *Webster's Dictionary,* Ottenheimer Press, 1975.

Allen, Frederick Lewis. *Since Yesterday: The 1930s in America: September 3, 1929 - September 3, 1939.* New York: Harper & Row, 1940.

Appalachian Trail Guide to New York-New Jersey, 4th ed. Harpers Ferry, West Virginia: Appalachian Trail Conference, 1998.

Berg, Shary Page. *The Civilian Conservation Corps: Shaping the Forests and Parks of Massachusetts - A Statewide Survey of Civilian Conservation Corps Resources.* Boston: Department of Environmental Management, 1999.

Blum, John, Edmund Morgan, Willie Lee Rose, Arthur Schlesinger, Kenneth Stampp, C. Vann Woodward. *The National Experience: A History of the United States since 1865,* 3rd ed. New York: Harcourt Brace Jovanovich, 1973.

Carr, Ethan. *Wilderness by Design: Landscape Architecture & The National Park Service.*

Lincoln, Nebraska: University of Nebraska Press, 1998.

Cohen, Stan. *The Tree Army: A Pictorial History of the Civilian Conservation Corps, 1933-1942,* rev. ed. Missoula, Montana: Pictorial Histories Publishing Company, 1996.

Cutler, Phoebe. *The Public Landscape of the New Deal.* New Haven, Connecticut: Yale University Press, 1985.

Cutright, Paul Russell. *Theodore Roosevelt: The Naturalist.* New York: Harper Brothers, 1956.

Daniels, Jane, ed., *New Jersey Walk Book.* New York: New York-New Jersey Trail Conference, 1998.

Daniels, Jane, ed., *New York Walk Book.* New York: New York-New Jersey Trail Conference, 1998.

Dupont, Jr., Ronald J. and Kevin Wright. *High Point of the Blue Mountains.*

Newton, New Jersey: Sussex County Historical Society, 1990.

Frome, Michael. *Whose Woods These Are: The Story of the National Forests,* Garden City, New York: Doubleday & Company, 1962.

Guide to the Appalachian Trail in New York and New Jersey, Publication No. 2, 7th Edition. New York: New York-New Jersey Trail Conference,1972.

Helms, Douglas. Ed., *Preliminary Inventory of the Records of the Civilian Conservation*

Corps. Washington D. C.: National Archives and Records Administration, 1980.

High Point Park Commission. *High Point Park: On the Roof of New Jersey.* Newark, New Jersey: The Essex Press, 1928.

Hoyt, Ray. *We Can Take It: A Short Story of the CCC.* New York: American Book Company, 1935.

Hunt, John Gabriel. ed., *The Essential Franklin Delano Roosevelt: FDR's Greatest Speeches, Fireside Chats, Messages and Proclamations.* New York: Gramercy Books, 1995.

Honeyman, A. Van Doren. ed. *Northwestern New Jersey: A History of Somerset, Morris, Hunterdon, Warren and Sussex Counties. vol. iv.* New York: Lewis Historical Publishing Company,1927.

Kennedy, David M. *Freedom from Fear: The American People in Depression and War 1929-1945.* New York: Oxford University, 1999.

Kennedy, Steele com., Bertrand Boucher, John Cunningham, Patricia Merlo, *The New Jersey Almanac 1964-1965.* Upper Montclair, New Jersey: The New Jersey Almanac, Inc, & Trenton Evening Times, Trenton, New Jersey, 1964.

King, Lawrence, ed. *Our Wantage Heritage: By People of Wantage.* Baltimore, Maryland: Gateway Press, 1976.

Leuchtenburg, William E. *Franklin D. Roosevelt and the New Deal.* New York: Harper and Row, 1963.

Matchette, Robert B., com., Anne B. Eales, Lance J. Fischer, Brenda B.

Kepley, Judith A. Kouchky, *Guide to Federal Records in the National Archives of the United States, Volume 1, Record Groups 1-170,* 2nd edition. Washington, D.C.: National Archives and Records Administration, 1998.

Merrill, Perry H. *Roosevelt's Forest Army: A History of the Conservation Corps 1933-1942.* Barre, Vermont: Northright Studio Press, 1981.

Moley, Raymond. *The First New Deal.* New York: Harcourt, Brace & World, 1966.

Nixon, Edgar B, ed., *Franklin D. Roosevelt & Conservation 1911-1945.* 2 vols.

Washington: US Government Printing Office, 1957.

Osborne, Peter *The Port Jervis Area Heritage Commission Salutes The Gilded Age of Port Jervis.* Port Jervis, New York: Port Jervis Area Heritage Commission, 1992.

Perkins, Frances, *The Roosevelt I Knew.* New York: Harper and Row,1946.

Pinchot, Gifford, *Breaking New Ground* Washington D.C.: Island Press, 1987.

Pinkett, Harold T. *Preliminary Inventory of the Records of the Civilian Conservation Corps,* Preliminary Inventory No. 11. Washington

D. C.: The National Archives of the United States, 1948.

Raynor, D. N., & R. B. Coler, *Where the Rivers Meet: Golden Jubilee 1907-1957.* Port Jervis, New York: Golden Jubilee Committee, 1957.

Reiger John F., *American Sportsmen and the Origins of Conservation.* New York: Winchester Press, 1975.

Roosevelt, Eleanor. *This I Remember.* New York: Harper Brothers, 1949.

Roosevelt, Elliot. ed. *FDR His Personal Letters: Early Years.* New York: Duell, Sloan and Pearce, 1947.

Rosen, Eliot, *Hoover, Roosevelt and The Brains Trust: From Depression to New Deal.* New York: Columbia University Press, 1977.

Rybczynski, Witold, *A Clearing in the Distance: Frederick Law Olmsted and America in the Nineteenth Century.* New York: Scribner, 1999.

Salmond, John A. *The Civilian Conservation Corps, 1933-1942: A New Deal Case Study.* Durham, North Carolina: Duke University Press, 1967.

Terkel, Studs. *Hard Times: An Oral History of the Great Depression.* New York: Pantheon Books, 1986.

Your CCC: A Handbook for Enrollees. Washington, D.C.: Happy Days Publishing Co., Inc., 1940.

Watkins, T.H. *The Hungry Years: A Narrative History of the Great Depression in America.* New York: Henry Holt & Co., 1999.

Wurst, William J., *At the Top of New Jersey: A Brief History of the High Point State Park.* Sussex, New Jersey: Friends of High Point State Park, 1994.

Articles

Dale, Frank. "Good Guys, Bad Guys, Memories of the Civilian Conservation Corps." Book No. 8, *Warren County Chronicles.* (Washington, NJ: Eckert Printing, April 1999).

Dupont, Jr., Ronald J. "Vandalism at High Point Not A New Thing." (Vernon, New Jersey: *Advertiser-News*, North Edition December 11, 1997).

_____. "Off-limits Lake Rutherford Rich In Beauty, History." Vernon, New Jersey: *Advertiser-News,* North Edition, April 16, 1998.

"High Point - Conservation Practiced In The Blue Mountains." (Port Jervis, New York: *The Union Gazette*), February 27, 1992.

Leake, Fred, and Ray Carter, *Roosevelt's Tree Army: A Brief History of the Civilian Conservation Corps,* 6th ed, St. Louis, Missouri: National Association of the Civilian Conservation Corps Alumni, 1987.

Management Assistant to Superintendent, "Civilian Conservation Corps activities in Morris County," July 14, 1983, CRM Archives, Central File Box 5, CCC, 1933-1940, (Morristown, New Jersey: Morristown National Historic Park.)

Promised Land State Park. "Interesting CCC Facts." Greentown, Pennsylvania, undated.

"Sharing Memories," Walpack News, Walpack, New Jersey: Walpack Historical Society, March 1989.

White, E. B. "One Man's Meat." *Harpers: An American Retrospective, Writing from Harper's Magazine 1850-1984.* ed. Ann Marie Cunningham.

New York: Harper's Magazine Foundation, 1985.

Reports & Unpublished Manuscripts

Dupont, Jr. Ronald J., "*A History of Mashipacong Pond.* 1994.

_____., "High Point: New Jersey's First State Park."

_____., "Nomination for Inclusion of High Point State Park on the Register." National Register of Historic Places, Registration Form, Sussex County Historical Society, Newton, New Jersey, 1992.

Hubbard, Adam, *"Gifford Pinchot's Influence on FDR and the Formation of the Civilian Conservation Corps,"* Capping paper, Marist College, 1996.

Kuser, Dryden. *Report on High Point State Park.* 1958.

_____., *History of High Point State Park, Sussex County, New Jersey.* 1960.

Olmsted Brothers, *Landscape Architects. High Point Park, New Jersey: A Report Concerning Its Development.* Brookline, Massachusetts. 1923.

Osborne, Peter. ed. "We Can Take It: The Roosevelt Tree Army at High Point State Park 1933-1941: Interviews With Former Civilian Conservation Corps Enrollees, Camp Kuser, Companies 216 & 1280." vol. 1. rev. ed. 2000.

_____., "We Can Take It: The Roosevelt Tree Army at High Point State Park 1933-1941: Interviews With Former Civilian Conservation Corps Enrollees, Camp Kuser, Companies 216 & 1280." vol. 2. rev. ed. 2000.

Newspapers & Magazines

Advertiser-News, Vernon, New Jersey, 1997-1998.

Hotel World-Review, 1937.

Newark Sunday Call, Newark, New Jersey, 1937.

Newark Evening News, 1936-1937.

New Jersey Herald, Newton, New Jersey, 1933-1946.

New York Evening Post, 1936.

New York Herald Tribune, 1937.

New York Post, New York, New York, 1936-1937.

New York Times, 1937.

Port Jervis Union Gazette, Port Jervis, New York, 1933-1941.

Sussex Independent, Sussex, New Jersey, 1933-1941.

Sussex Register, Newton, New Jersey, 1933-1941.

Wantage Recorder, Wantage, New Jersey, 1933-1941.

Unidentified newspaper clips in the High Point State Park archives and the Minisink Valley Historical Society archives

Letters

Dupont, Jr., Ronald J., Letters to author, January 2000 - August 2001.

Fuller, Florence. Letter to author, undated.

Keator, John, Letters to author, January 2000 - September 2001.

Malina, John P. to William Cerynik, Superintendent, High Point State Park, June 2, 1982, CCC Files.

Mastriani, Albert. Letters to author, January 2000 - July 2001.
Stapler, Mead. Letter to author, August 21, 2001.
Strain, Rick. Letter to author, March 5, 2001.
Toltin, Joseph to High Point State Park, September 24, 1982.

Oral Interviews

Bello, Nancy Interview by author. January 7, 2000.
Cherepy, Louis. Interview by author. Telephone, January 26, 2000.
Conklin, RoseMary, Interview by author. Telephone, October 26, 2000.
Crine, Leslie. Interview by author. January 7, 2000.
Hanisak, Nicholas. Interview by author. Tape recording. December 17, 2000.
Innella, Zita. Interview by author. January 13, 2000.
Keator, John. Superintendent, High Point State Park, Interviews by author.
January 2000 - January 2001.
Lutz, Peter. Interview by author. May 2, 2000.
Sacco, Red. Interview by author. March 12, 2000.
Segar, Thomas. Interview by author. August 19, 2000.
Slate, Ronald. Interview by author. January 8, 2001.

Theide, Neil. Interview by author. October 24, 2000.

Maps

High Point to Mid-Kittatinny. Appalachian Trail Map Set No. 5. New York-New York: New Jersey Trail Conference for the Appalachian Trail Conference. 1998.
Map of High Point State Park. Dryden Kuser, 1947.
North Kittatiny Trails. New York: New York-New Jersey Trail Conference, 1988.
Olmsted Plan Map. 1923, HPSP.
Port Jervis South Quadrangle, Topographic Map, United States Geological Survey, Washington, D.C., 1906.
Port Jervis South Quadrangle, Topographic Map, United States Geological Survey, Washington, D.C., 1969, photo-revised 1983.

Archives

Center for Research Libraries, 6050 S. Kenwood Avenue, Chicago, Illinois. The Civilian Conservation Corps Camp Papers. Civilian Conservation Corps Company 216 & Company 1280.
Department of Environmental Protection.

501 East State Street, Trenton, New Jersey
Division of Parks of Parks & Forestry,
State Parks Service, New Jersey
    Official Park & Forest Files
    Statewide CCC History Files
New Jersey Historic Preservation Office
    High Point National Register Nomination Files
    Statewide CCC Files
Aerial Photo and Map Library
Tidelands Management Bureau
Trenton, New Jersey
    1939-1974 Aerial Surveys of New Jersey

Franklin Delano Roosevelt Library, Hyde Park, New York.
    Official File on the Civilian Conservation Corps, OF 268, 1933-1942.
    President's Personal Files, 1933-1945.
High Point State Park, Visitors Center,
Route 23, Sussex, New Jersey.
    Audio tapes of former CCC enrollees
    Annual Reports, 1923-1941
    CCC History Files
    CCC Maps and Blueprints Collection in CCC map cabinet General Park History Files.
    Guides to park's trail system - 1980 - present
    Map of High Point State Park, Dryden Kuser, 1947.

Minutes, Commissioners of High Point Park, 1923-1945.
Olmsted Plan Map, 1923.
Park brochures - c.1937 - 2001.
Photograph archives
Plot Plan, Insurance Schedule Layout, October 1933.

Minisink Valley Historical Society,
138 Pike Street, Port Jervis, New York.
CCC At High Point Collection
CCC History Files
High Point State Park History Files
Photograph Archives

Morristown National Historic Park,
31 Washington Place, Morristown, New Jersey
Central File Series - CCC 1933-940
Superintendents Monthly Narratives 1939-1947
Superintendents Annual Reports 1939-1967,

National Archives and Records Administration, 8601 Adelphi Road, College Park, Maryland
Records of the Civilian Conservation Corps, Records Group 35
General Records of the Emergency Conservation Work and Civilian Conservation Corps,1933-1942
Work Progress Reports, 1933-1942
Division of Investigations, Camp Inspection Reports, 1933-1942

We Can Take It!

Records of the CCC Liquidation Unit - 1933-1953

Records of the National Park Service, Records Group 79

Superintendent's Reports, 1933-1942

National Personnel Records Center, 111 Winnebago Street, St. Louis, Missouri.

Individual Service Records for CCC Enrollees

Wayne McCabe Collection, 83 Main Street, Newton, New Jersey

High Point Park Commission Correspondence, 1923-1924, High Point State Park Post Card Collection Records of the High Point Park Commission & High Point State Park

Videotapes

"The CCC in Idaho." Boise, Idaho: Idaho Public Television, 2001. Videocassette.

"The CCC: Roosevelt's Tree Army - The Story of the Civilian Conservation Corps during the Great Depression." Atlanta, Georgia: State of Georgia epartment of Natural Resources, 1997. Videocassette.

World Wide Web Sites

Civilian Conservation Corps Resources on the Internet. (Cited September 1, 2001,

http://pages.prodigy.com/reunion links.htm.)
Idaho Public Television, (Cited September 1, 2001) www.idahoptv.org/outdoors/shows/ccc/index.html.
James F. Justin Civilian Conservation Corps Museum, Justin Oral History Center, (Cited September 1, 2001) http://members.aol.com/famjustin/cccroster.html.
National Association Civilian Conservation Corps Alumni,
(Cited September 1, 2001) http://www.cccalumni.org.

CCC Alumni Organizations

National Association Civilian Conservation Corps Alumni, 16 Hancock Avenue, St. Louis, Missouri 63125
Brotherhood of XCCCers, 17833 Jameston Way, Lutz, Florida 33549-6678

Regional CCC Museums

New York State CCC Museum, Gilbert Lake State Park, Laurens, New York.
Northeast Civilian Conservation Corps Museum, Shenipsit State Forest, Connecticut Department of Environmental

Protection 166 Chesnut Hill Road Stafford Springs, Connecticut.

Pennsylvania Lumber Museum, Galeton, Pennsylvania.

Promised Land State Park, Park Museum, Route 390, Greentown, Pennsylvania 18426.

Miscellaneous

High Point State Park. *"Historical Chronology,"* 1974.

Promised Land State Park. *"Interesting CCC Facts."*

Population Data 1920-1940, Sussex County, Sussex County Department of Planning, Development and Human Services, Newton, New Jersey.

Program, 50th Anniversary Event, Rededication Ceremony: CCC Statue, June 5, 1999, Stokes State Forest, Branchville, New Jersey.

ACKNOWLEDGMENTS

A project of this magnitude could not have been accomplished without the help of many people, institutions, government agencies and organizations. First and foremost I must acknowledge my wife, Janis, who edited this copy, read microfilmed copies of newspapers, drove to many Civilian Conservation Corps projects with me and endured my constant dinner conversations about President Franklin Delano Roosevelt, the New Deal and the CCC. She gave up parts of vacations to visit archives that had CCC materials in them. Without her interest, forbearance and letting me slide on some of my chores, this book would not have been possible.

I must also mention my son Ryan who had to listen to history lessons about the CCC, visit CCC sites and was the only student in his social study class who knew what the *Roosevelt Tree Army* was when his teacher asked. My stepdaughter Megan has also become increasingly enamored with President Franklin Roosevelt and Eleanor Roosevelt in the last few years as I have often talked about my project.

I am in the debt of John Keator, superintendent of High Point State Park who was always gracious and helpful during my many visits to his office and the park during the project. He was willing to share his knowledge and make the park's resources available to me. His staff was helpful and patient in spite of my repeated visits and inquiries. They include Carol J. Forbes, Renee Bonham, Philip Fancher and Kate Monahan.

I am especially grateful to Ron Dupont for many professional courtesies extended to me over the years. His book, *High Point of the Blue Mountains,* co-authored by Kevin Wright, is the single best resource on the general history of the park. His nomination to place High Point State Park on the United States Department of Interior's National Register of Historic Places was a most valuable source of information when I began this project. That inventory of existing structures and those long gone, will be valuable to researchers for generations to come. In many ways, his work is the foundation on which this project rests. His research serves well those who love state history. He offered countless pieces of information, photocopies, e-mails, insight and his advice without reservation. If this book is my child, then he is its uncle.

William Wurst, formerly a member of the Friends of High Point, and Debbie Fritter, formerly a naturalist at High Point, did a wonderful job of interviewing former CCC enrollees, most of whom were in their late 60s or early 70s when they spoke with them in the late 1980s. The audio tapes offered a unique

Peter Osborne

perspective of what it was like to be in the CCC at High Point. They deserve our collective thanks because most of the men who were interviewed are now gone. If Bill and Debbie had not taken time to find and interview these men, those memories would have been lost forever. Bill's history of the park was a delight to read and provided my first insights into what the CCC did at High Point.

The Friends were enormously helpful in other ways as they purchased the only known copies of the company newsletters and have been working steadily on organizing the large collection of photographs in the archives, many of which are CCC era. Myra Snook and Roberta Bramhall spent hours with me sorting through the large collection of photographs and assisting me in my quest for information. Myra also shared clips from her personal archives and Roberta was kind enough to make slides of many of the photographs that allowed for the creation of a new slide show for the Minisink Valley Historical Society. They also provided insights from their own recollections of the park.

When I first began to write to people who had served at High Point during the CCC era, only a few people answered my queries. One of them was Albert Mastriani, the National Park Service foreman and later designer for Company 1280 from 1933 to 1941. He designed some of the projects that were built and supervised the construction of most of the important projects that remain today. We have carried on a correspondence by e-mail, and he has been a wealth of information. Our regular letters are reminiscent of the recent best seller *Tuesdays With Morrie*. His memory is remarkable, and his insights and recollections were invaluable. Without them this book would not be as accurate as I wanted it to be.

Former CCC enrollees who were stationed at High Point and were helpful include Peter Lutz who was interviewed twice and whose memories of the camp and love for the CCC were touching. Barbara Sagursky Pohl, daughter of enrollee Michael Sagursky, was kind enough to provide photos and her father's service records. "Red" Sacco, a member of Company 216 gave his recollections as well. Thomas Segar of Company 1280 and I spent a delightful hour at Promised Land State Park talking about his memories of High Point. Neil Thiede and I spent a wonderful fall morning talking about his time in the CCC and his memories of the boundary survey are found in the text. I am appreciative of Nicholas Hanisak, former Technical Services clerk, who was generous with his time and insights into the CCC's operation at High Point.

I am grateful to the board of directors of the Minisink Valley Historical Society in Port Jervis who allowed me to work on the project and take a day off occasionally to deal with research. They also allowed me to use their computer equipment and archives. As always, my friend Bill Clark, a volunteer at the Society, got roped into the act as he was enlisted to build a new archives case for CCC blueprints and project files at the park office.

Kelly Millspaugh, an intern at MVHS, transcribed audio tapes of former CCC boys recorded at High Point over the years. She did an excellent job, and most of the quotes from the C boys are a result of her work. MVHS member Margie Sierski earned incredible numbers of gold stars because she volunteered to go through years of newspapers and cull CCC articles. This effort proved to be extraordinarily helpful and many details of the camp, enrollees and their activities would not have come to light without her research. Almost every footnote that refers to a newspaper article comes from her work. Nancy Vocci also found newspaper clips for me.

Other MVHS members who helped include Les and Jean Crine who have many recollections of the park's long history and, in fact, are a part of it. They were kind enough to share them with me. Irene Cosh and Stella Kelsch, whose memories of the park and first tented CCC camp at Lusscroft farms, proved to be valuable early on and they provided recollections of John Gibbons. Charles King, Miral Haubner, Susan Stanton and Nancy Bello provided reference materials and Mary and Mead Stapler, my old friends, offered encouragement and thoughts on Franklin D. Roosevelt and spent a lovely evening with Albert Mastriani and me as we talked about my research. The Bello family, including Michael, Nancy, Jeremiah and Victoria, all graciously gave up computer time while I scanned photographs for the final draft of the book.

Also of assistance from the state's Department of Environmental Protection were Gregory Marshall, Director, from the Division of Parks of Parks & Forestry, Louis Cherepy, Regional Superintendent, Northern Region; Paul Sedor, Regional Superintendent, Shore Region; Chuck Sary, Superintendent, Monmouth Battlefield; Paul Taylor, Supervising Historic Preservation Specialist; Beverly Weaver, Principal Historic Preservation Specialist; both with the State Park Service; Terry Karschner, New Jersey Historic Preservation Office and Michael Ryan, Tidelands Management Bureau. David Vecchioli, the archivist with Morristown National Historic Park in Morristown, New Jersey, provided insights into the internal workings of the NPS at Morristown during the years of the CCC.

The staff and members of the National Association of Civilian Conservation Corps Alumni who provided materials, St. Louis, Missouri; Julie Kemper; Joe Toltin, the Brotherhood of X'CCCers; the staff of the Port Jervis Free Library and RoseMary Conklin, St. Mary's Church, Port Jervis, New York. Congressman Benjamin Gilman and his staff assistant Brian Walsh, and Gene Morris, along with the staff at the National Archives and Records Administration facility at College Park,

Peter Osborne

Maryland, all helped me access the voluminous records of the CCC as they pertained to the camp at High Point State Park. Without Gene's help and insightful advice, I would have spent many weeks looking for things in the archives.

Of great help were Marilyn L. Nelson, Senior Research Librarian, Information Research Division, Congressional Research Service at the Library of Congress and Raymond Teichman, Supervisory Archivist, Franklin Roosevelt Presidential Library, Hyde Park, New York. Pictorial Histories Publishing Company, Missoula, Montana gave permission to use previously copyrighted materials. James Simon from the Center for Research Libraries in Chicago assisted me in getting the High Point camp newsletters. The illustrations from the camp newsletters are reproduced from *CCC Camp Papers* held by the Center for Research Libraries, and for their permission to use them, I am grateful. Wayne McCabe was kind enough to let me review his collection of High Point materials which were very helpful and provided some important information.

Also, Jane Proctor; Rick Strain; Ronald Slate; Alicia Batko, Montague Association for the Restoration of the Community History; Robert Longcore, Sussex County Historical Society; Steve Bates, The Nature Conservancy and Trailblazers Camp; Len Peck, Walpack Historical Society; the Sussex County Department of Planning, Development and Human Services,

Newton, New Jersey; Donald Eby; Florence Fuller; Joseph Ryan; Lois and Andy Fortune; Walter Gochenour; Helen Cuddeback; Pat Governale; Frank Toth; Paul Lighty; Gerald Tomlinson; Florence Gray; Dick Heiney, Promised Land State Park, Greentown, Pennsylvania; Sandra Schultz, Acting Superintendent, National Park Service, Upper Delaware Scenic and Recreation River; Helen Connelly and Ann Marino all provided information. Zita Innella, my mother-in-law, reflected upon her not being allowed to date CCC boys when she was a young woman and was gracious enough to allow me to use photographs of her. My years associated with the Pinchot Institute for Conservation and Grey Towers gave me my love and admiration for Gifford Pinchot and my knowledge of him and President Theodore Roosevelt.

And, finally, I have to thank the people who were helpful in producing the final product. My readers, John Keator, Kate Monahan, Ron Dupont, Mead Stapler, Myra Snook, Roberta Bramhall, Leslie and Jean Crine and Albert Mastriani all were kind enough to read the original manuscript which was over 430 pages. They made corrections, additions and suggestions. Whatever mistakes remain in this book, however, are mine and mine alone. The publisher and the wonderful people who work there, the 1st Books Library, did a wonderful job in designing, laying out and publishing the book.

Peter Osborne

I am also so grateful to Mary and Mead Stapler who provided a generous matching grant to the Minisink Valley Historical Society that allowed for the initial design and printing of the book. Without their help the book would not have been possible. Allison and Charles Gillinder provided additional funding that also allowed the Society to purchase the first printing run.

Without these people, institutions and agencies I could not have completed this work which has, over the last year, become a labor of love and consumed my life. To all of you, I offer my heartfelt thanks. We are finally acknowledging the work of the Civilian Conservation Corps at High Point State Park in a way that will never be forgotten.

About the Author

Peter Osborne has been the full-time executive director of the Minisink Valley Historical Society for twenty-two years and the historian for the City of Port Jervis for the last ten years. He has a Bachelor of Arts in American History from Rutgers - The State University of New Jersey. He has long been interested in preserving the Upper Delaware River's heritage, is a community activist and has written extensively about the region's history. He has received the Tri-State Chamber of Commerce's Citizen of the Year Award, the Upper Delaware Heritage Alliance's Merit and Repeat Offender awards and the Upper Delaware Council's Cultural Achievement Award.

Osborne was involved with the restoration of the Port Jervis Erie Depot an 1892 building listed on the National Register of Historic Places, the Port Jervis Erie Turntable and Fort Decker, a 1793 stone house museum. In addition to his work at the society he has served on the board of directors of the Orange County Historical Society and the Pinchot Institute for Conservation. He is married to Janis Osborne who is the editor of the weekly newspaper, TheGazette in Port Jervis, New York and has a son Ryan.

The author continues to collect information on the activities of the CCC at High Point and the men who served there. Readers with additional information can contact the author at the Minisink Valley Historical Society, Post Office Box 659, Port Jervis, New York, 12771 or the superintendent at High Point State Park, 1480 State Route 23, Sussex, New Jersey 07461-3605.

Printed in the United States
696000002B